HYPERTEXT: from Text to Expertext

ROY RADA

Department of Computer Science
University of Liverpool

McGRAW-HILL BOOK COMPANY

London · New York · St Louis · San Francisco · Auckland
Bogotá · Caracas · Hamburg · Lisbon · Madrid · Mexico · Milan
Montreal · New Delhi · Panama · Paris · San Juan · São Paulo
Singapore · Sydney · Tokyo · Toronto

Published by
McGRAW-HILL Book Company (UK) Limited
SHOPPENHANGERS ROAD · MAIDENHEAD · BERKSHIRE · ENGLAND
TELEPHONE: 0628 23432
FAX: 0628 770224

British Library Cataloguing in Publication Data
Rada, R. (Roy)
    Hypertext: from text to expertext.
    1. Computer systems. Software packages
    I. Title
    005.3

ISBN 0–07–707401–7

Library of Congress Cataloging-in-Publication Data

Rada. R. (Roy),
    Hypertext: from text to expertext/Roy Rada.
        p.   cm.
    Includes bibliographical references and index.
    ISBN 0-07-707401-7
    1. Hypertext systems.   I. Title.
    QA76.76.H94R33   1991
    005.75′4–dc20   90-20812
    CIP

12345 CUP 94321

Typeset and printed and bound in Great Britain
at the University Press, Cambridge.

HYPERTEXT: from Text to Expertext

Contents

Preface

Book chapter

The declining costs of digital computing along with the information explosion necessitate a reassessment of the principles and systems which may be united to serve the information age. In particular, the links within a document, among people, and among documents must come together. The disciplines of **human–computer interaction**, **computer-supported collaborative work**, **information storage and retrieval**, and **artificial intelligence** should complement one another in the new discipline that studies hypertext. — *motivation*

This book was written with the help of a special computer system for multiple authors. Students from classes at George Washington University and University of Liverpool contributed to the book through the computer system. Additionally, the system supported a model of a document as a **network** whose nodes are labeled with semantically meaningful terms and whose edges point to paragraphs. This book was produced by a traversal of the network. — *how this book was written*

This book was written for **students** and **practitioners** of information science. Exercises and references are provided. Anyone interested in combining text and high technology will benefit from this book. Text is synonymous with document and includes personal letters, novels, computer programs, medical records, legal contracts—everyone needs text. — *audience*

This book includes chapters on — *preview*

1. Text
2. Small-volume hypertext
3. Large-volume hypertext
4. Collaborative hypertext, and
5. Intelligent hypertext.

I will concentrate on These as Guide & HyperTies book are small-volume hypertext systems. You might even try!

Psychological models of reading and writing are presented in Chapter 1 on **Text**, where the structure of a traditional document and word-processing software are described. A document may be abstractly represented as a network of concepts, and how this network within a single document may be represented and browsed is the focus of Chapter 2, Small-volume hypertext. Typically, small-volume hyptertext systems are easy to use and run on personal computers. — *Text and Microtext*

To facilitate the handling of massive document collections, institutions collect and provide access to the documents. A **large-volume hypertext** system may store hundreds of millions of documents and principally supports search. — *Macrotext and Grouptext*

as is case with Guide & HyperTies

Human–human, as well as human–computer communication, is supported by a collaborative system, and manipulation of a few documents by a few people is the focus of Chapter 4 on **Collaborative hypertext.**

Expertext

The major problem with hypertext is that in dealing with text that contains many links people become disoriented. Expert guidance in the form of **intelligent hypertext** may lessen the disorientation. Instilling life into document systems, by adding procedures which will respond to different users in different ways, one has a greater chance of creating documents which will succeed in influencing others. The combination of expert system and hypertext system features increases the utility of each system.

what is missing?

Since this book focuses on conceptual structures and functions, chapters on **hypermedia** and **hardware** are missing. A chapter on hypermedia would further examine the role of audio and video, stating, for instance, that not only is animation important but also that three-dimensional animation should be used. Rapid three-dimensional animation, however, requires massive computational power. Special hardware is needed to support hypermedia; in a hardware chapter, topics, such as high-density television and optical disks, would be covered.

Now go to conclusion p. 182-186

Book available in hypertext

This book is available in four hypertext systems: Emacs-INFO, Guide, HyperTies and SuperBook. Emacs-INFO is public domain software, whereas the other systems are sponsored by corporations. In all cases the hypertext version of the book is made available to you at no cost other than the cost of reproducing the material and sending it to you.

To acquire the Emacs-INFO or HyperTies versions please contact Roy Rada at either his British or American addresses:

Department of Computer Science   724 Corona
University of Liverpool   Denver
Liverpool L69 3BX   Colorado 80218
UK   USA
email rada@uk.ac.liverpool
Telephone: 051-794-3669

To acquire the Guide version contact Office Workstations at either their British or American addresses:

144 Broughton Road   2800 156th Avenue SE
Edinburgh EH7 4LE   Bellevue
UK   Washington 98007
    USA

A version of this book in SuperBook form is available from Bellcore. A commerical version of the SuperBook software is currently being developed but is not yet available at the time of printing. For information on obtaining the SuperBook Research Prototype software, contact Bellcore Customer Service at:

60 New England Avenue
Piscataway
New Jersey 08854-4196
USA

or telephone 1-800-521-CORE. Ask for reference number SUP001. Information
is also available by electronic mail: mlittman@bellcore. com.

Tradenames
The following tradenames used in this book are acknowledged:

Augmentation System	Linkway
Apple Computer	MacIntosh
Drexel Disk	MacPaint
Dynabook	MacWrite
FRESS	Microsoft
Guide	NoteCards
Emacs-INFO	PicturePhone
HyperCard	SMART
HyperTies	STAIRS
Intermedia	SuperBook
InterNote	ThinkTank
KMS	WordStar
KnowledgePro	WordPerfect

1

Text

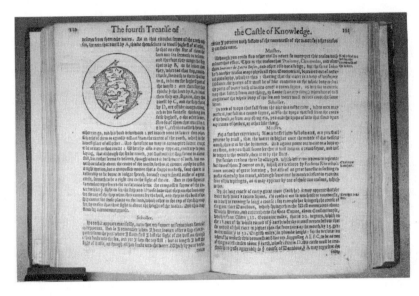

Figure 1.1 This book, *Castle of Knowledge*, was written by Robert Recorde and published in 1596. While a printing press was used, the typography and some of the layout was intended to suggest a hand-written document. Observe the notes in the margins of that book, and the notes in the margins of this book.

The term hypertext is related to the term 'hyperbolick space' introduced in 1704 and popularized by the 19th century mathematician F. Klein (Kane, 1990). Klein used **hyperspace** to describe a geometry with many dimensions. Human mental processes have been modeled in such multi-dimensional spaces. Ted Nelson coined the term hypertext in 1967 because he believed that text systems should reflect the hyperspace of concepts implicit in the text (Nelson, 1987).

hyperspace

Hypertext is multi-dimensional text. The internal structure of a text is one dimension. Along another dimension the relations among texts are important. Along yet another dimension people communicate with one another as they manipulate text. Each of these **dimensions** corresponds to a **chapter** of this book (see Fig. 1.2).

hypertext dimensions

Along all of its dimensions, hypertext is an extension of **text**, and to understand hypertext one must first understand text. What is the definition of text? What is its history? Which psychological models are relevant to explaining how people read and write text? Are there standards for representing text on the computer? What types of computer programs exist to support authors of text?

questions about text

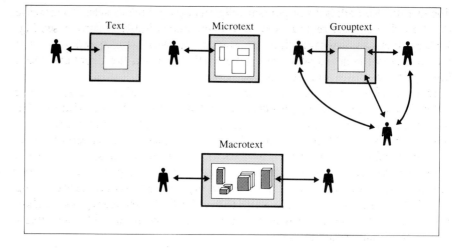

Figure 1.2 Dimensions of hypertext. The large rectangles represent the technological medium. The mid-sized rectangles encompass the document material. Microtext contains pieces of one document, while macrotext contains many documents. In the grouptext situation, people communicate directly.

If one is better able to understand the answers to these questions, one is better able to understand hypertext.

definition of text

Text is a recorded body of information. The terms text and **document** are synonymous, and while they predominantly contain natural language in the form of alphabetic characters, they also contain graphics. Text is a medium for the transmission of culture and science and may be of arbitrary size. Mail, recipes, reports, papers, books, and software documentation are examples of text.

ancient history

Text has a **history** of thousands of years. Six thousand years ago a Sumerian might, for instance, have kept a **record** on clay of the number of sheep he owned. The Egyptians made records on papyrus at around the same time. These

Figure 1.3 Stone with hieroglyphics. This stone is a fragment from the wall of the Tomb of Akhethotep in Sakkarah. It was written in about 2400 BC. The hieroglyphics were the written alphabet of the day.

documents also addressed important religious and political issues. To increase the durability of these records they were sometimes chiseled into stone (see Fig. 1.3). Egyptian documents such as the *Book of the Dead* were so important that already several hundred years before the birth of Christ, the Egyptians had a library for such books in Alexandria.

Documents prepared in the Middle Ages often included complex, artistic letter forms, as they were painstakingly written by hand. To reproduce such a document manually was a time-consuming task. The **printing press** was developed about 600 years ago and allowed copies of a document to be produced efficiently. In the early days of the printing press, the printers continued to use complex letterforms. Furthermore, they used erasers and paintbrushes to doctor what the printing press produced, so that the text would look like an old-fashioned manuscript (Dam, 1988). Many years passed before printers accepted that the new documents did not need to look like documents which had been written by hand.

Middle Ages

The history of text shows how gradual was the change. Some text written on papyrus was only transcribed to stone 500 years later. In the first century of the printing press, text continued to look like it had before the printing press appeared. The lesson to be learned from history is that change occurs slowly. A new **technology** for producing text may take root slowly because society has an enormous investment in traditional text methods.

gradual change

1.1 Principles

People write text in order that others may read it. Good writers must appreciate the reading process. The processes of **reading** and **writing** both involve complex interplays among many levels of structure and function. Reading and writing are inverses: reading takes text into the mind, and writing puts the mind into the text.

reading and writing

1.1.1 Reading model

The understanding of language may be viewed at the **lexical**, the **syntactic**, the **semantic**, or the **pragmatic** level (see Sec. 5.1.2.1). At the lexical level one determines for each word its definition. At the syntactic level the subject, action, and object of a sentence are determined. At the semantic level the meaning of a sentence is determined. The pragmatic interpretation of text depends on the integration of the text's semantic meaning into the reader's model of self and of the world.

lexical, syntactic, semantic, and pragmatic levels

In a simplistic model of text processing, people proceed from the lexical to the syntactic to the semantic and to the pragmatic levels in that order. More realistically, these levels interact continuously, as no interpretation at one level can be made independently of other levels. For instance, pragmatics affects everything. The meaning of a word may depend on the world model which a reader holds. The correct syntactic and semantic interpretation of a sentence may depend on the role the sentence plays in some real world situation. Thus, while in a certain sense readers proceed from words, to sentences, to paragraphs,

interacting levels

and to the overall document, in another sense the progress is more to and fro. For instance, only after scanning the structure of a document, might a person start to read the first paragraph word by word. **Feedback** between less and more complex units is continual (Dijk and Kintsch, 1983).

1.1.1.1 Structures

text translated into propositions

The words and phrases that make up a text are the raw material from which a mental representation of the meaning of that text is constructed. This mental representation initially takes the form of **propositions** or relationships. For example, the propositional representation of the sentence 'The incumbents have won the elections' is 'have won (incumbents, elections)'. The 'have won' proposition takes two arguments, namely who has won and what was won. In one simplified account of reading, the reader has a store of propositions, such as 'have won', in memory and, in reading, retrieves and uses the appropriate ones.

local coherence

Many sentence-based models of language do not go beyond the representation of propositions from a sentence. **Local coherence**, however, is established across sentence boundaries and is established in short-term memory (see Sec. 2.4.2.2). Language users must establish coherence as soon as possible; otherwise, they cannot effectively move information from short-term memory to long-term memory. Readers immediately attempt to link propositions from one sentence with related propositions from another sentence.

larger structures built from propositions

The language user makes preliminary **hypotheses** about local coherence from the titles, thematic words, and first propositions of the text and from knowledge about global situations. The long-term memory contains these global situations and hence interacts with the short-term memory to guide the filtering of information. Hypotheses are continually generated as to what the text is intended to say. These hypotheses are refined as the text proceeds, and **propositions** are combined into larger structures (Dijk and Kintsch, 1983). Many text types exhibit an overall form that determines the larger structures. For instance, stories usually have a Setting, Complication, and Resolution, while scientific papers usually have an Introduction, Method, Results, and Conclusion. Language users try to activate the largest, relevant structure from memory as soon as a cue is available. They use this hypothesized **superstructure** to guide subsequent processing of text by providing constraints on the set of propositions which may be extracted from the text.

1.1.1.2 Functions

control system

A **reading control system** supervises processing in short-term memory, activates more general knowledge, and decides what information to move to where in long-term memory. Large amounts of knowledge are needed for the interpretation of text. The text may be seen as translated into propositions which the reader first organizes into locally **coherent** patterns. The control system is continually invoked during the reading process to try to translate the locally coherent information into globally coherent information.

The reading control system uses **spreading activation** to process propositions (see Sec. 5.1.1.1). In memory each proposition is connected to a number of other propositions (Kintsch, 1988). After an initial reading has identified some propositions to represent the text, further propositions may be obtained by a process of activating neighboring propositions. The spreading activation process is repeatedly applied as reading continues and determines both what is added to and removed from the interpretation of the text. If activation ceases to go to some propositions that were considered relevant to the text, then those propositions are subsequently ignored. This process continues until further spreading activation does not change the propositions used to represent the text.

spreading activation

Readability means the relative ease with which texts can be read and remembered. Traditional readability models deal primarily with surface variables, such as sentence length. For instance, a readable text has short sentences. More interesting measures of readability relate to the construction of complex memory structures. Such measures note that the number of inferences required to construct a complex structure is inversely proportional to the readability of a text. For instance, when two adjacent sentences invoke similar propositions, then the number of inferences required is much less than when the adjacent sentences invoke completely different sets of propositions. An adequate model of readability must account for the cost of constructing complex memory structures.

readability depends on coherence

1.1.2 Writing model

The ancient Greek philosopher, **Aristotle**, emphasized that a text has basically two parts: stating the case and proving it. Reluctantly, he recognized the role of an introduction and epilogue. The introduction shows the aim of the speech. The **audience** must be motivated to read the rest of the text. The epilogue may be used to secure the good disposition of the audience and refresh the audience's memories (Magill and McGreal, 1961).

state the case and prove it

1.1.2.1 Framework

Successful writing is constrained by **goal** and **audience** (Frederiksen and Dominic, 1981). The author is guided by a goal but is constrained by what the audience is prepared to accept (see Fig. 1.4). The writer must view his knowledge from multiple perspectives to find the organization that best suits the audience and the goal (Langer, 1984).

goal and audience

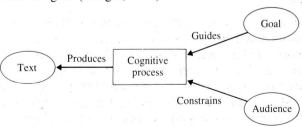

Figure 1.4 Environment of cognitive writing process.

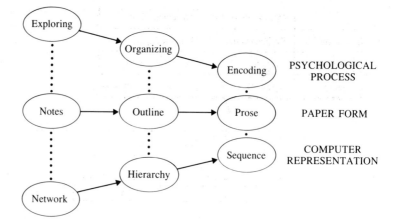

Figure 1.5 Three phases of writing. The top row shows the sequence of cognitive processes through which a person writes a document. The paper items in the middle row reflect the activity in the top row, while the underlying structural representation is given in the bottom row.

explore, organize, and encode

The three phases of writing a document are: **exploring**, **organizing** and **encoding**. In the exploration phase knowledge is acquired—brainstorming occurs, and unstructured notes are made. Next, the unstructured notes are organized into an outline. In the encoding phase the prose for the final document is written (see Fig. 1.5). Some writers progress through this model of the writing process in a linear fashion, going from rough notes to outline to prose. Other writers may begin in the middle of the process and write an outline before making any notes. The writing process not only varies from one author to another, but the sequence of events may also vary from time to time for a single author (Rada, 1989a). Authors like to move freely from one phase to another and back again.

novice versus expert

Novices and experts write differently (see Exercise 1.1). **Novice** or in-experienced writers find writing a tedious chore of translating what they already know onto paper. They do little effective reorganization of their ideas and feel that after the writing exercise that they know no more than they knew before the writing exercise. **Expert** or experienced writers have the opposite experience. As they go through the various phases of making notes and outlines and prose, they continually examine what they have suggested relative to how they expect it to impact on their intended audience. Experts have a good reader or audience or user model and continually adjust what they have to say after feeding it through their reader model (Scardamalia and Bereiter, 1987). After an expert has written a document, he feels that he has gained insight about ways to look at the subject of the document; his **reader model** has criticized his thinking and helped him to develop a better document.

1.1.2.2 Extended writing model

structured and unstructured

The phases of exploring, organizing, and encoding can be further elaborated by considering unstructured and structured representations at each phase. An **unstructured** text item is isolated. A **structured** text item shows connectivity. During the unstructured subphase of the exploratory phase, brainstorming is represented by scattered idea labels. In the note-taking subphase of the

	Unstructured item	Structured item
Exploring	Brainstorming	Note-taking
Organizing	Argument	Organizing notes
Encoding	Linear planning	Drafting and revising

Figure 1.6 Structured versus unstructured. The cells of the matrix indicate the cognitive process which occurs for each type of item and each phase of writing (Sharples *et al.*, 1990).

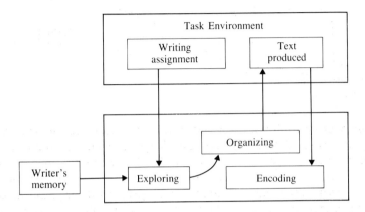

Figure 1.7 Goal-oriented writing model. Writing process relative to memory and task (adapted from Hayes *et al.*, 1987).

exploratory phase the idea labels are elaborated as notes. In the unstructured subphase of the organizing phase, argumentations lead to relationships being sketched among idea labels. In the structured subphase of the organizing phase, various groupings of notes are made. In the unstructured subphase of the encoding phase, groupings of notes are viewed as sequences of notes. In the structured subphase of the encoding phase, the linear sequence of notes is polished into final form. Given the matrix of unstructured and structured items versus exploring, organizing, and encoding phases (see Fig. 1.6), the writer may proceed from one box of the matrix to another in any order which suits him. For example, the plan–draft–revise strategy of writing proceeds first from the unstructured organizing phase, then to the unstructured encoding phase, and finally to the structured encoding phase.

A writing model can emphasize **goal-oriented** behavior. The goal of writing is to operate on one's memory so as to produce text which satisfies some writing assignment. In the context of goal-seeking (see Fig. 1.7), the exploratory phase finds connections between the assignment and the memory (Hayes *et al.*, 1987). The organizing phase takes material from memory and transforms it into networks of loosely-structured text. In the encoding phase the text is revised until it satisfies the goal.

writing is goal-oriented

Hypptext Chapter

1.2 Systems

The use of text systems to support the reading and writing of text files has been one of the prominent uses of computers for years. Of the hours spent by people in front of computer terminals, more have been spent with **editors** or

text systems: prominent computer usage

Document logic
Text
Layout
Image
Visual–verbal integration

Figure 1.8 Visual–verbal integration. The image of a document is influenced by the layout, while the impact of the text content depends to a large part on the document logic. The proper balance of images and text depends on the document type.

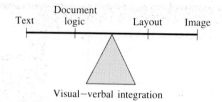

word processors to access or create text files than any other use. Languages have been developed and standardized for representing the layout of documents. Numerous writing tools have been developed which are supposed to help writers deal with the creative challenge of organizing text.

1.2.1 Text structure

abstract and physical forms

To convert the abstract form of a text into a concrete visualization, the author needs a **layout language**. This can be embedded in a text file so that a computer program can produce an attractive, physical form of the text. Text should have an appearance which immediately means something to the reader. Text systems must help users specify and appreciate both the abstract and the physical form of text.

continuum from text to image

A document integrates words and **images**. The integration can be usefully viewed as a continuum of meaning from text-based to image-based. The **visual-verbal** fulcrum point should move along the continuum in concert with the type of document being produced (see Fig. 1.8).

poetic license

Poets have a special license to organize text on the page so as to combine both visual and verbal messages. An extreme example of an unusual image is provided by an Ezra Pound poem from the early 1900s (see Fig. 1.9). Pound juxtaposes discrete images—the image being not an idea but rather 'a radiant node or cluster ... from which, and through which, and into which, ideas are constantly rushing' (Slatin, 1988).

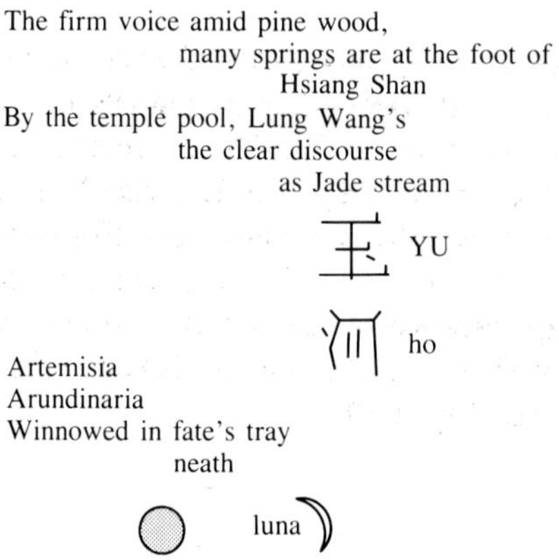

The firm voice amid pine wood,
many springs are at the foot of
Hsiang Shan
By the temple pool, Lung Wang's
the clear discourse
as Jade stream
YU
ho
Artemisia
Arundinaria
Winnowed in fate's tray
neath
luna

Figure 1.9 Poetry. Excerpt from Ezra Pound's Canto CXII. This shows how one poet represented abstractions that are atypical in more traditional text.

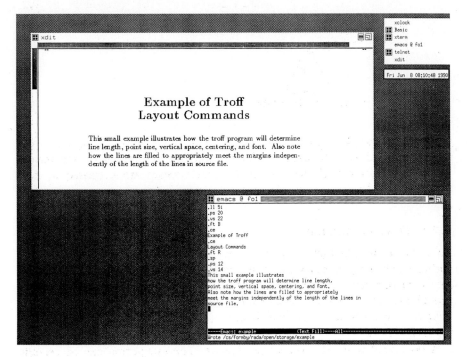

Figure 1.10 Troff commands. In this screen the window on the lower right shows the source text with embedded troff commands. The size of characters is described in points, and the command '.ps 20' means to make point-size-20 characters. The vertical height of a line is determined by the '.vs' command and '.vs 22' means to make a vertical height of 22 points. The bold font of the title comes from the '.ft B' (font bold) command. The window in the upper left shows how the text appears after processing by troff.

1.2.1.1 Physical document structure

The languages for the specification of **physical** document structure come in, at least, two generic formats. One approach is to manipulate directly the physical appearance of a document with a 'What You See Is What You Get' (WYSIWYG) system. A command in a WYSIWYG system is interpreted immediately upon being expressed. For instance, a command to center a line immediately centers the line on the screen. The center command is never explicitly visible in the text. An alternative approach to document layout requires commands embedded within text. For instance, the command '.ce' may be inserted in a text, and when the text is processed by the document formatter, the '.ce' command causes the next line of text to be centered on the page.

embedded commands versus WYSIWYG

One popular example of a layout language based on embedded commands is **troff**. A document with embedded troff **formatting commands** can be automatically translated into a physical representation. The commands determine how the text should be placed on the printed page (see Exercise 1.2). One form of command begins with a period followed by two characters. For instance, the '.sp' command creates a blank line (space) in the physical representation. Various parameters control the appearance of text on the printed page. For instance, the size of the text (point size) and the spacing between lines of text (vertical spacing) are parameters (see Fig. 1.10).

embedded command language example

Hierarchical structure	
Command	Result
.NH 1 'Writer'	1. Writer
.NH 2 'Single author'	1.1. Single author
.NH 2 'Types of network'	1.2. Types of network

Figure 1.11 Heading macro. A sequence of new heading (.NH) commands results in section headings within text.

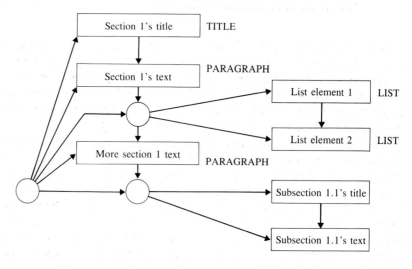

Figure 1.12 Hierarchical logical document representation.

1.2.1.2 Logical document structure

troff macros

Troff includes facilities for writing computer programs or macros. By building onto troff with **macros**, one may control the logical structuring of a document, as well as its physical structuring. For example, the new-heading '.NH' macro command signals the beginning of a new section (see Fig. 1.11). This command keeps track of outline levels and computes the proper index for a heading, such as '1.1. Single author', based on the indices of preceding headings.

hierarchical representation

Document processing systems that logically structure a document may address units such as sections, paragraphs, and lists. One logical document structuring language uses a **hierarchical representation** for which the text itself is contained entirely in the leaves of the hierarchy (see Fig. 1.12). The internal nodes of the hierarchy are not distinguished from each other.

STANDARD GENERALIZED MARKUP LANGUAGE

what is SGML?

To make electronic information more exchangeable, standards of logical document structure are useful. The Standard Generalized Markup Language (SGML) is a language for logical document structure and is an international standard for publishing (International Standards Organization, 1989). SGML is based on the Generalized Markup Language developed at IBM. The concepts on which it is based were approved by the American National **Standards Institute**, then the International Standards Institute, and published in official

Sample from SGML		
Element	Tag	Attributes
Starter document	<sd>	sec= and status=
Title	<td>	
Heading level 1	<h1>	id= and st=
Paragraph	<p>	
Heading reference	<hr>	pn and rid=

Figure 1.13 A few SGML elements, tags, and attributes are given. Any tag may have several attributes, as is the case for heading reference.

form in 1986 (Smith, 1986). SGML is based on the generic **markup** of the structural elements of a document without regard to their presentation, which is regarded as a separate issue. It is based on the principles of the generic encoding of documents and 'marks up' a document's logical structure and not its physical presentation. SGML contrasts to typographic markup, since font and style are not considered during document markup.

The **syntax** of SGML is based on tags that occur in a sequence with certain constraints. The **tags** mark the beginning of logical components of the document. For example, the first tag to be entered in a document would be ⟨sd⟩, signifying that what follows is a general document (see Fig. 1.13). Security for the document could be set through the 'sec=' attribute. This might, for instance, be useful for a confidential report. The title of the document would be represented by ⟨td⟩. A heading at level 1 is specified with ⟨h1⟩. A heading can be given an identifier next to 'id=' and a short title next to 'st='. The short title might be printed on every page that is in the section marked by the heading. Cross-reference may be made in the text to a heading via the ⟨hr⟩ marker. The reference identifier 'rid=' says what the identifier 'id=' of the header is. If the 'pn' attribute is given, then the page number on which the referenced header occurs will be printed along with the reference. For instance, somewhere in the text there may be a reference as follows '⟨hr rid=Apes pn⟩'. When the text is processed, this reference may be formatted as '(see Sec. Apes on page 3909)', although the **format** in which the reference appears is not the concern of SGML.

SGML syntax

The appeal of SGML is that a document prepared with SGML should be immediately useful to many other groups because they will be prepared to deal with it. SGML applies to

SGML applications

- computer-assisted publishing where the final product is a typeset document (hard copy),
- electronic publishing where the document appears on the screen (soft copy), and
- database publishing where document elements are retrieved in combination with other elements.

Many **publications**, be they books, manuals, reports, directories, or messages may be represented in SGML. Graphics and scanned images may be included in an SGML-marked document.

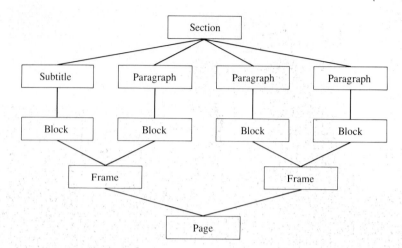

Figure 1.14 Office Document Architecture. Specific logical and layout structures coming together (Brown, 1989).

OFFICE DOCUMENT ARCHITECTURE

logical and layout structure

The Office Document Architecture (ODA) is an alternative or an extension (depending on one's view) to SGML. The **ODA** representation simultaneously applies two abstract structures to a document's content—a logical and a layout structure (International Standards Organization, 1988). The logical structure defines the composition of document **objects** into successively larger logical components, and the layout structure defines the composition of document objects on the page (Furuta, 1989). There naturally arises a mapping between the logical and layout structures (see Fig. 1.14).

logical structure

In the ODA **logical structure** an object in the hierarchy may have an attribute that describes how the object may be made from subordinate objects. These indicate that **subordinate** objects may be optional or required and that a group of objects may occur in a given sequence or in any order. Some of the logical objects with which ODA deals are 'section', 'subtitle', and 'paragraph'. A section must have one subtitle at the beginning and any number of paragraphs afterwards.

layout structure

The ODA layout structure divides a text into pages, frames, and blocks. **Blocks** are the lowest level areas and contain actual text. A frame is a rectangular area with blocks within it. By example, a paragraph is a block, and a frame might represent a column of text that is divided into paragraphs.

1.2.2 Reading tools

reading, browsing, and searching

In many situations a single text must serve a wide range of users, and the user's needs determine the style of access. Reading, browsing, and searching are three different styles of access to text.

- **Reading** implies the traditional sequential, line-by-line coverage of a document from page 1 to the end.
- **Browsing** involves jumping from place to place and only reading small segments in each of those places.

Figure 1.15 Paper and the computer. The author has a copy of a document on the computer screen, but since paper has many advantages, pages of the document are scattered around the computer. Notice the stand which holds some pages on one side of the computer, as well as the pages on the other side of the computer and on the chair. The author thus gains perspectives on the document which are difficult to achieve on the computer screen. To achieve comfortable positioning, the author holds the keyboard on her lap and has elevated the screen to eye level.

- **Searching** occurs when a person knows the label for some information and wants only that specific information.

Most studies have determined that reading from **paper** is faster than reading from **computer screens.** In experiments with a personal computer screen of 14 cm by 20 cm and a workstation screen 25 cm by 25 cm, the larger screen consistently supported better reading and writing behavior (Hansen and Haas, 1988), but was not as good as paper. Text on computer screens can take 30 per cent longer to read than text on paper with roughly equal comprehension (Shneiderman and Kearsley, 1989). If the studies include the confusion over page-turning commands and anxieties that some users have in reading from a computer, then the time required to read a text on the computer can double relative to the time required to read the same text on paper (see Fig. 1.15). Higher resolution displays and larger displays may eliminate the disadvantages associated with on-line reading.

paper is better

Directly observable attributes of hardware and software that affect **reading** are page size, legibility, responsiveness, and tangibility (Hansen and Hass, 1988). Together, these constitute a kind of physical readability:

physical readability

- **Page size** is the amount of text visible at one time. It can affect reading by limiting the context and thus burdening short-term memory.
- **Legibility** has strong influence on reading speed but is itself a consequence of many factors such as font design, spacing, and edge sharpness.
- **Responsiveness** is the speed of system response. The psychological impact of a slower response depends on the user's state of completion as the action is performed. In scrolling, the user is anticipating new information and can do nothing until it appears.

- **Tangibility** is the extent to which the state of the system is visible and modifiable via physical apparatus. Text on paper has high tangibility: the sheets have a layout and are stacked together. As the user reads, the shifting stack gives tactile position cues. This contrasts with the viewing options on some computers which require keystrokes. A scrollbar displays an analog representation indicating which portion of the document is visible and thus provides some tangibility.

In general, computers are weak relative to paper along the dimensions of page size, legibility, responsiveness, and tangibility. Improving the presentation of text along these dimensions would, therefore, improve the attractiveness of computers as reading tools.

1.2.3 Writing tools

value of computer
writing tools

Computer writing tools have replaced pen and paper for some people. In some situations, students who write with computers get higher grades for their writing products than students who write with pen and paper (Griffey, 1986). What are the methods for writing text with a computer?

task level

In writing a document with a computer text editor as the **medium**, writers must manifest multiple **levels** of understanding of the medium. At the **task level**, writers must integrate smoothly, at least three kinds of activity:

- They must recognize that the document will be stored as a file and know the details of the save command.
- At a more detailed level, they must recognize the mechanism for beginning, writing, and ending a sentence.
- At the primitive level, writers must comprehend the motion of the cursor on the screen and know which keys to press for each letter.

These three levels of interaction with the computer should ultimately occur at the skill or instinctive level, if users are to be comfortable with the computer as a writing medium.

cognitive model

While models of writing with the computer may focus on physical parameters such as keystrokes required to effect a certain change in the text, the fact that the user is busy with physical motions should not cloud the importance of cognitive processes. Such processes are not directly observable as physical motions, but ultimately appear as such. A **cognitive model** of writing with the computer might incorporate the presentation of the computer, the writing problem or task, and the user problem-solving strategy.

1.2.3.1 Editors

editor characteristics

In the 1950s, a computer editor was a program that was accessed via punched cards which said how a file should be edited. Modern editors are often **display editors** with advanced functions and self-documenting features. In a display editor the text being edited is visible on the screen and is updated automatically as one types commands. Usually, after each character or pair of characters that the user types, the display is updated. An advanced editor provides facilities that go beyond simple insertion and deletion. Filling of text, viewing two files at once, and dealing with sentences and paragraphs as units are typical advanced features. With a self-documenting editor one can type a special character, the 'Help' key, either to learn about the options, or to discover the meaning of any command.

A powerful computer text editor is customizable and extensible. With a customizable editor one can change the definition of the editor's commands in little ways. For example, if the user wants to change the keys which are associated with the up, down, left and right motions, it can easily be done. An extensible editor buys further flexibility—one can write new commands in a special programming language. The **programming language** of an extensible editor may give the user the power of a general-purpose programming language and also have special editor-related functions. **Emacs** is the best known, on-line, extensible editor, and is divided into functions that call each other, any of which can be redefined in the middle of an editing session (Stallman, 1981).

extensible

The translation between a text file with embedded physical formatting commands and the document's final layout may be a complex one which the author has trouble visualizing. Some editors allow the document structure to be changed, but also facilitate viewing of the formatted layout of the document. An editor which allows the author immediately to see the final layout is called a 'What You See Is What You Get' (WYSIWYG) editor (see Sec. 1.2.1.2). **WYSIWYG** document preparation systems use an uncomplicated, physically-oriented document structure. WYSIWYG editors have the advantage of immediacy or tangibility. One sees the text as it will be in its final form.

WYSIWYG advantages

While WYSIWYG editors have substantial appeal to novices who are most familiar with writing on paper (which is the primordial WYSIWYG medium), some argue that WYSIWYG interferes with writing by experts (Engelbart, 1984). WYSIWYG provides an advantage in the final process of converting a computer-held document to a formatted paper copy, but can have a negative impact on logical structure. WYSIWYG constraints of lines and pages and other formatting geometry do not necessarily contribute to matters of content and structure. An editor which facilitates reordering by **logical structure** would be difficult to provide in a purely WYSIWYG environment. Since the logical structuring of the document is a more difficult task than the physical structuring of the document, an editing tool should not rely exclusively on WYSIWYG features.

WYSIWYG disadvantages

The media of **paper** and **computer editor** support different writing functions (Sharples *et al.*, 1990). In writing with paper, note cards play a special role. Note cards are smallish pieces of paper which are used to contain text that is easily reordered. A writing medium can be characterized according to whether it supports full-text, portability, reordering, non-linear organization, reusability, or annotating (see Fig. 1.16).

paper versus computer

- **Full-text** means that both images and text are accommodated.
- A **portable** medium can be carried into the bed and onto the train.

Medium versus Property						
	Full-text	Portable	Reorder	Non-linear	Reusable	Annotations
Paper sheet	yes	yes	no	debatable	no	yes
Text file editor	no	no	yes	no	yes	no
Note cards	no	yes	yes	yes	no	no

Figure 1.16 Medium versus property. Paper and note cards have more yes's than does a text file editor. But the text file editor can be more easily extended.

- With the reordering facility the user can move a block of text from one place to another in the document.
- **Non-linear organization** is illustrated by a map-like distribution of note cards on a table top.
- A medium supports **reusability** when copies of arbitrary parts are easily generated.
- A text medium supports **annotations** when a colleague can take the text and easily mark on it so that the marks will subsequently guide the original author in revisions.

Paper is arguably good for full-text, portability, and annotations (see Fig. 1.17). It is not good for reordering or reusing (nor for deletions and insertions). Computer editors are best for reordering and reusing. While paper and note cards have positive attributes that text file editors lack, the computer medium can be more easily extended than can either paper or note cards.

1.2.3.2 Word processing and desktop publishing

program, menu, and screen levels

Editors are incorporated into word processing packages which in turn are extended into desktop publishing packages. **Word processing packages** may be

Figure 1.17 Portability. This small newspaper stand is in the entrance to a local train station and is continually busy with the sale of papers. People grab something to read while they travel from place to place—paper is portable.

EDIT MENU				
Cursor	*Scroll*	*Erase*	*Other*	*Menus*
E up	W up	G char	J help	O onscreen format
X down	Z down	T word	I tab	K block and save
S left	R up screen	Y line	V turn insert off	P print controls

Figure 1.18 Word processing edit menu.

seen as having three major levels of organization: **program level**, **menu level**, and **screen level**. The typical program package may include an editor program, a formatting program, a print program, a dictionary, and a mail listing program. Most popular word processing packages are directly based on menus or are menu-driven. With a menu system the user directly selects commands from a menu. In a menu-driven system the user types a command in one window after reviewing options from a menu in another window. At the screen level the video display of most word processing packages is organized into several specialized areas. For example, the edit screen for the WordStar word processing package has a status line at the top which tells the user first the name of the file and then the page number, line, and column of the cursor. Next on the WordStar screen is a menu which specifies the edit options (see Fig. 1.18). In the formatting or printing phases, other menus would be shown.

desktop publishing

Desktop publishing systems allow an organization to produce publications that look as though they were produced by a professional publishing company (see Exercise 1.3). A **desktop publishing system** includes:

- A personal computer with a hard disk and a laser printer.
- Word processing, graphics, and page makeup software.

The page makeup program helps the user develop the format of each page by automatically adjusting the amount of text on a page and appropriately sizing headings. Desktop publishing software is designed to be used by people who may have no previous computer experience and who may only use the computer for publishing. Accordingly, the interface is made easy to understand, and menus help direct the user into the appropriate actions.

1.2.3.3 Outliners

manipulating outlines

Whereas desktop publishing systems extend word processing in the realm of a sophisticated physical presentation, outliners emphasize the organization of ideas. Outliners provide a diagram of the **logical structure** of the document—a hierarchical table of contents—to help readers and writers visualize the structure. An outliner treats text blocks as objects and supports manipulation of text which coincides with a cognitive model of how one manages ideas. Advanced features of an outliner may qualify as hypertext system features.

COMMERCIAL OUTLINERS

history and features

While the Augmentation System of the 1960s included outliner capabilities, the first well-known commercial outliner, **ThinkTank**, was released in 1984. Most outline processors, such as ThinkTank, are designed for personal computers. Modern word processing packages may also include outliners. For instance, Microsoft Word is a popular word processing package that allows the user to manipulate outlines and to see in one window of the computer screen the outline alone and in another window the full text. When a heading in the outline is moved from one place to another, its associated text automatically moves with it.

the outliner automatically numbers sections

WordPerfect is another popular word processing system with some outliner capabilities (WordPerfect Corporation, 1990). Each section of a document is given an outline label that corresponds to a relative position in the outline, and a section can be as small as a single paragraph. The author signals the next section label with one of three options; the next label will be (assume the previous label is 2.2):

- the same level as the previous section (Sec. 2.3),
- one level deeper than the previous section (Sec. 2.2.1), or
- one level shallower than the previous section (Sec. 3).

The author can browse the document by jumping from section to section within the outline. In particular, one command directs the computer to move backward to a section at the same or a shallower level as the current section, while another command directs the computer to move comparably forward. An outline family is a section with all its subordinate levels and can be moved, copied, or deleted without the author needing to worry about the section labels, because WordPerfect automatically adjusts them.

OUTLINE WITH TEXT BLOCKS

structure

While typically, the components of an outline are terms or headings, the components of an outline could be blocks of text (Watt, 1988). The formal structure of an outliner whose nodes are text blocks can be defined in terms of text blocks and emphasized terms (see Fig. 1.19).

- A **text block** is a small unit of internally coherent information, which contains text and any number of emphasized terms.
- An **emphasized term** is a label in one text block which points to another text block.

initial difficulty for writers

The recommended process of writing outliner text blocks differs from normal expository writing. Each text block must be complete within itself, and then

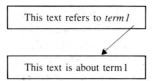

Figure 1.19 Text outline structure based on highlighted terms.

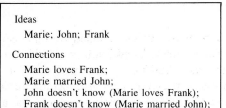

Ideas
   Marie; John; Frank

Connections
   Marie loves Frank;
   Marie married John;
   John doesn't know (Marie loves Frank);
   Frank doesn't know (Marie married John);

Figure 1.20 Ideas.

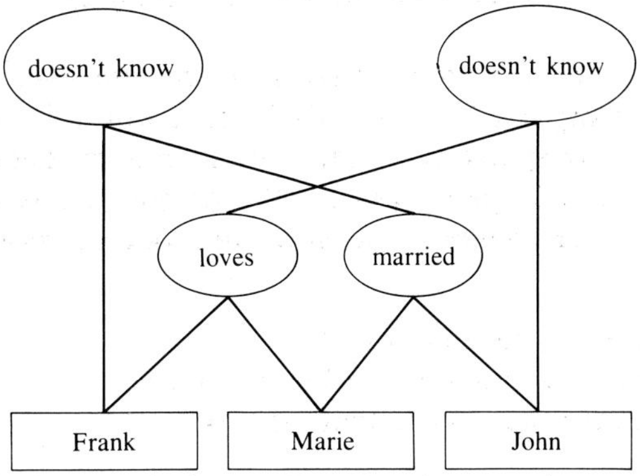

Figure 1.21 Ideas graph. Boxes are Ideas; ellipses contain relation-type. Graph structure depicts Connections.

must be linked to less abstract text blocks. This process of writing a set of text blocks is like writing 'top-down' programming code. Writers have initial difficulty in writing text blocks. However, the creators of one system that supports the writing of hierarchies of text blocks and emphasized terms claim that the system helps writers (Watt, 1988).

OUTLINE LOGIC

In one outline system the author enters Ideas and Connections (Wayner, 1988). **Connections** draw together pairs of Ideas. A program can generate a **graphical representation** of the Ideas and Connections. A different node represents each idea. The program adds a connection to the graph by generating a new node with pointers to the two nodes it connects. This new node is 'higher' than the two nodes it connects (see Figs 1.20 and 1.21).

graphical components

The outliner program next **traverses** the graph in generating instructions which the author is then asked to follow. The program starts at some top level connection and proceeds downward from that until two Ideas are located. The program then backtracks as it combines the Ideas via the Connections. The author would then be given a list of instructions for material to be written, as in Fig. 1.22.

traversal

To produce Ideas and Connections the writer must think clearly about the logical content of the document (see Exercise 1.4). Some **users** of such an outline logic system have reported that prior to their use of the system their outlines were lists of ideas without firm connections between them (supposedly, after using the system their ideas had firm connections!). The creators of the system

user satisfaction

```
Describe: Marie
Describe: John
Show how: Marie married John
Describe: Frank
Show how: Frank doesn't know (Marie married John)
```

Figure 1.22 Ideas guides.

believe that it frees the author from worrying about the overall structure, because the machine does the organizing (Wayner, 1988).

1.3 Epilogue

reading versus writing

While reading and writing must share large amounts of world knowledge and are both broadly speaking problem-solving or communicating exercises, they do not necessarily involve the same cognitive steps. Readers look for cues as to the meaning of a text. The text must present clearly the main points in such a way that from the specifics the reader can build a **model** that incorporates the generalities. Writers undergo the reverse process as they start from a general model and must provide adequate details to support the main claims. A reader has to determine in complex ways what the topic of the text is, whereas the writer already knows the topic before the writing starts. The first and major task of the writer is to construct a reasonable large-scale structure or plan. The reader, on the other hand, begins with local interpretations and must build towards a large-scale structure.

writing

Writing is one of the more challenging tasks which people perform. Models of the writing process can take many different perspectives, but all must agree that the author does not begin with a complete mental image of each word and its position in a text. Tools to support writing bring the medium closer to the cognitive events of the user. A good writing tool should facilitate the development and **organization** of ideas. A document that is well-structured logically will, in turn, be more easily read.

reading

In reading, a person constructs a representation in memory to reflect the significance of what has been read. While this understanding process occurs in real-time, the ability to understand text assumes that the reader has a **world model** into which the text information somehow fits. In this way, the impact of the text depends on wide cognitive and social frameworks in the reader. The analysis of meaning and of the significance of a text must ultimately be couched in terms of these models which the reader brings to the text and how these models are changed after the text has been read.

large screens

For simple tasks of reading a page the computer is inferior to paper. The look and feel of **paper** should be simulated on the screen. Text systems should support large, high-resolution screens. This is also true for writing, since the writer wants to see many notes and possible organizations at once. Quality screens that can simulate the desktop help a writer to manipulate both logical and physical representations.

training needed

People need training in how to read and write with computers. The creators of a system often note that people have difficulty adapting to the system but after some time become fond of it. Unfortunately, these testimonials are often anecdotal and what remains clear is that training for a system is important (Sullivan, 1988). Systems should be designed to be easy to learn, and should include **training aids** that are adaptable to different types of users.

1.4 Exercises

1.1   Observe a novice and an experienced writer preparing a short document. *observing authors* Do they use notes and an outline before producing prose? What are the differences in method between the novice and experienced writer? (2 hours)

1.2   A formatting language may include commands like centering a line and *layout* changing the size of characters. What other document layout would be useful for formatting a page? Give an example. (30 minutes)

1.3   Compare and contrast the features of an extensible editor with those of *editor* a desktop publishing system. (20 minutes)

1.4   Convert the following Ideas and Connections to a writing guide that is *outline logic* a sequence of instructions such as 'Describe: KGB' and 'Show how: Hans cooperates with KGB'. (20 minutes)

Ideas
      Hans; KGB; FBI

Connections
      Hans cooperates with KGB
      Hans cooperates with FBI
      KGB has secrets from FBI
      KGB does not know that (Hans cooperates with FBI)
      FBI does not know that (Hans cooperates with KGB)

2
Small-volume hypertext

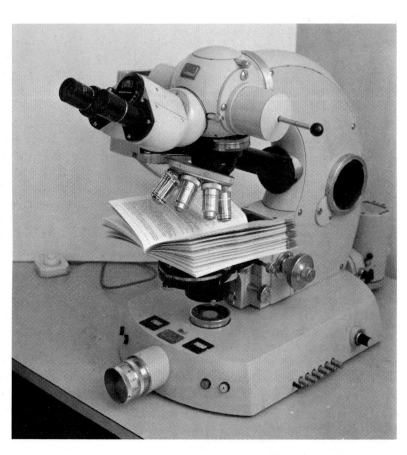

Figure 2.1 Microscope. Microtext involves a detailed look into the structure of a text.

what is small-volume hypertext?

Small-volume hypertext or microtext is a single document with explicit **links** among its components. One has to examine carefully, microscopically, a document to construct these links (see Fig. 2.1). A small-volume hypertext system provides a computer medium for manipulating the links of **microtext**. The popular usage of the term hypertext refers largely to microtext, and in this document the terms may, when no confusion should result, be used interchangeably. In this document a **microtext system** manages a single document and is intended to be used in stand-alone fashion by one person.

2.1 History

Authors for centuries have tried to create implicit, non-sequential links in their documents. The efforts to use electronic **computers** to facilitate the creation and access of linked text is necessarily much more recent. A fascinating hypertext system was developed in the early **1960s** but not made widely available in part because of the costliness of associated hardware. In the **1980s** the use of computers to deal with text in richly linked ways has become commonplace.

from 1960s to 1980s

2.1.1 The 1960s

The first hypertext system, the **Augmentation System**, was developed in the 1960s by Douglas **Engelbart's** group (Engelbart and English, 1968). The facilities for browsing text were particularly sophisticated. The hardware facilities were also impressive for the time. Among other things, the **mouse** was invented to support this hypertext system.

Augmentation System

The working information in the Augmentation System was organized into files, with flexible means for users to set up indices and directories, and to hop from file to file by display-selection or by typed-in file-name designations. The system's creators believed that the symbols one works with are supposed to represent a mapping of one's associated concepts, and further that one's concepts exist in a network of relationships as opposed to the essentially linear form of actual printed records. Accordingly, the concept-manipulation aids derivable from real-time computer support were enhanced by structuring conventions that made explicit the various types of **network** relationships among **concepts**.

concept network

In the late 1960s the **Hypertext Editing System** was developed on a mainframe computer. At the time the normal technology for editing on mainframes was batch cards. The Hypertext Editing System supported branching text and automatically arranged branches into menus. Authors could specify which branches to follow when printing was to occur.

Hypertext Editing System

The Hypertext Editing System failed in the **marketplace**. In 1968 the Hypertext Editing System was demonstrated to staff at two major **publishing corporations**, whose staff felt, however, that the Hypertext Editing System was too complex. The idea of sitting behind a computer terminal and authoring and editing was more than the managers at that time were willing to believe (Dam, 1988).

marketplace

2.1.2 The 1970s

The microtext history of the 1970s was marked by the continued development of ideas that were first implemented in the Augmentation System of the 1960s. Major advances corresponded to the availability of more sophisticated **hardware,** such as rapid, touch-screen terminals. Commercial success remained, however, limited.

extending the 1960s

development stimulated by rapid response terminals

One system, called **ZOG** (for no obvious reason) and developed at Carnegie-Mellon University in 1972, allowed users to interact with programs through a menu-selection interface (Akscyn *et al.*, 1988). The slow-response terminals were, however, inadequate for comfortable use. The availability of rapid-response, touch-screen terminals in the mid-1970s renewed the interest of the developers, and several versions of the system were developed in the late 1970s.

FRESS

The File Retrieval and Editing System (**FRESS**) was implemented in the early 1970s (Dam, 1988). Outline and cross-reference files could be viewed and edited. **Editing** of the outline file (or cross-reference file) would cause the document file to change appropriately. Likewise, editing the document file would change the outline file (or cross-reference file). Every edit was saved in such a way that an undo command could be executed at any time to undo the effect of the edit. In applications of FRESS, the users could follow outlines and cross-references easily, but had difficulty amending the outline or cross-references.

Dynabook

Also in the 1970s the **Dynabook** was developed to support reading and writing of text. Most of the interface was manipulated by pointing at the screen, rather than by typing. By selecting an icon on the screen, the reader could change the level of detail. Furthermore, the author could connect any section of the text to an icon and specify what actions should take place after the reader had selected that icon. In one Dynabook display the current page was displayed in the context of the links which that page had to other pages. On the left of the page was a filmstrip of all the pages from which one could have come, and on the right was a filmstrip of all the places to which one could go. Selecting any of these miniature icons took one to the page represented by the icon. Despite its many features, the Dynabook was difficult to use.

hypertext visionary

The term hypertext was actually coined by Ted Nelson in the 1970s. His visionary ideas ranged through such diverse topics as stores into which people stopped to get information and Stretchtext which one could fold or unfold. **Nelson** published books that were structured as small blocks of text with many links to other blocks of text (Nelson, 1987). Some of the issues which he raised are still topics of research today.

2.2 Principles

database, interface, and semantic network

Microtext may be represented as a database of **text** and **links**. A microtext system supports, via a graphical interface, the creating and accessing of the database. The links and text blocks constitute a special kind of semantic network, while the user perception of the system functionality is determined by the interface.

2.2.1 Database

object-oriented versus relational

A natural representation for hypertext uses nodes, links, and attributes. This representation is particularly well-suited for graphics. The node, link, and attribute model is part of the **object-oriented** approach to databases. However, most work on databases has been done for numeric information which is conveniently stored in tables with columns of fixed width. This popular tabular, or **relational**, database model can be adapted for hypertext.

2.2.1.1 Object-oriented database

An object-oriented design for microtext well suits the character of microtext (Campbell and Goodman, 1988) and uses basically three objects, nodes, links, and attributes:

- A **node** contains arbitrary data, including text or images.
- A **link** defines a relationship between two nodes.
- **Attributes** can be attached to nodes or links. An attribute could include the name of the creator of the node or link to which the attribute is connected or could include a complex procedure which is executed under certain conditions.

components

The basic operations on an object-oriented database include create, destroy, change, and get. These operations all act on the data whether it be an object, a link, or an attribute. The **create** operation creates new data; the **destroy** operation removes data; the **change** operation modifies data; and the **get** operation retrieves data.

basic operations

What basic unit of the document—**word**, **sentence**, **paragraph**, or **section**—is most appropriately displayed to a reader? A reader is unlikely to want to see only one sentence, and the linking of a document would be excessively tedious, if it had to go at the sentence level. But a paragraph intuitively seems to be the right size for presentation in a window and for linking.

paragraph as basic unit

The **granularity** of data affects its utility. If only a large file can be changed, then costs of moving and updating the file are substantial. When one knows in advance the size of object which is most likely to be needed for access and change, then one should try to have the system operate with objects of that size.

granularity

Since the properties of objects may get augmented as work with a system continues, representations should be **extensible**. Traditional database management systems solve some of the problems of extensibility and granularity but not at the right level of abstraction. For instance, the operations which one wants to perform on paragraphs may change as a document is elaborated, and the definition of the paragraph object should permit such changes.

extensibility

2.2.1.2 Relational database

A relational database stores the network of hypertext in relations or **tables**. For instance, a network of nodes and links may be represented in a table with two columns, where two nodes are in one row of the table when they are connected by a link. Typically, these columns have a fixed width or, in other words, store a certain limited amount of information. Graphics and text blocks do not naturally fit into the tabular form.

constraint of column width

Text blocks may be stored in a relational scheme which contains three columns for a **Unique Identifier**, the **Text**, and **Sequence Numbers**. Text may be

text relation

UI	Text	SN
1	Text blocks were stored in a relational scheme which	1
1	contained three columns labeled UI, Text, and SN.	2
1	Text was defined as a field of width	3

Figure 2.2 Text in relational database form. UI is short for Unique Identifier; SN is short for Sequence Number.

defined as an 80-character alphanumeric field (see Fig. 2.2). The text in a given text block may be displayed by sorting all text fields with the same unique identifier by sequence number.

graphics

Some graphics may be described as alphanumeric sequences (Gehani, 1986). For instance, a picture with two ellipses connected by an arrow might be described as 'ellipse1, ellipse2; arrow from ellipse1 to ellipse2'. Such an object-oriented **graphic** may be treated as a paragraph, and each line describing the graphic becomes a row in the paragraph table with the appropriate sequence number and unique identifier. If the graphic must be described by a **bit-image**, then storing it directly in a relational database is impractical. Instead, the bit-image is stored in a file, and the relational database includes a pointer to that file.

network in relational form

The network of microtext may be viewed in the **relational form**. For instance, if the nodes of the network contain terms but point to paragraphs, then the following two relations might be used:

- **Network** (term$_1$, term$_2$), means that term$_1$ is connected to term$_2$.
- **Point** (term, Unique Identifier), means that the text paragraph identified by Unique Identifier is to be associated with the term.

Through a combined view of these two relations, a user could follow a network term to the text about that term.

2.2.1.3 Attributed graph

definition of attributed graph

The links within a document may be represented as the edges of a graph. An attributed graph associates with each **node** or **link** of the graph an arbitrary number of **attribute/value pairs**. For example, an attribute type might be 'text block', and the value of the 'text-block' attribute might be a paragraph. The logical structure of microtext may be viewed as an attributed graph.

nodes and text blocks

Two blocks of text connected by a link may be represented as two nodes with an attribute of **text block** and a link between the nodes. In the presentation of a text block on the screen, the link will be indicated by a highlighted term or symbol within the text block (see Fig. 2.3). Internally, the system must know a **label** for the target but externally it just shows the entire text block rather than its label.

buttons

In the screen presentation the labels for links are often called **buttons**. This name originates from the convention of activating the link by guiding the mouse to the label and then pushing on the button on the mouse. The screen presentation, the way the text is actually stored internally, and ways of logically

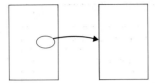

Figure 2.3 Nodes and text blocks. A node is 'embedded' within a block of text and its target node is invisible.

viewing the structure may all be different. In Fig. 2.4 the screen shows a text block with labeled links. Internally the text is a flat file with markup commands (see Exercise 2.1). In one logical view text fragments are the leaves of a tree whose branches are the labeled links. While the screen presentation does not give an explicit name to the text block itself, such a name exists and in the figure is label 0.

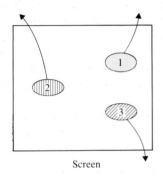

Screen

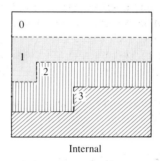

Internal

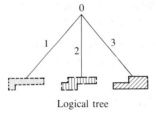

Logical tree

Figure 2.4 Buttons. The screen presentation on the left corresponds to the internal representation as a marked-up text on the right. An alternative logical representation of the marked-up text is as a tree where the leaves are fragments of text.

2.2.2 Interface

The interface is critical to the success of a microtext system. The interface should be easy to use, but there are no well understood methods for creating such interfaces. Particular guidelines have been developed for browsing and writing in a microtext context.

easy to use

2.2.2.1 Human-computer interaction

Semantic and syntactic models of user interaction and interface design exist. Since **semantic knowledge** about computer concepts has a logical structure, this knowledge is expected to be relatively stable in memory. When using a computer system, users must maintain a profusion of **syntactic knowledge**. Syntactic details include the knowledge of which key erases a character (delete, backspace, ctrl-h, right-most mouse button, or ESCAPE), and what command

semantic and syntactic models

inserts a new line in a text editor. Such syntactic knowledge may be arbitrary, system dependent, and ill structured and, unless regularly used, may fade from memory.

interaction styles

Four of the popular interaction styles involve menu selection, command language, natural language, and direct manipulation:

- **Command language** is flexible but requires substantial training.
- **Menu selection** shortens learning and structures decision-making but may slow frequent users.
- **Natural language** relieves the burden of learning syntax but requires clarification dialog (see Exercise 2.4).
- **Direct manipulation** visually represents task concepts and may be easy to learn.

While menu selection systems are attractive because they can eliminate training and memorization of complex command sequences, direct manipulation seems to be the best alternative for a wide variety of users (Shneiderman, 1986). By the use of direct manipulation rather than command language a novice may begin using a system immediately. Direct manipulation eliminates the possibility of errors from incorrectly typed commands.

diversity of users

Designers should recognize the diversity of interaction styles. **Novice** users have no syntactic knowledge and little semantic knowledge of computer issues. For them, the system should have few options. **Expert** users demand rapid response and great flexibility. Designing for one class of users is easy; designing for several is much more difficult.

diversity over time

Research on information display design has repeatedly shown the need to model dynamically the human cognitive processes that occur when the information is being displayed. Factors positively affecting acceptance at one point in the interaction may have negative effects at other points (Normore, 1984). In a **dynamic system**, the information available to the user at any one time preserves the context of interest to the user, rather than forcing some static display on all situations (Mitchell and Miller, 1986).

speed

User interface experiments of more than a decade past showed that as the **response time** of the computer improved from 20 seconds to 0.1 second, the user satisfaction increased. At that time, faster response times were not feasible, but the hypothesis was that yet faster response would be better. However, the somewhat unexpected result now indicates that response time can be too fast. Users generally prefer response times of about **0.1 second**; response times of less than this can cause confusion because screen changes may be difficult to perceive (Shneiderman and Kearsley, 1989). Unfortunately, the common problem is not that the response time is less than 0.1 second, but rather it cannot be made that short. No matter how elegant the system, if the response time is slow, the system will not be acceptable to users.

2.2.2.2 Browser interface

definition of browsing

Browsers may have no clear indication of the type of information that they want. **Browsing** may be defined as 'the art of not knowing what you want until you find it' (Cove and Walsh, 1988). There are different types of browsing depending on whether the user has many unrestricted options or not. Success in the less restricted type of browsing depends in some ways on serendipity, or luck.

The layout of a hypertext screen should draw attention to important pieces **link standards** of subject matter (information content), as well as the links (structure information). A bold word should not indicate a button at some times but simply indicate an important term at other times. Links always take the reader somewhere else, but do so for different reasons. Each **link type** should have a distinct and **standard style** (Hardman, 1988). For instance, a button that takes the user to the beginning of the document might consistently be represented with a picture of a house, while a button that takes the reader to the next page, might be represented with an arrow pointing to the right.

With electronic media, it is not automatically apparent how much **hierarchical view** information is available, how it is structured, and where the reader currently is. In a **hierarchical view**, the reader gets to see a high-level, tree-structured index in one window, and by pointing at an item the user can view the contents of that document in another window. The stability of the text and the simple cognitive model make the hierarchical view attractive (Shneiderman and Kearsley, 1989).

The concept of the fisheye view is based upon the analogy to a fisheye camera **fisheye view** lens, which distorts the image so that the nearest objects are seen in detail and distant objects are compressed (see Fig. 2.5). In the context of a document, a **fisheye view** shows full details of the immediate location and outlines of other parts of the document (see Exercise 2.5). Although the fisheye approach solves some problems, it can be disconcerting. As the user moves the focus of attention,

Figure 2.5 Fisheye view. This photo of a corner of a building was taken with a fisheye lens and from the curb of the street. The windows which are close to the corner are much larger than the ones a few removed from the corner.

the screen changes drastically, and the user must reorient. In one approach to the microtext interface two hierarchical views are presented and provide a kind of fisheye view. The reader sees a page of text and next to that page a hierarchy for the top level of the document and the hierarchy around the current page (Nielsen, 1990a).

travel metaphor

Text menus or semantic graphs may be inadequate metaphors for browsing. To provide the kinesthetic or tangible feel which people appreciate on paper or in person–person interactions one might exploit space and time metaphors (Dillon *et al.*, 1990). For instance, a guided tour across a town with the help of a map and a tour company suggests the **travel metaphor**. In an interface that exploits the travel metaphor, guided **tours** are initiated when the user selects a coach icon labeled with the topic of the tour (see Fig. 2.6). The user is then guided round a sequence of frames on the topic until the tour ends, at which point the starting point is again reached. In experiments contrasting hypertext interfaces with and without travel metaphors, users of bare hypertext thought they saw the most material, but in fact they saw the least (Allinson and Hammond, 1989). Guided tours allowed more accurate overviews of the available material and resulted in a higher rate of exposure to new, rather than repeated, information. Furthermore, a range of access tools was used with no apparent cost in terms of user indecision.

spaghetti versus museum layout

In one experience a massive semantic net was first presented as a graph. The editing/browsing interface soon became too cluttered and tangled (like a bowl of spaghetti) to be useful (see Fig. 2.7). To avoid the **spaghetti layout**, local instead of global placement of nodes was attempted, but that did not help. Accordingly, the interface was improved to include a 'spatial museum room' editor that maps frames metaphorically into floorplans of rooms (Travers, 1989). In a **museum layout** system a reader may select a point on a map to reveal enlarged detail in the neighborhood of that point (see Exercise 2.6). For an actual museum this is done by using a diagram of a museum with various subjects in each part, such as art, science, geography and media. The user looks

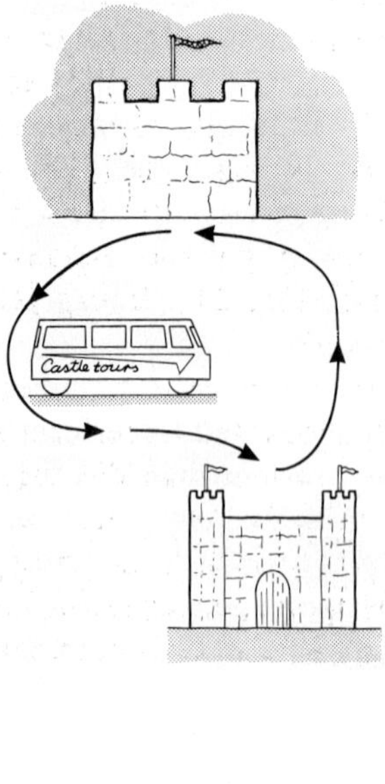

Figure 2.6 Travel metaphor. When the user selects the bus labeled 'Castle Tours', the user is taken to text blocks about castles.

Figure 2.7 Spaghetti and museum. Plate of spaghetti on left, and museum floor plan on right. The plate of spaghetti suggests the disorder that can be perceived when dealing with hypertext whose network looks like spaghetti. The museum layout suggests the orderliness and understandability that might derive from a network view projected as a museum layout.

at the map and has to move to the relevant place using commands, such as forward, left and right. The user then sees a picture relating to the topic of interest and can select further information by using a mouse on the picture itself. Subsequently, menus may be displayed.

2.2.2.3 Usability

One would like to be able to say that a certain interface style is best for a certain class of **users** and **tasks**. Many papers have been written about the user response to various presentations of hypertext on various tasks. As one surveys these papers, the question continually arises of 'what can be said in the general case?'

relating task, user, and interface

One researcher compared the results of 30 studies on microtext (Nielsen, 1989). For each study the performance of a control group was compared to a test group. In most cases the difference between the test and control group was slight, but in one case the difference was an order of magnitude. This enormous effect was due to age: when the test group was young, its members found hypertext very attractive, whereas when the test group was middle-aged, its members were disinclined to use microtext (see Fig. 2.8). **Young people** will accept hypertext more readily than will old people.

positive effect of youth

The other most significant factor in the survey of microtext studies was the **motivation** of the user. Users who were highly motivated to perform a certain task interacted much more with the hypertext system than did those whose motivation was less. While this result seems intuitively clear, it has not received enough attention. Microtext system characteristics, such as screen size or pointing device, have a relatively insignificant impact on user satisfaction when compared to the impact of user characteristics, such as age and motivation.

user characteristics are most important

Figure 2.8 Youth like microtext. In one survey of microtext results, the age of the user had most impact on user satisfaction.

2.2.2.4 Interface hardware

screens

The variety of display terminals on microcomputers presents a dilemma to the designer of microtext. The type of display chosen constrains the graphics and screen formats. Screen resolution might range from 200×200 pixels to 1200×1000 pixels, and colors may range from monochrome to 16 million shades.

input modes

There are four ways to enter information into a computer system: **typing**, **direct manipulation**, **scanning**, and **voice recognition** (Shneiderman and Kearsley, 1989). The keyboard allows input of about 100 words per minute but is error-prone. Direct manipulation does not accommodate data entry. Relatively inexpensive scanners for personal computers can translate a page of printed text or an illustration into a computer file. A computer can reliably recognize about 1000 spoken phrases from an individual, but the general capability to recognize discourse does not exist. For short, text-oriented documents, typing is the most common input method.

2.2.3 Imagery

visual formalisms

This book focuses on the links of hypertext from a semantic or abstract perspective. Yet, much of the attractiveness of hypertext is based on its visual appeal. Can one deal with this **visual** aspect in a semantic or **abstract** way?

2.2.3.1 Role of images

icons

Icons are visual symbols for entities or actions. Icons can be used to represent information powerfully. For instance, an icon of a gray cloud could be used on

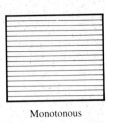

World   Discordant   Monotonous

Figure 2.9 Role of images (Price, 1988).

a weather map and be linked to a description of the rain forecast. The opportunity to link part of an image to an elaboration of that part is attractive. For instance, a town on a map may be linked to the enlarged map of that town. In a neuroanatomy tutorial this feature may allow the reader to navigate through the different levels of the brain (Hardman, 1988).

types of images

The role of **imagery** in hypertext is major but unclear. Should text live in a separate box or should text and imagery be together—for instance, a description of the world could be found inside the picture of the world (see Fig. 2.9)? If one can navigate freely among different kinds of images, then how restricted will one feel to see only line drawings? What is a discordant or monotonous image?

diagrams versus text

A consistent role for images in human communication is sometimes difficult to determine. When asked to place instructions on paper for someone crossing town from one landmark to another, most people write **text** and do not use **diagrams**. Yet, when asked, hypothetically, whether they would include a diagram if giving such information, most say yes. Furthermore, when asked how they would like to be given such information, people say they would like a diagram (Wright and Lickorish, 1989).

graphics extend memory

Human **memory** can be viewed as consisting of three types: **long-term memory**, **short-term memory**, and **external memory** (Simon and Newell, 1972). The external memory may come in the form of a computer graphics screen. Psychological research suggests that individual differences in cognitive style significantly affect the way in which a graphics screen can help a problem solver. Subjects who score high on certain psychological tests are called analytics and are good at imposing structure on a problem. Those who get a low score on this psychological test tend to rely more on intuition. In one set of experiments, short-term memory limitations prevented analytics from solving a problem that non-analytics could solve. With a graphics screen to augment their short-term memory capacities, the analytics solve the problem more quickly than non-analytics (Pracht, 1986).

2.2.3.2 Visual formalisms

Visual formalisms are visual because they may be generated and comprehended by humans, but formal because they may be manipulated and analyzed by computer. Two of the better known visual formalisms are graphs and Venn diagrams. **Hypergraphs** extend graphs so that links are no longer necessarily

hypergraphs and Venn diagrams

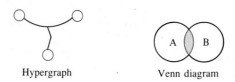

Hypergraph

Venn diagram

Figure 2.10 The hypergraph shows three nodes connected by one edge. The Venn diagram represents two sets, A and B, which have an intersection represented by the shaded region.

binary—a link may connect several nodes. **Venn diagrams** appeal to the principle that closed curves, such as a circle or blob, may partition the plane into inside and outside regions (see Fig. 2.10). A set may be represented by the inside of a closed curve. Thus while graphs may be interpreted so as to represent arbitrary links, Venn diagrams are good for representing sets and relations. In numerous computer-related applications both capabilities are needed.

higraphs

  Higraphs combine the characteristics of hypergraphs and Venn diagrams (Harel, 1988). Every set of interest is represented by a blob—these give the Venn diagram characteristic. A hypergraph characteristic is obtained by allowing links to connect any number of blobs. In this way, the hierarchies which are important in human cognition can be visually captured by nested blobs, while the flexibility of hypergraphs is kept (see Exercise 2.7). **Zoom out** capabilities suppress low-level details by removing blobs that are contained within other blobs and are useful for capturing abstraction in the hierarchy. A link to a blob within a blob is replaced by a link to a short bar when 'zoom out' occurs (see Fig. 2.11). Psychological experiments suggest that a higraph-like visual formalism is useful (Green, 1982), and microtext systems are being developed whose visual presentation is based on the higraph formalism.

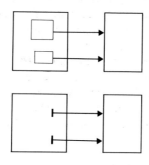

Figure 2.11 The higraph formalism shows hierarchies by including one blob within another. Zooming-out from the large blob (upper left) leads to another higraph in which the smaller blobs within the large blob are replaced by small vertical bars (lower left).

2.2.4 Conceptual model

representing the mind

How can the **conceptual model** of hypertext be related to the computer model? When what people have in their mind is elicited and compared to various computer representations for hypertext, the semantic net representation often proves particularly convenient (Jonassen, 1990). As one might expect, different semantic net types are appropriate for different tasks (Stanton and Stammers, 1990). By looking at paths through a hypertext semantic net, one can come to higher-level abstractions, such as those of plots in a novel.

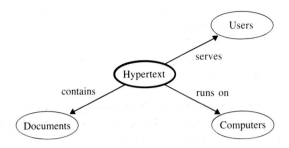

Figure 2.12 Semantic net example.

2.2.4.1 Semantic net

The abstraction of a document as a network of concepts and relations is a   intuitive meaning
semantic net. In a semantic network, concepts are defined by their relationships
to other concepts in the network. For example, the meaning of 'hypertext' may
be defined by saying that it contains documents, runs on computers, and serves
users. The link types in this example are 'contains', 'runs on', and 'serves'. The
nodes are 'hypertext', 'documents', 'computers', and 'users'. Semantic nets are
a **model of memory**. They lend themselves to graphic display, and their meaning
tends to be **intuitively clear** (see Fig. 2.12). The disadvantage of semantic nets is
that the meaning or semantics of the net may be difficult to formalize.

The best understood semantic net link types manifest **inheritance properties**.   formal meaning
For instance, if the network connects the node 'student' to the node 'person'
with the link 'is a', then one can infer that the properties of a student can be
inherited from those of a person. Inheritance is a type of **transitivity**. If a student
is a person and a person is an animal, then by transitivity, a student is an animal.
Transitivity also applies to the 'cause' link. For instance, if viruses cause
infection and infections cause fever, then viruses cause fever.

The semantic net of microtext may be **independent** or **embedded**. In the   independent versus
'independent' case the nodes and links are tagged with concepts represented by   embedded
terms (Collier, 1987). Each node of the net points to text blocks, but the links
between nodes can be seen without necessarily seeing the text blocks. In the
'embedded' case a document chunk is at the end of a link (see Fig. 2.13). In

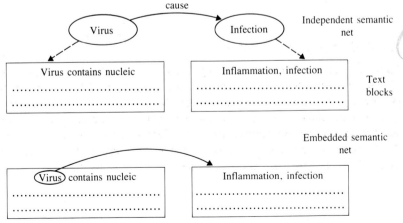

Figure 2.13 Independent versus embedded semantic net. Top: sketch of semantic net a level above the document itself. Bottom: sketch of semantic net embedded within the document.

traversing an embedded semantic net microtext, the user has to visit a text block (see Exercise 2.2).

2.2.4.2 Link taxonomy experiment

experimental method

What kinds of links do microtext authors tend to create? By analyzing microtext, one could collect **data** about the links created. The **link types** in one microtext **experiment** are reported here. In a document creation exercise a class of students was divided into four teams and asked to write a four-part hypertext. The students used a tool with which each text block may contain nodes which link to other text blocks. The students spent two months on the writing exercise and repeatedly revised their hypertext.

outline links

One particularly interesting text block created by the students is duplicated in Fig. 2.14. The text block depicted a tree of six nodes. This tree had labels on the edges. For instance, the node 'Evaluation' is connected by the 'has' relation to the node 'Advantages'. Activation of a topic in the tree would take the reader to the beginning of the subsection about the topic. The **nodes** of the **tree** which the readers directly see actually correspond functionally to links in the hypertext from the text block to another text block.

link types

The collection of links the students created can be classified into a handful of types: sequence, outline, reference, and embedded.

- A **sequence** link shows a linearity between two text blocks x and y—it means that text block x is sequentially or linearly followed by text block y.
- An **outline** link goes from an outline to the beginning of the section which elaborates on that portion of the outline. The link is itself part of an outline on a single text block which shows the reader the hierarchical structure of the document. The outline is indicated by a tree in which the hypertext links are the nodes of the tree. The edges of the tree constitute a type of metalink, although these edges do not cause any change on the screen when the reader points the mouse at them.
- A **reference** or citation link goes from a point in text block x where an author's work is discussed to the text block y where that author's citation is detailed.

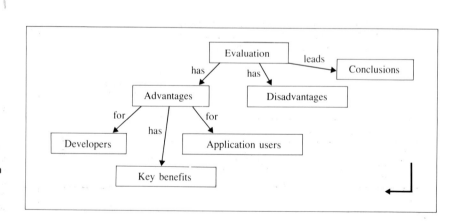

Figure 2.14 Outline links. A card that began a section on 'The Evaluation of HyperCard' contained this outline.

- An **embedded** or cross-reference link is in the text of a text block and takes the reader from a concept in the text block to another text block which has information related to that concept.

For every link there can be its **inverse** ($link^{-1}$). For instance, an $outline^{-1}$ link goes from a text block to the conceptually nearest broader outline link. A tally of the link types in this experiment showed an emphasis on embedded links and $outline^{-1}$ links (Rada, 1989a).

The embedded link might be expected to be comparable to a **non-hierarchical relation** which explores a new, but related, topic. A non-hierarchical link would go from a concept in one text block to a text block which was about a different concept, but that was non-hierarchically related, as for instance in going from the concept 'infections' to a text block about viruses (where viruses cause infections). An embedded link of the hierarchical type would take the reader to a text block which goes into more detail on the topic from which the link started. One might expect that most of the **embedded links** would be of the non-hierarchical type, since the outline links depict hierarchical relations. Surprisingly, however, in this study all the embedded links conveyed a **hierarchical**, rather than a non-hierarchical relation.

Furthermore, the embedded links had two distinct hierarchical flavors. Some buttons pointed to a straightforward elaboration of the concept as it was represented in the button. For instance, the button 'windows' on one text block connected to a text block which described what windows are and that description of windows could have fit into many different contexts where windows were of interest. The other type of embedded button pointed to an elaboration of the concept in the button that was heavily biased by the context in which the button occurred. For example, on one text block there was a discussion about semantic nets which contained a button for 'graphical representation' (see Fig. 2.15). The path to this text block came from a text

embedded hierarchical links

context dependency

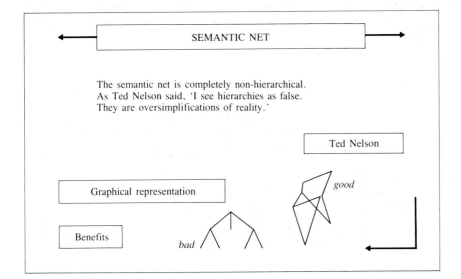

Figure 2.15 Context-sensitive hierarchical button. The 'graphical representation' button led to a very specific discussion of the graphics of semantic nets, rather than to a more general description of graphical representations.

block about a particular hypertext product. The 'graphical representation' button linked to a text block which was not about graphics in general, but was very particularly about semantic nets graphically represented in that specific hypertext product. Thus two types of embedded links were used: **context-independent** hierarchical and **context-sensitive** hierarchical.

individual differences of authors

Do authors prefer to use context-sensitive or context-independent embedded buttons? While a little more than half the embedded buttons were of the context-sensitive type, closer inspection showed a **surprising distribution** of button types by authors. About 90 per cent of the embedded buttons written by one group were of the context-sensitive type, while about 80 per cent of the buttons created by another group were of the context-independent type. This seemed to reflect the different **preferences** of the groups of authors, rather than a different intrinsic character of the topics which the groups addressed (Rada, 1989a). In other words, certain authors had a tendency to use context-independent embedded buttons and others to use context-sensitive embedded buttons.

2.2.4.3 Plots

whole network versus individual link

While the link between two text blocks in a microtext should be understood, the significance of a **whole network** must also be considered. If the reader does not appreciate why **multiple paths** between two nodes exist, he or she feels lost. What studies are relevant to the understanding of entire networks of text blocks? Plots of stories provide one well-studied abstraction about the whole network within a document (Meehan, 1981). Fiction writers have for centuries appreciated the importance of allowing the reader to see a meaningful multiplicity of paths in a story.

exploratory model

Laurence Sterne's 18th century *Tristram Shandy* shows many alterations in the narrative flow and provides a rich network of plots (Sterne, 1912). However, for authors less skilled than Sterne, a complex network of linear text may be obscure to the reader and places a heavy burden on the reader to form a conceptual model of the network. An abstract example of alternating narrative is the novel with many subplots that might look something like:

ABACADBACEBAD EACEFAFAB ...

where 'A' is the 'main' plot and B–F are subplots. The link may be common characters or settings. This type of implicit network creates an **exploratory** text. The difficulty with this style of presentation is that the reader may be repeatedly asking himself 'what is the author trying to say here?'.

developmental model

The alternative to the exploratory model is the **developmental model**. This differs from the exploratory model in how the links are built and traversed (Howell, 1990). The developmental model adds directional chains of links, or **storylines**. Essentially, these are links which are related in that from the beginning to the end of the chain a story is told and comes to closure. A storyline gives reader satisfaction at the end as well as motivation to read further along a different vein.

twists in fiction

When is the network within a story particularly exciting to read? An interesting story should provide a **twist** to one's normal expectations (see Exercise 2.3). When one reads **fiction**, one expects to suspend one's critical reality-based functions. Nevertheless, the story must take advantage of some model which is at least partially consistent with some real world. One key to success for a story is to lead the readers along the path of a model and at some point to help them appreciate that a path could be followed which they would never have expected.

For **non-fiction** the lessons which have been learned from the study of fiction *surprise in non-fiction* apply in many ways. An interesting non-fiction must still tell the reader something new—something which augments his model of the world. For non-fiction the role of surprise is less than in fiction. The author must lead the readers along the path of a pre-existing model but then help them appreciate that the path goes somewhere new. However, unlike the fiction case, the non-fiction case requires the new path to be consistent with all the constraints of the real world.

Both ? Good bridging point from book overview to systems.

2.3 Systems

Microtext systems can support creating and accessing microtext (Begoray, *authoring and* 1990). Some of the prominent microtext systems attempt to provide a modeless *browsing* interface, in which **authoring** and **browsing** are performed within the same screen, and minimal overhead is incurred in changing between authoring and browsing mode. Other systems are primarily available as browsing tools.

2.3.1 Writing systems

The number of microtext authoring systems is growing rapidly. Some of these *wide range of writing* systems sharply constrain the types of links that can be used, while others *systems* impose minimal constraints. In one, the windowing options are endless, while in another only one window can be on the screen at a time. KMS, NoteCards, HyperCard, and Intermedia are microtext systems that are particularly well known for their support of writing.

The microtext authoring systems have different features: *system philosophies*

- **KMS** encourages the use of hierarchical link types, and the screen presents two windows, as in an open book with two pages viewable.
- **NoteCards** and **HyperCard** allow any number of windows on the screen and any link types.

2.3.1.1 KMS

KMS, or Knowledge Management System, is a commercial microtext system *long history* which is a successor to the ZOG system developed at Carnegie Mellon University from 1972 to 1985 (Akscyn *et al.*, 1988). The 1972 version provided a menu-select interface to a few computer programs. A 1983 version was installed in a nuclear-powered aircraft carrier to support interactive management of complex tasks.

KMS is based on **frames**, where each frame is a unit of text and pointers to *methods* other frames (McCracken and Akscyn, 1984). The database consists of linked files each of which corresponds to a frame. While any kind of link can be used, KMS particularly supports **hierarchical links**. Users interact with the database by navigating from frame to frame, manipulating the contents of frames, and creating new frames. Tools also exist for inheriting characteristics from one frame to another and for importing material from other sources, such as text files, into frames.

frames

Each frame may have six different functional parts: frame title, frame name, frame body, tree buttons, command buttons, and annotation buttons (see Fig. 2.16). The **frame title** describes the frame topic. The frame name is a unique identifier for the frame, as a page number is a unique identifier for a page in a book. The frame body expands on the topic of the frame. **Tree buttons** link to frames at the next lower level of the hierarchy. **Command buttons** initiate actions, such as exiting KMS. **Annotation buttons** begin with an '@' and provide notes or cross-references. A frame may contain text and figures. The workstation screen is normally split into two windows, each of which shows a frame.

link types

The **source** for a KMS link is an individual item in a frame. The **destination** for a link is a whole frame. A frame is considered to be a small enough unit that the whole frame, rather than any part of it, can sensibly serve as the link destination (Akscyn *et al.*, 1988). In KMS there are two types of links: **tree** and **annotation**. Tree links point to lower-level frames in a hierarchy, such as a chapter of a book. Annotations point to peripheral material, such as comments. These two link types distinguish between structural relationships and purely

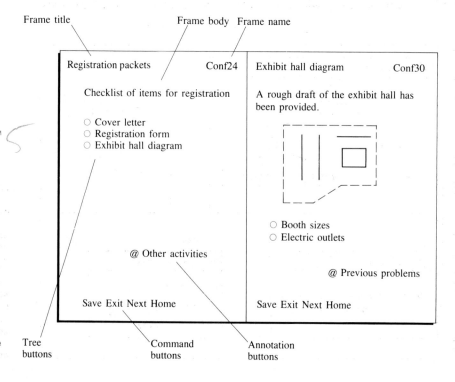

Figure 2.16 KMS screen. An illustration of a prototypical screen in KMS (Akscyn *et al.*, 1988). Tree buttons are preceded by a hollow circle, while annotation buttons are preceded by an '@' sign.

associative relationships. Links may be more than one line of text and allow the author to provide substantial semantic information about the link.

The KMS user interface is based on the **direct manipulation** paradigm. Users navigate from frame to frame by pointing the mouse cursor at an item linked to another frame and clicking the mouse button. Editing and browsing are done in the same mode. By exploiting contextual constraints, over 90 per cent of the user's interaction requires a single point-and-click. The average time per meaningful operation is less than it would be for pull-down menus.

ease of user interaction

In addition to specifying within a frame the children of that frame, KMS provides only one other view of the contents—a listing of the entire hierarchy of frame titles. There is no **graphical browser**. The outline of the database is not presented on the screen as a two-dimensional graph. In early versions of KMS graphical views were available, but studies showed that the graphical views were rarely used (Akscyn *et al.*, 1988).

no graphical views needed

2.3.1.2 NoteCards

Creating 'notes on cards' corresponds to the first stage in document writing. An early microtext technology was developed by Xerox Corporation to support writing notes. The product, called NoteCards, supports editing and browsing on an electronic generalization of the paper **notecard** (Trigg *et al.*, 1986).

electronic notecard

Every notecard can be displayed in a window and edited. It can contain text or graphics and is connected to other cards by links. In addition to the general notecard, **browser cards** and **filebox cards** may be used (see Fig. 2.17). A browser card contains a graph where the labels on nodes correspond to titles of

card types

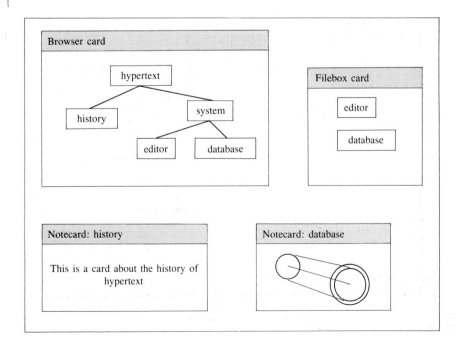

Figure 2.17 NoteCards screen. The largest box is the screen of the computer and encloses four notecards. The browser card shows the network of links among other notecards. Each boxed label within the browser card refers to a notecard. The two labeled boxes within the filebox card are also pointers to other notecards. The two notecards that do not contain labeled boxes are primitive notecards—one has text in it and the other has graphics.

notecards and links between nodes represent links between notecards. A browser card can be edited to change the structure or labeling of a network of notecards, or it can be used as a traversal guide. Selecting a title inside the browser card causes the corresponding notecard to appear in a window on the screen. **Filebox cards** can be used to categorize notecards. The NoteCards system requires the title of every notecard to occur in, at least, one filebox card.

Links are used to connect individual notecards. Each link has a label and connects a source card and a **destination card**. A link is anchored by an icon at a specific location in its source card but points to its destination card as a whole. Clicking the mouse in the link icon retrieves the destination card.

When a history graduate student wrote a term paper for one of his classes with NoteCards, he needed several hundred **notecards** and fifty **filebox cards** (Halasz, 1988). The student kept on his screen at all times a **browser card**, which contained an outline of the notecards. The experience of the student shows the importance of the browser and filebox cards as organizers of information.

NoteCards was designed to help people work with networks of ideas. It is first and foremost an authoring system for creating and modifying networks of cards which represent ideas. NoteCards' intended users are authors, researchers, and designers.

2.3.1.3 HyperCard

One of the most frequently used personal computer products is HyperCard. While Apple Computer Incorporated does not advertise HyperCard as a microtext system, it has several features of a microtext system. Since 1987 HyperCard has been delivered automatically with every new purchase of a **Macintosh** personal computer from Apple Corporation. HyperCard takes advantage of the user-friendly interface of the Macintosh and incorporates features of some of the successful authoring software on the Macintosh (Goodman, 1987). In 1989 IBM began marketing a software product called LinkWay which is very similar to HyperCard (Darby and Miller, 1990).

HyperCard presents information on cards and several cards may appear on the screen at one time (Kane, 1990). The **What You See Is What You Get** authoring tools, MacPaint and MacWrite, have been largely included within the HyperCard armamentarium and allow one to mix graphics and text freely in a card. Each card has a background which describes the kind of information which can appear in each part of the card. Cards are logically organized into **stacks**, and cards within a stack may, by default, have the same background. Icons or buttons may be inserted in a card to link the button to another card. A **link** between two cards in a stack is created by entering link mode, defining a button in the one card, and then pointing at the other card. Links from a card in one stack to a card in another stack are not easily created. The meaning of a link can be extended beyond 'goto that card' by adding a procedure to the description of the link (see Sec. 6.1.5, Expertext procedures).

HyperCard allows many people to experiment easily with visually powerful linking tools and to choose preferred methods of expression. For instance, authors commonly specify that in going from one card to another the reader

links

distribution of card types

networks of ideas

market penetration

cards

links

standard images

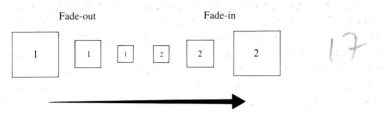

Fade-out   Fade-in

Figure 2.18 Fading. The card with a '1' in it is fading from the screen before the card with a '2' in it fades into the screen.

should see a fade-out from the source card and a fade-in to the destination card (see Fig. 2.18). The **visual effects** of fading to and from cards may constructively give the impression that one is going down a pathway to a final destination, which will have to be exited by the same route. One of the predefined **icons** in HyperCard is the 'question mark' icon. Popular usage of this icon has it point to information to help a confused user. HyperCard usage may suggest standards for the association of images with the meaning of links.

2.3.1.4 Intermedia

Intermedia was developed in the mid-1980s at Brown University **Institute for Research in Information and Scholarship**. Intermedia facilitates the creation of highly graphical microtext and complex filtering of text links (Yankelovich *et al.*, 1985). Intermedia was designed to work on personal computers more flexible than but similar to the **Macintosh**. Its development was sponsored by several industrial firms that could not agree on a fair way to market it until late 1989.

> history and goals

A document is created with Intermedia in a **direct manipulation** environment. Cutting and pasting can be done from one application to another. Links may be created between any two blocks. A block is defined as any material which the user selects within a document. One selection provides the source of a link and another selection determines the destination block. A **bi-directional link** is created which can then be followed in either direction by user choice. Intermedia supports the creation of graphics and animation. Keywords applied to links allow the user to attach one or more attributes to a link. Paths can also be defined as a sequence of links.

> links

The keywords on links can be used to filter searches. Only links with certain attributes will subsequently be viewable. **Views** can be generated at different levels including the document–document level, document–block, and block–block level. Since views can be generated dynamically, based on filtering criteria, one user can request different views of the same document in one sitting.

> views

2.3.2 Browsing systems

How should microtext be browsed? Several microtext browsing systems, the Augmentation System, Emacs-INFO, Guide, HyperTies, and Drexel Disk are described in this section. The Augmentation System demonstrates the basic features of a **hierarchical browser**. Emacs-INFO and Guide also emphasize the role of hierarchical relationships. HyperTies does not favor a constraint towards hierarchies—links may go from any node to any other node. The Drexel Disk emphasizes graphics in hierarchical browsing.

> hierarchies in browsing

2.3.2.1 Augmentation System

pioneering system

The Augmentation System was developed in the **1960s** and introduced many features of hypertext. Some of these features are still not generally available on commercial systems. The system emphasized the hierarchical structuring of text and a flexibility of viewing this structure.

AUGMENTATION SYSTEM BROWSING

hierarchy

The Augmentation System team adopted for several years the convention of organizing all information into explicit **hierarchical structures**, with provisions for arbitrary cross-referencing among the elements of a hierarchy. The principal manifestation of this hierarchical structure was the breaking of text into statements, each of which bore a number showing its serial location in the text and its level in an outline of the text. The paper which reports on the Augmentation System was written with this structure, and part of the manifestation of the approach was the use of labeled, indented sentences or paragraphs (Engelbart and English, 1968). Section 3 was called 'The User System', 3a was 'Basic Facility', and 3a1 was 'As seen by the user, the basic facility has the following characteristics' (see Fig. 2.19). By convention, the first word of a statement was treated as the name of the statement, if it was enclosed in parentheses. References to these names could be embedded anywhere in other statements. This naming and linking when added to the basic hierarchical structure yielded a flexible, general structuring capability.

selection

In browsing a document, the user could select the **start point** and the **form of view**. In work with paper the first operation is straightforward but the second often requires scissors and staples. In the Augmentation System the display start could be specified in several ways, for example:

- By direct selection of a statement which is on the display—pointing with the mouse accomplishes this.
- By selecting a marker to text elsewhere.

After identifying a statement by one of the above means, the user could request to be taken directly there for his next view. Alternatively, he could request instead that he be taken to some statement bearing a specified structural relationship to the one specifically identified.

view

The normal **view** was like a frame cut from a long scroll upon which the hierarchical set of statements was printed in sequential order. Otherwise, three independently variable, view-specification conditions could be applied to the construction of the displayed view: level clipping, line truncation, and content filtering.

Figure 2.19 Paper about Augmentation System. This hierarchical structure was explicit in papers produced by the Augmentation System team.

3. The User System.
   3a Basic Facility.
      3a1 As seen by the user, the basic facility has the following characteristics.

- **Level clipping** meant that given a specified level, the view generator would display only those statements whose depth was less than or equal to that level.
- The **line truncation** parameter meant that the view generator would show only the first T lines of each statement being displayed.
- Given a specification for desired content, the view generator could be directed to display only those statements that had the desired content. For example, one could ask for all statements that had the word 'memory' within five words of the word 'association'. This is **content filtering**.

The user could also freeze a collection of statements in the upper portion of the screen. The remaining lower portion was treated as a reduced-view scanning frame (see Fig. 2.20). Any screen-select operand for any command could be selected from any portion of the display.

RESULTS

What has the **user response** to the Augmentation System been? The system was a success in the eyes of those who created it (Engelbart and English, 1968):

user response

> We have found that in both off-line and on-line computer aids, the conception, stipulation, and execution of significant manipulations are made much easier by the structuring conventions. ... We have found it to be fairly universal that after an initial period of negative reaction in reading explicitly structured material, one comes to prefer it to material printed in the normal form.

On the other hand, users who had not helped build the Augmentation System proved less willing to learn the novel features of the interface. The technology on which the system depended was ahead of its time, but the average firm could not afford the high cost of an Augmentation System.

The commercial rights for the Augmentation System were transferred to a large corporation in the 1970s. In the current system, files are hierarchically structured, and graphics and text can be embedded in the same file. The screen may be divided into arbitrary, rectangular windows. Various selection and viewing facilities are supported. The hardware for the system is no longer particularly expensive, but the system is still not widely used and could be considered a **commercial failure** (Rosenthal, 1990).

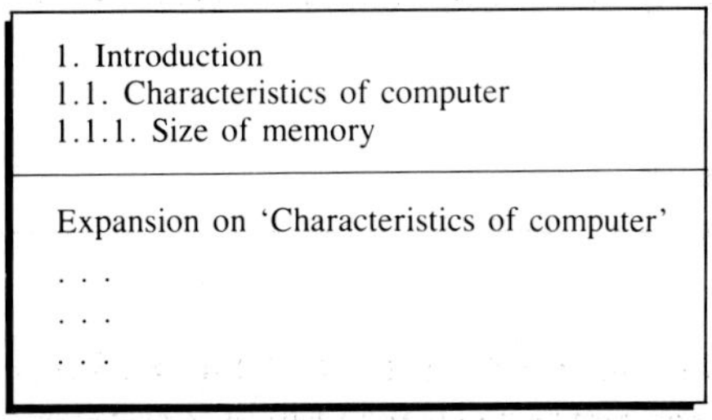

commercial failure

```
1. Introduction
1.1. Characteristics of computer
1.1.1. Size of memory

Expansion on 'Characteristics of computer'
. . .
. . .
. . .
```

Figure 2.20 This split screen view in the Augmentation System allowed the user to keep some information fixed while scrolling through other information. In this example, the user has selected the topic 1.1. from the upper half of the screen.

2.3.2.2 Emacs-INFO

on-line help system

Emacs is a powerful editing system which may be freely copied—it is **freeware**. Many people have contributed software to the Emacs system, and the system is heavily used in research facilities that run the UNIX operating system. One of the many interesting components of Emacs is its **on-line help** system, called Emacs-INFO (Stallman, 1981). The text for INFO is stored in nodes which also contain links to other nodes. The interface provides a simple set of commands (often issued by typing a single letter) to activate a link and retrieve another node.

links

In Emacs-INFO a link to text that is an expansion of a particular topic may be presented on a **menu**, which consists of a list of node names. When a menu item is selected, the INFO program searches for the required node and displays it. At the top of a node, call it node X, are labels that begin with either **Prev:**, **Next:**, or **Up:** (see Fig. 2.21). Following the colon is the title of another node. 'Prev:' points to a node meant to be sequentially previous to the node X. Conversely, 'Next:' points to the node sequentially following X. The 'Up:' label is followed by the name of the node that contains the menu entry for X. An option exists to jump to any node in the system by giving its node name. Additionally, the user may request via a 'previous-in-time' command to see the node last visited. If the user had been at node Y before going to node X, then activating the 'previous-in-time' option returns the user to node Y (see Exercise 2.8).

2.3.2.3 Guide

history begins 1982

Guide began as a research project at the University of Kent in Canterbury, England in 1982. In 1984, **Office Workstations Limited** implemented Guide as a commercial product (Brown, 1987). The commercial product is available for a wide range of personal computers. In one example of a Guide application an

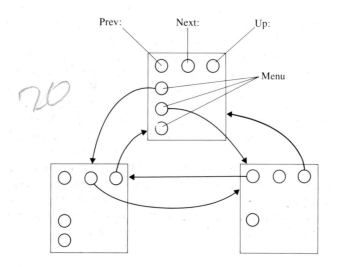

Figure 2.21 The Emacs-INFO structure is suggested by these three rectangles which represent nodes of text and links. The links are indicated by circles and arrows. The straight lines go from the name of a link type to the placement of that link in a node.

automobile company uses the system to distribute training manuals to dealerships. The research work at the University of Kent continues in parallel with the commercial development.

The developers of Guide have emphasized the **hierarchical structure** of a document and the possibility of folding and unfolding entries in the hierarchy or outline. In an unfolding event, the user selects a term in an outline and the text associated with that term replaces the term. Later, selection of the text causes folding, and the text is replaced by its associated outline term. The two principal buttons in Guide implement unfolding in different ways:

folding and unfolding

- **Replacement** buttons when selected with the mouse lead to an in-line replacement of the material linked with that button. The intent is that the replacement material will expand on material around the button.
- **Note** buttons are an extension of replacement buttons, but display the additional material to which the note button points in a separate window of a split screen.

Both buttons keep the original material surrounding the button on the screen after the button is activated, and in both cases selection of the new text causes that text to disappear from the screen (to fold into the document).

goto

The developers of Guide have reluctantly found it necessary to use a third type of button, called a reference button. **Reference** buttons cause a jump to a different point of the document or point to a new document. These buttons have a **goto** effect unlike that of the replacement and note buttons. These reference buttons may lead readers into corners and leave them disoriented. But the flexibility that reference buttons allow seems indispensable for some purposes.

Guide maintains a document in scrollable form. As the user moves the mouse over the screen, the shape of the cursor changes to indicate the type of link available at that point. A book called _Hypertext: Theory into Practice_ has been placed into Guide, and samples of screens from one chapter in that book are presented here (Baird and Percival, 1989). The first screen illustrates the use of the **note** button: when over the name 'Baird', the cursor is represented by an asterisk, and after depressing the mouse button, the user is shown a small box of text in the upper right of the screen (see Fig. 2.22). This small box provides some details about Baird and remains on the screen only so long as the button on the mouse is depressed. Upon scrolling into the document one next sees more of the outline of the chapter. When the mouse points to one of the bold headings in the outline, the cursor appears as a circle with an '×' in it. By depressing the mouse button, the user gets a **replacement** or an unfolding of the chapter so as to see more detail about the section whose heading was underneath the circled '×' (see Fig. 2.23). When the cursor rests over the unfolded text, the cursor's shape changes to that of a box (see Fig. 2.24), and selection of the button would fold the text and return the user to the situation before the unfold was initiated. Scrolling downward and sliding the mouse over the screen, the user next sees a cursor shaped like a right-pointing arrow. This indicates a **reference** or goto button (see Fig. 2.25). Activating the reference button over 'Table 1' leads to a new window with the full drawing of 'Table 1' in it (see Fig. 2.26).

example session

change to Rada book & give Rada book screendumps

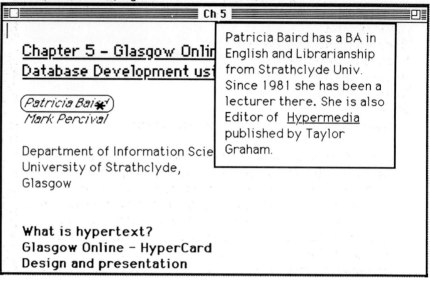

Figure 2.22 Guide note button.

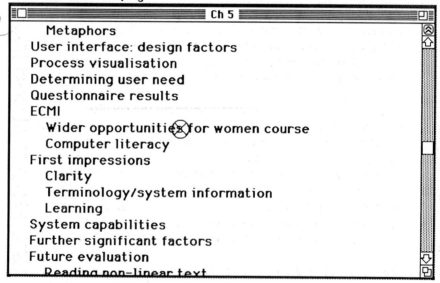

Figure 2.23 Unfold button.

2.3.2.4 HyperTies

The development of HyperTies began in 1983 at the University of Maryland. A commercial version is available from **Cognetics Corporation**. The first microtext to be published simultaneously in electronic and paper form was prepared in HyperTies. The microtext is called *Hypertext Hands-On* and was published in 1989 (Shneiderman and Kearsley, 1989).

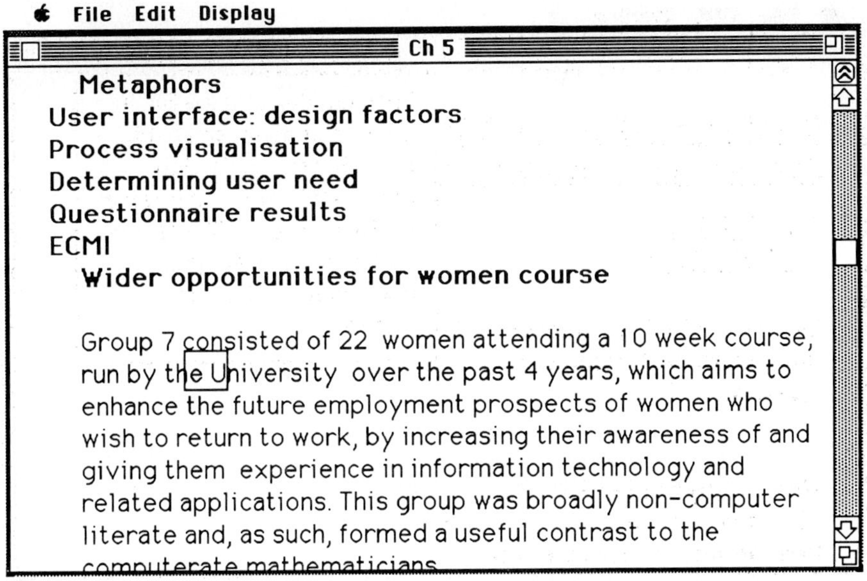

 File   Edit   Display

=== Ch 5 ===

   Metaphors
User interface: design factors
Process visualisation
Determining user need
Questionnaire results
ECMI
   Wider opportunities for women course

Group 7 consisted of 22 women attending a 10 week course,
run by the University over the past 4 years, which aims to
enhance the future employment prospects of women who
wish to return to work, by increasing their awareness of and
giving them experience in information technology and
related applications. This group was broadly non-computer
literate and, as such, formed a useful contrast to the
computerate mathematicians

Figure 2.24 Fold button.

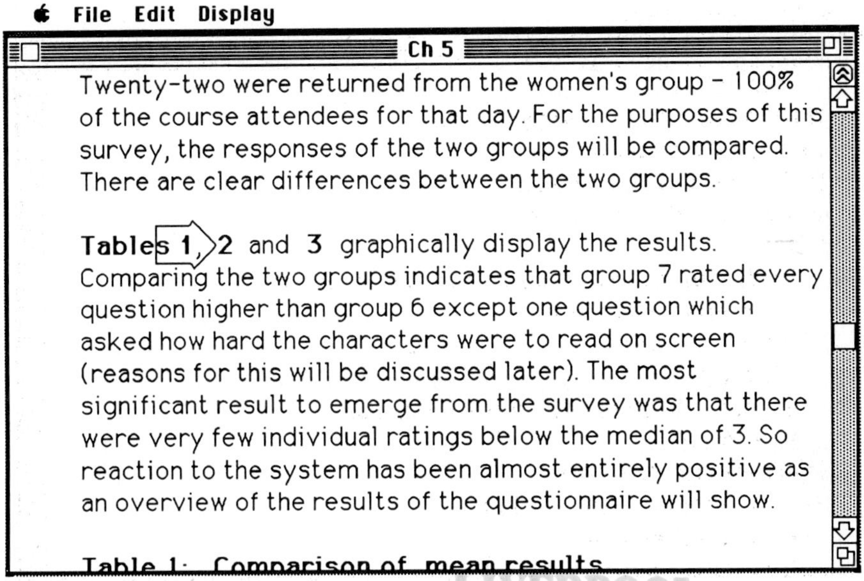

 File   Edit   Display

=== Ch 5 ===

Twenty-two were returned from the women's group – 100%
of the course attendees for that day. For the purposes of this
survey, the responses of the two groups will be compared.
There are clear differences between the two groups.

Tables 1, 2 and 3 graphically display the results.
Comparing the two groups indicates that group 7 rated every
question higher than group 6 except one question which
asked how hard the characters were to read on screen
(reasons for this will be discussed later). The most
significant result to emerge from the survey was that there
were very few individual ratings below the median of 3. So
reaction to the system has been almost entirely positive as
an overview of the results of the questionnaire will show.

Table 1: Comparison of mean results

Figure 2.25 Goto button.

The overall model of a HyperTies database is based on the metaphor of the   architecture
'electronic encyclopedia'. The database consists of a set of short **articles**, related
to one another by links, which are displayed as user-selectable highlighted
strings within the body of the article (Koved and Shneiderman, 1986). Each
article is divided into three fields: a title, a definition (which briefly describes the
article), and the body of the article. When a user selects a HyperTies link, the

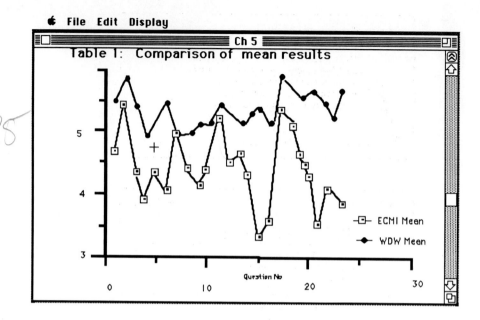

Figure 2.26 Result of following goto button.

destination article's title and short description are shown in a separate window. Confirming the selection causes the source article's display to be replaced by the destination article (see Fig. 2.27). An article about a topic may be one or more screens long. As users traverse articles, HyperTies keeps the path and allows reversal. Users can also select articles from an index.

arrow-jump keys

Readers may use arrow keys, touch-sensitive screens, or the mouse to move the cursor to highlighted strings. Several experimental studies have been conducted to test certain design alternatives with HyperTies. **Arrow-jump keys** allow the cursor to jump to the closest highlighted string in the direction pressed. In the study comparing the arrow-jump keys to the mouse, the arrow-jump keys proved to be an average of 15 per cent faster and preferred by almost 90 per cent of the subjects (Shneiderman and Morariu, 1986). The conjecture is made that when there are a small number of highlighted strings on the screen, arrow-jump keys can provide a good mechanism for selection.

general public needs

HyperTies has been implemented in diverse environments, but the experiences in a **museum application** best illustrate the special needs of the general public. The museum users often had no prior computer experience and had no obligation to use Hyperties. A surprisingly wide variety of ways to touch a screen were observed. Some users rubbed the screen, some touched with three fingers, some swished elegantly with a fingernail (Shneiderman et al., 1989). Since swishing elegantly with a fingernail did not initiate a response from the computer, the computer instructions or interface should be improved for the 'fingernail' user.

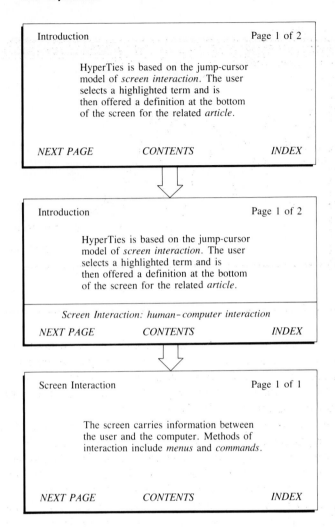

Figure 2.27 HyperTies example. In the top screen the italicized (highlighted) terms are 'screen interaction', 'article', 'NEXT PAGE', 'CONTENTS', and 'INDEX'. If the user selects 'screen interaction', then the next screen differs from the first only by the addition of a brief note near the bottom of the screen about 'screen interaction'. If the user now activates this brief note, then the next screen is the article with that term as its title.

2.3.2.5 Drexel Disk

Drexel University has for years required all entering freshmen to have access to a personal computer. One need created by this policy was that of introducing students to the capabilities of their computers. To this end the University created a **consulting service** of which the 'the Drexel Disk' was a part (Hewett, 1987). The Drexel Disk was distributed to all freshmen at Drexel University from 1984 to 1989.

history

One design goal of the Drexel Disk was to create landmarks to orient users. Another goal was to place the burden of communication and organization on the computer, rather than on the user. The menu structure was shallow and wide. Multiple paths to each point were provided. Graphics were extensively used to provide information about space and time. No documentation was given to the user, since the system was intended to be self-explanatory. The

design goals

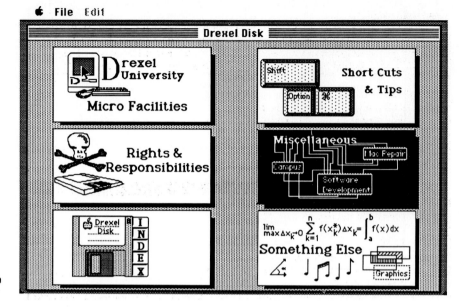

Figure 2.28 Early choice with the Drexel Disk.

design of the Drexel Disk followed good principles of **human–computer interaction**.

The Drexel Disk provides an attractive **interface**. In one example of someone using the Drexel Disk, the user first chooses the button called 'Miscellaneous' (see Fig. 2.28). Next the 'Campus' button is chosen and the user is taken to a map of the campus. If instead the 'Index' button had been chosen first, then the user could have reached the same map by activating the 'see Campus Buildings in Miscellaneous' button in the Index (see Fig. 2.29). Once in the map, the user sees the university with streets labeled and buildings numbered. When a building is selected, then the name of that building first appears in the lower window (see Fig. 2.30). After the mouse is clicked a second time over that building, further information about that building appears on the screen (see Fig. 2.31).

examples of Drexel Disk use

The Drexel Disk has been successfully used by students to obtain information about personal computer facilities at Drexel University. However, since the software was developed there and was not widely used elsewhere, Drexel remains responsible for any modifications to the software. Additionally, as with any such directory service, the directory information itself must be regularly updated. For instance, the hours of operation of the library may change, and the information in the hypertext about the library would also then need to be changed (see Fig. 2.31). Since **maintenance** of the Drexel Disk was expensive, the developers decided in 1989 to switch to a standard software system, namely **HyperCard**. Sophisticated users could then take advantage of the well-documented and popular features of HyperCard to implement updates to the information system themselves and propose that the updates become part of the next release of the directory. The university was also no longer responsible for the development of the system software because Apple Computer Incorporated

high maintenance costs prompt move to HyperCard

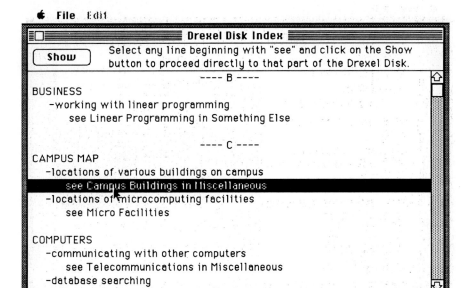

Figure 2.29 Drexel Disk index.

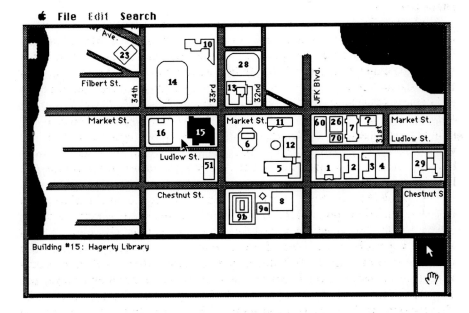

Figure 2.30 Drexel map.

continues the development work on HyperCard. In the academic year 1989–1990 all Freshmen at Drexel University were given the campus computer directory in a HyperCard environment (Hewett, 1990).

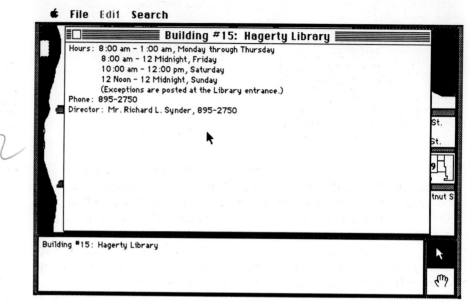

Figure 2.31 Details of one building.

2.3.3 Software engineering environments

documents

There are many documents in the **software life cycle** including requirements documents, design documents, software, and software documentation. Software is a special type of document because it must be read by both people and machines. The other documents of the software life cycle are written exclusively for people.

software engineers use computers and need links

People who work with software documents have access to and depend on **computers** in a way that other authors typically do not. Computer environments to support people in the development of documents in the software life cycle are called software engineering environments. Many interconnections exist among components, but these interconnections are hard to maintain in paper forms. Hypertext makes it practical to connect all the pieces.

2.3.3.1 Onion structure

onion structure

A typical structure for a software engineering environment is built around a layered system like an **onion**, where there are a number of layers of functionality provided by the different levels in the system. The model includes the following layers (see Fig. 2.32):

1. Operating system
2. Database system
3. Object management
4. Tools interface
5. User interface

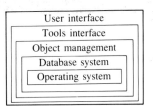
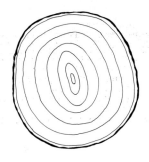

Figure 2.32 Onion structure. The layers of a software engineering environment are depicted on the left and a sketch of a real onion slice is shown on the right.

The operating system is the innermost layer in the computer system. The outermost layer is the user interface. While some software engineering environments use special-purpose operating systems tailored to software life cycle documents, the need for portability has meant that most systems depend on a standard **operating system** for the innermost layer. More particularly, the majority of software engineering environments have been built on top of the UNIX operating system. UNIX is widely available and has many functions that are well suited to managing the needs of software engineers.

operating system

The database layer provides a low-level model for all data. A **database management system** supports efficient storage and retrieval. Many people can simultaneously access or change the database without accidentally destroying data. The concerns of the database layer are not peculiar to the application of software engineering.

database system

The **object management** layer recognizes the entities of the software life cycle. Broadly, the object management layer allows software documents to be named, to exist in a number of different versions, and for relationships to be recorded between documents. Its ability to keep track of the links among document components is one of the most critical functions of the software engineering environment.

object management

The **tools interface** supports the tools which do specific things, such as retrieve the latest version of a document or create a new link between the software and the software documentation. The most integrated tools intimately exploit the abilities of the object management layer. A tool that is foreign to a particular software engineering environment was not built with that software engineering environment in mind. In order to work, this foreign tool must communicate directly with the operating system and the user interface.

tools interface

The final layer in the software engineering environment is the **user interface** layer. In an integrated system the tools communicate through the object management layer to the database and then to the operating system. It is equally important that the tools should be integrated at the user interface level, so that users are not faced with the daunting task of learning different tool interfaces. Each tool should have interface conventions which coincide with those of the other tools. For instance, if typing '?' brings help when one is trying to formulate a query to the retrieval tool, then typing '?' should also invoke help when one is trying to create a link with the authoring tool.

user interface

2.3.3.2 Object management

nodes, links, and
attributes

An object management system for software engineering environments may be based on **nodes** which store data and **links** which connect nodes (Bigelow, 1988). **Attributes** label the types of nodes and links. Furthermore, a link or node can have any number of attribute/value pairs. The attribute 'projectComponent' can have any value from the set of project components, namely, requirements, design, code, tests, or documentation. The attribute 'relatesTo' is applied to links and can have any value from the set {leadsTo, comments, refersTo, callsProcedure, followsFrom, implements, or isDefinedBy}. By example, a node with a projectComponent value of 'requirements' would have a 'relatesTo' value of 'implements' with the node whose 'projectComponent' value was 'code'. A node may contain any amount or type of information. A link is not restricted to pointing to an entire node but can point to any place within a node.

contexts define
workspaces

Contexts are defined by grouping nodes and links with certain values. For instance, nodes with the 'projectComponent' value of code are implicitly grouped into a context. Contexts allow the partitioning of a project and the definition of **workspace**. Local workspace allows the software engineer to abstract a subset of nodes and links from the project workspace, make local modifications, test these modifications against the rest of the project, and when satisfied merge the changes back into the global workspace. Ideally, the partitioning of workspaces between engineers should be disjoint, but in practice it may transpire that two or more are working on the same nodes concurrently. In order to allow this, the object management system must resolve concurrent update conflicts and not allow the work of one engineer to be overwritten by that of another when local workspaces are merged back into the project workspace.

documentation

Traditionally, comments are interspersed throughout the source code of a program. Placing **comments** within the source code often means that they are too terse to be useful, or if they are more elaborate, they destroy the flow of the program's code. The object management system allows documentation and source code to co-exist in separate linked nodes. The use of a suitable windowing user interface would allow source code and comments to be viewed simultaneously by using comment links. Linear traversal is also possible and source code and documentation may be viewed in sequence by following the appropriate links.

2.3.3.3 Program editing

editing is primary
activity

Program and document preparation is the primary activity of software engineers. **Text editors** enable users to create and modify files, and most environments used for software development offer a number of different editors. Because this is such a common activity, the power of the editor contributes significantly to the productivity of the software engineer.

language-oriented
editors

To support the preparation and editing of programs, some work has been done in developing **language-oriented** editors, which are designed to prepare and modify programs in a specific programming language (Arefi *et al.*, 1990). An example of such a system is the Cornell Program Synthesizer which is designed to help beginners prepare programs. Rather than manipulate unstructured text, the system actually manipulates a tree structure representing the program. Such systems may be valuable for beginners wrestling with the idiosyncrasies of programming languages.

A system with **multiple windows** may present different parts of a program and allow interaction in terms of program concepts. For example, one window might show the code for a procedure, with the program declarations in another window. Changing one part of the program results in related parts being immediately identified and presented for modification. Multi-window program preparation systems offer such productivity advantages that they are likely to supplant the use of general purpose text editors for the preparations of programs, specifications, and software designs.

multiple windows

A program editing system must present a user interface that intuitively shows the relationships among the parts of the program (see Exercise 2.9). In one program editor, a **box** represents a unit of information, and hierarchies of boxes are visually presented (DiSessa, 1985). A box may contain other boxes or text or graphics. A program is a box that contains some boxes with input and output variables and others that specify behavior. Alternative views of boxes are available. Cross-referencing is done through a port which gives a direct view of the destination. The destination box appears as a window on the screen within the origin box.

screen design

2.4 Text and microtext

The world of text remains largely a linear world. If microtext is to be successful, the ability to **translate** easily between text and microtext is essential. Under what conditions can text be automatically restructured as hypertext? Conversely, how can a microtext be traversed so as to create a coherent linear document? If algorithmic methods do not exist for assessing the quality of text or microtext, how could an algorithm be demonstrated to do a good job of translating between text and microtext?

translation and evaluation

2.4.1 From text to microtext

To map a text into microtext, one must decide how much text to associate with a node or link (Glushko, 1989). If the text is various short messages, then each message may be associated with its own **node**. For large documents some more clever breakdown is required. Two distinct classes of **links** are important. Structural links enforce the mapping between the conventional document and the microtext skeleton. These links may be automatically generated from a formatted document. The second class of links give non-sequential and non-hierarchical paths and may be difficult to extract from text. Two classes of text should be distinguished: clearly structured and implicitly structured. Clearly structured text has obvious structural links, whereas implicitly structured text does not.

paragraphs and links

2.4.1.1 Clearly structured text

directory

A prime example of clearly structured text is a **directory**. Technical manuals, dictionaries, encyclopedias, course catalogs, and bibliographies are like directories. The embedded commands in the electronic versions of these texts can be readily translated into a form that a microtext system exploits.

manuals, dictionaries, and encyclopedias

The documentation for the operating system UNIX has been converted into the microtext format of Guide (Brown and Russell, 1988). Each section heading within the documentation was automatically converted into a Guide replacement-button. The Prototype Electronic Encyclopedia was developed in the early 1980s for browsing encyclopedias. From tapes which contained the typeset for the encyclopedia, the microtext was semi-automatically derived (Weyer and Borning, 1985). The *Oxford English Dictionary* has been placed on the computer to support browsing (Raymond and Tompa, 1988). Many companies are currently creating hypertext versions of **manuals**, **dictionaries**, and **encyclopedias**.

translation algorithm

A graph can be used to represent the text to hypertext translation algorithm. The edges of the graph indicate a string which must occur in the text in order that the translator progresses from one node to another. At each node the **translator** takes some action of moving text into a hypertext form. For example, a bibliography is considered which gives for each document a title, authors, and abstract. This bibliography is prepared with troff commands. Since troff is more a layout language than a logical structure language, some additional logical structure is inferred from expressions in the bibliography, such as 'author' (Furuta *et al.*, 1989b). The description of expressions is incorporated into the edges of the 'translation' graph (see Fig. 2.33).

2.4.1.2 Implicitly structured text

requires substantial human effort

Implicitly structured text refers to text whose explicit logical structure is minimal. The extreme case is an **essay** which has no subdivisions or other logical decomposition. A **novel** likewise may often be an extended stream of consciousness for which the logical structure is not suggested in the layout of the document and is not indicated by the markup language which may have been used on the computer. To translate implicitly structured text into hypertext

Figure 2.33 Conversion. This rough sketch of the 'translation' graph shows that markers for title, author, and abstract are detected. The text between markers is collected in the small cyclical loops. With the larger cycle the algorithm proceeds from one bibliographic entry to the next.

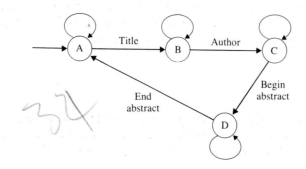

requires substantial human effort to be invested in characterizing the relations among components of the document.

The July 1988 issue of *Communications of the Association of Computing Machinery* had eight papers about hypertext. The papers were independently written for journal publication—in linear form with minimal cross-referencing. Those papers were converted into several microtext products, including HyperTies. The **HyperTies** effort illustrates the complexity of the task. The eight papers were first divided manually into about 100 HyperTies articles. An overview was added that offered a set of links to topics that were covered in several papers, because the papers did not provide the links. The **conversion process** required several person-months of effort. While some portions of the conversion could be automated, it seems likely that conversion of a similar collection of scientific papers would require a similar amount of overall effort (Furuta *et al.*, 1989a).

example difficulty

2.4.1.3 Conversion tools

In converting text to hypertext, software tools may be applied to restructuring the source text and to polishing the target hypertext. However, intervention may be required at various points. **Secondary authors** might read documents and annotate them with hypertext links. In one system, part of the hypertext structure was inferred from the source document formatting commands. Then an expert in the domain of the document read the document and interacted with the system in the course of augmenting the network with links which could not be inferred from the formatting commands in the document (Price, 1982).

secondary authors

One example of a text to hypertext translator is **SuperBook**. The SuperBook software analyzes the words and the heading structure of a text. Pieces of the text are presented in a print-like format in one or more arbitrary-sized windows which can be scrolled (Egan *et al.*, 1989). The hierarchy in which the text was embedded appears at the top of each window in which text occurs and is changed as the text is scrolled. Appearing in a separate window is a Table of Contents, which is automatically constructed by SuperBook, based on the formatting commands in the marked-up document.

example translator

2.4.2 From microtext to text

Tools for converting microtext into text could be useful for authors in the intermediate stages of writing. The **writer** could see how the microtext might be traversed. For **readers**, the opportunity to get a linear view and perhaps a paper copy might often be invaluable. Yet, how this linearization should be done remains an open question.

linearization

2.4.2.1 Linearization

A traversal of the links of a microtext that visits every text block once and only once has effectively linearized the text. **Printing** these blocks as they are visited can produce a paper product. How should these traversals be done?

traversal

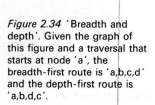

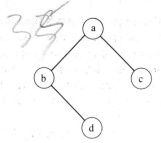

Figure 2.34 'Breadth and depth'. Given the graph of this figure and a traversal that starts at node 'a', the breadth-first route is 'a,b,c,d' and the depth-first route is 'a,b,d,c'.

breadth- or depth-first

Two popular ways to traverse a graph are a **breadth-first** and a **depth-first** traversal (see Fig. 2.34):

- A breadth-first traversal starts at a node and visits all the nodes directly connected to it before proceeding in a similar fashion from one of the recently visited nodes.
- A depth-first traversal starts at a node, visits one of the nodes directly connected to it, and then repeats this process from the last visited node.

Both breadth-first and depth-first methods backtrack when a node is reached all of whose directly connected nodes have already been visited (see Exercise 2.10).

KMS

The microtext system **KMS** (see Sec. 2.3.1.1) supports printing. Since the text is divided into frames which are embedded in a hierarchy, concatenating the contents of frames from the hierarchy in depth-first order produces a document. Annotations can specify modifications to the layout of the frame. This approach is a hybrid between 'What You See Is What You Get' and markup, as directly printing the frame as seen on the screen constitutes 'What You See Is What You Get', but the annotations give a markup ability. A new system has been developed as a combination of KMS and a word-processing system and supports large-scale document engineering.

framework

In one approach to **depth-first** printing of microtext, a text block associated with a link in a **semantic net** is printed as the link is traversed in a modified depth-first search of the net. The semantic net may be described as a set of frames where each frame has a name of a node and has slots for the links emanating from the node. Each slot in turn has several attributes, called link, target, deadend, order, and paragraphs (see Fig. 2.35). The value of the link

Figure 2.35 In this example two links are described. The terms in single quotes are the attribute values. The value of the paragraph attribute points to a paragraph of text.

```
frame name: 'hypertext system'
    link: 'begin'
            target: 'preview'
            order: 1
            deadend 'yes'
            paragraphs 'p₁'
    link: 'past'
            target: 'hypertext history'
            order: 2
            deadend: 'no'
            paragraphs: 'p₂'
```

attribute specifies the type of link. The value of the target attribute is the name of the node to which the link points. Deadend 'yes' signifies that when the traversal reaches this link, the traversal should not continue to the target but instead should resume from the frame node. Conversely, deadend 'no' means that traversal should continue to the target. The value of the order attribute tells the traversal program the priorities among the links in that frame (see Exercise 2.11).

If the **traversal** begins with the node 'hypertext system' shown in Fig. 2.35, then it first crosses the 'begin' link and prints the paragraph 'p_1'. Since the 'preview' node is a deadend, the algorithm returns to 'hypertext system' and looks for the next branch. The process recurs this way as the linear document is created through a modified depth-first search of the semantic network.

The traversal program guarantees that every edge in the graph is visited exactly once. The program begins at the edge that the user declares as the starting edge and maintains a variable which holds the current depth of the tree that is being generated. This variable is used to calculate the **numeric indices** of entries in the outline. (This book was produced using the traversal program.)

The strict depth-first traversal chooses randomly from the edges emanating from a given node. By ordering the link types, an additional constraint may be placed on the traversal (see Exercise 2.12). A **constraint-based traversal** of the graph in Fig. 2.36 might apply an ordering on link types of caused-by ⟩ explained-by ⟩ part-of ⟩ has-part. If the start node is 'hypertext', the depth-first search then follows the link 'explain' to the node 'new opportunity' and then makes an arbitrary choice between the two links exiting from 'new opportunity'. The final traversal touches these nodes, from first to last: hypertext, new opportunity, new technology, history, hypermedia, writer, reader. To print the document associated with the network another algorithm would select the blocks of text associated with the network and place them in sequence according to the sequence determined by the traversal of the network.

example traversal

computer program

constraint-based traversal

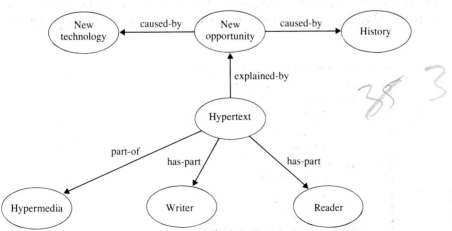

Figure 2.36 Example semantic net for ordered link types; this illustrates one linearization algorithm.

2.4.2.2 Linearization evaluation

cohesiveness

Given a network to which text is attached, many traversals may exist which produce a linear document. The 'best traversal' generates the most coherent document. **Cohesiveness** is a measure of how well a document can be perceived as a whole, rather than as an amalgamation of disjoint paragraphs. But how is coherence assessed?

pronoun referent gives cohesive tie

Language is richly composed of many references which set up a commonality of theme between different parts of text or speech. There exist many different types of **cohesive tie**, but one of the most common is the pronoun. Pronominal substitution is one of the several methods to link sentences and paragraphs and to allow the perception of an overall text. For example:

> '*The golfer hit the ball well. It soared into the air.*'

Within these two sentences, the situation is easily understood and explained. The *it* in the second sentence refers back to *the ball*. The two sentences are bound together by a cohesive tie (see Exercise 2.13).

automating count of cohesive ties

By studying the number of occurrences of **cohesive ties** and their locations, one can begin to gain an indication of how well-formed a text is. Assessing the ties manually is time consuming, so if applied to a document comprising more than just a few sentences or paragraphs, automation would be invaluable. It is possible to resolve automatically many of the cohesive ties within a text (at least reducing the amount of work that investigators would have to undergo) and thus provide a method of quantifying coherence of the linearized text (Ghaoui et al., 1991).

optimal paths

Cohesiveness can be assessed from a more abstract level than the pronoun reference level. If a **semantic net** represents an abstraction of the network of text and a traversal of this net produces a linearized text, then this network structure can be directly related to the cohesiveness of the **linearization**. If the traversal goes from node X to a node directly connected to node X, then the associated text should seem related or cohesive. If the traversal goes from a node X to a node that is several edges distant from node X, then the linear cohesiveness will seem less. The **minimum path length** between two nodes X and Y is the number of edges that must be crossed in going between X and Y and directly corresponds to the amount of cohesiveness. The cohesiveness of a linearized text may thus be directly proportional to the length of the paths in the semantic net which the traversal algorithm had to follow (see Exercise 2.14). In a network

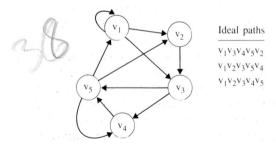

Figure 2.37 Ideal paths.

with n nodes, the minimal cost traversal of the entire network must cross paths with a total length of, at least, $n-1$; these ideal paths are illustrated in Fig. 2.37 (Ghaoui *et al.*, 1991).

2.5 Epilogue

In the early 1960s Douglas Engelbart's group developed the first **microtext system**, using graphical workstations for the creation and browsing of documents (Engelbart and English, 1968). The mouse was developed to make the information on the screen easier to navigate. At the same time, van Dam's group was developing the Hypertext Editing System. Both systems had technical features which today are still not generally available but which are desirable. When one reads the current literature, one finds discussions of technical possibilities, as though no one had imagined those possibilities. Yet, a careful look at their history should foster understanding of the difference between technical possibility and commercial acceptability.

How did users respond to the **Hypertext Editing System**? A patent document system was implemented within the Hypertext Editing System. While the implementors were able to browse the patent documents easily, other users could not. The problem of being lost while **navigating** among text blocks was significant. To quote one of the creators of the Hypertext Editing System (Dam, 1988):

> We already started getting the notion that the richer the hypertext, the greater the navigational problem. But we arranged careful demos in which we knew exactly where we had to go, and people were impressed [with the demonstrations].

Outside the carefully arranged demonstrations, however, the meaningfulness of links among document components was not clear to users.

The requirements for microtext are difficult to delineate as the evidence is sometimes conflicting. The explanation for this might be that different users with different tasks need significantly different microtext systems. Thus, in designing a system one needs either to clearly specify the target users and task or make a system with great **flexibility** which will readily appear in different situations as a different system.

A flow-control model, an attributed graph, or a semantic net are formalisms that can support microtext. All represent information with **nodes** and **links** and have obvious graphical representations. A general network of terms may provide flexibility but experience suggests that creators and accessors alike need hierarchies to help manage the complexity of microtext. For example, a table of contents may be necessary to complement a lengthy index.

The interface should never take the user to a situation from which the user does not appreciate the options. In particular, the system should be tailored so that novice users have few decisions to make. For a window with highlighted buttons or nodes, the user should be able to point to those with a mouse, to use arrow-jump keys to circulate among the options, or to type a description of the desired target. Given that a window corresponds to a node, **window placement**

[margin notes]

history lesson

user response to Hypertext Editing System in the 1960s

different users need different features

representations

interface options

should be nested for hierarchically connected nodes and tiled for non-hierarchically related nodes. Any **traversals** by the user should be recorded so that the user can see where he has been. Reversal of path, either by the order of what the user has last seen (dynamic reversal) or by the author's structuring of the graph (static reversal), should be possible.

authoring guidelines

The authoring challenge is to design the structure of the hypertext to match the ways that a user might want to think about the topics. Text must be structured to support the mental models that readers may create when they use the hypertext system. Each node or edge of the document should be a small self-contained entity (Shneiderman and Kearsley, 1989). **Names** of nodes and edges should be **consistent**.

modeless

A microtext system should be modeless. **Modeless** microtext software supports editing or browsing from the same window. One can select certain browsing options, or one can immediately change the contents of the screen. Commands are directly effective rather than simply switching the user from one mode to another.

discipline

A robust microtext authoring tool should make it easy for the author to

- specify links and nodes,
- switch between author and reader mode,
- import and export text.

text to microtext uses markup

The system should give the author the option of using many different types of links but should encourage a **discipline** in link use. The meaning of hierarchical and non-hierarchical links should be clear. Similarly, the system should allow any number of windows to be created but there should be a discipline underlying their choice and placement.

The conversion of **text to microtext** should be supported by the computer. Providing the text has been prepared in a standard **markup language**, programs can automatically translate the text into, at least, a partial hypertext. The user can then access the text through hierarchical views. Moving clearly-structured text to microtext is straightforward, but less explicitly structured text, such as a novel, is very difficult to translate into microtext.

traverse network for microtext to text

Given that authors prepare microtext but that paper remains the most attractive medium for many purposes, a good microtext system should support the translation of **microtext to text** printed on paper. To convert microtext into text, a non-linear structure has to be reduced to a linear structure. The straightforward way for a program to do this is for it to **traverse** the network and print the associated text as it goes, though how to guide this traversal so that the resulting text is coherent is an unsolved problem.

marketplace based on work flow

The history of microtext shows that systems can be built with multiple functions, but not necessarily succeed in the marketplace. An economic analysis of this failure indicates not only that the system cost should be low, but also that the system must fit into the **work flow** of the users in a way that makes the computer decidedly more attractive than paper or other options.

repeatable experiments

People do not necessarily agree on what is needed for microtext. One person thinks WYSIWYG is bad, another thinks it is needed (Engelbart, 1984). One thinks that bi-directional links are crucial, another that such links are bad. This indicates that methods of evaluating microtext are not well established. The literature reports, often anecdotally, how a system helped or hindered performance on a task. Unfortunately, these **experiments** are often islands unto themselves, and their results are often impossible to compare. Tasks and measures of success should be **standardized** so that an experiment done by one group can be readily repeated by another group.

2.6 Exercises

2.1 The **Standard General Markup Language** and the Office Document Architecture focus on sequential and page-based layout. What additional features would be desirable to create a Hypertext Markup Language or an Office Hypertext Architecture? (40 minutes) — *hypertext layout*

2.2 Discuss translations between the **independent semantic net** microtext and the **embedded semantic net** microtext. Consider the relation between the terms in the semantic net and the terms in the text itself. Is it always possible to translate from one form to the other? (60 minutes) — *independent versus embedded*

2.3 From a model of Aesop's fable, one can generate a story. The model of **Aesop's fable** is that 'X has some goal which requires that Y be kindly disposed towards X, so X says something nice to Y, Y reacts accordingly, X achieves his goal but also causes Y to suffer'. The difficulty with the tales based on Aesop's fable is that they become dull after a time. First draw a semantic net which represents an Aesop-like fable and then change it to show a twist to Aesop's fable. (30 minutes) — *Aesop's fable*

2.4 What is the advantage to a **natural language interface**? (20 minutes) — *natural language*

2.5 A **fisheye view** may select information according to a 'degree-of-interest' function. The degree-of-interest may depend on the link types which emanate from the point of focus. Construct a small semantic net for a microtext and demonstrate different fisheye views based on different degree-of-interest functions. (30 minutes) — *fisheye view*

2.6 The depiction of a semantic net as a graph on the screen may give the impression of a tangled mass of **spaghetti**. The **museum layout** approach attempts to structure information so that users quickly appreciate the logical structure of the hypertext. Illustrate an interaction with a 'museum layout' interface. (20 minutes) — *museum layout*

2.7 While the network in a microtext may be encoded in a database system that makes no direct reference to **spatial relationships**, the visual representation of the network forces some spatial ordering on the network. For example, even though the network logically represented as 'infectious diseases are diseases and diseases cause suffering' does not say anything about spatial relationships, a visual representation of the network would have to show one node above, or to the side of, another node. Illustrate alternative ways to lay out a hierarchy. (25 minutes) — *visual formalisms*

2.8 A **link** with the name 'Previous' could mean several things. Describe the different semantics which Previous might have in microtext. (30 minutes) — *meaning of Previous* software engineering

2.9   Imagine that **software** code is nested. Say that parentheses are used to delimit functions or subroutines. Here two functions are nested within another:

(... (...) (...) ...).

One might want to read about the outside function without reading about either internal function. Develop an algorithm which allows one to select the left parenthesis of an innermost pair of parentheses and have everything from that parenthesis to its matching right parenthesis removed, leaving just the two parentheses. If one selects the second-left parenthesis in the above example, one would get

(... () (...) ...).

Next, extend the algorithm so that one can point to a left parenthesis of a () pair and have the material which was inside the parentheses appear. This is the inverse of the previous operation. The algorithm might associate a file with the contents of each innermost pair of parentheses and then fetch the appropriate file. If the user selected the second-left parenthesis from

(... () (...) ...),

the algorithm would produce

(... (...) (...) ...).

Discuss how this algorithm compares to an algorithm that would handle the fold and unfold operation of Guide. (2 hours)

depth versus breadth

2.10   To traverse a hypertext network, standard graph traversal methods may be used. Given a hypertext network, contrast the effect of a **breadth-first traversal** and a **depth-first traversal**. (20 minutes)

depth-first algorithm

2.11   Given a graph with edges that have two attributes: one attribute is 'deadend' and one is 'paragraphs', sketch an algorithm to do a modified **depth-first traversal** of a graph. Edges are to be visited only when they have a deadend value of 'no'. Paragraphs are to be printed as their associated edges are traversed. (45 minutes)

balanced trees

2.12   A spanning tree of a graph is a tree which is extracted directly from the graph and visits every node of the graph. The height of a node in a tree is the number of edges from the node to the most distant descendant of the node. In a balanced tree the height of siblings is the same or differs by only one. It may be that a balanced tree cannot be produced from a certain graph. Describe an algorithm that produces an approximation to a balanced tree. Discuss how this algorithm might be applied to linearizing hypertext. (2 hours)

pronoun references

2.13   Pronoun substitution links sentences and paragraphs to allow the perception of an overall text. Text also needs to activate mental models of the reader that help the text seem connected. For the example

Popeye hit Bluto on the nose. He soared into the air.

Explain the cohesive ties which are present. (20 minutes)

path costs

2.14   Assume that the cost of the traversal of a graph is equal to the number of edges which must be traversed. For the sample graph (see Fig. 2.38)

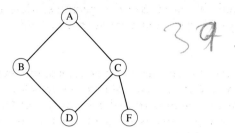

3 9.

Figure 2.38 Sample graph.

determine the cost of all **traversals** which start at node A and visit every node of the graph. Are breadth-first or depth-first traversals more costly? (25 minutes)

3

Large-volume hypertext

Figure 3.1 Library.

information storage and retrieval

Large-volume hypertext or macrotext emphasizes the links that exist among many documents rather than within one document. Typically, many people have contributed documents to macrotext and an institution is involved in maintaining the macrotext system. Maintaining the system involves maintaining both the interface to the documents and the connections among the documents. The many users of a given macrotext are searching for a few documents from

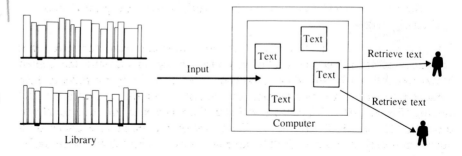

Figure 3.2 Macrotext. A general model of a macrotext system. Text from a library is fed into the computer; people retrieve text from the system.

a large set (see Fig. 3.2). Macrotext does not support the browsing of a single document—that is a microtext facility. Traditionally, the term **information storage and retrieval** was used when talking about storing and retrieving many documents.

3.1 History

Throughout history the **information explosion** has been perceived as outstripping people's ability to manage information. One partial solution has been to build archives of documents and to index the documents in a standard way. With the computer one can implement the **archiving** and **indexing** functions on a grand scale.

managing the information explosion

3.1.1 Paper indices

Bibliographies are pointers or links to documents. Simple **bibliographies** were published in the Middle Ages. By the 1700s, scholars had prepared bibliographies exhibiting a variety of approaches both by author and subject. The **Repertorium** is a subject index of the publications of the seventeenth and eighteenth centuries and took 20 years to publish, starting in 1801. However, the effort required to build the *Repertorium* was so great that it was hard to imagine how one could update such a subject index. In his annual report for 1851, the Secretary of the Smithsonian Institution in the United States called attention to the fact that 'about twenty thousand volumes … purporting to be additions to the sum of human knowledge, are published annually; and unless this mass be properly arranged, and the means furnished by which its contents may be ascertained, literature and science will be overwhelmed by their own unwieldy bulk.'

18th century bibliographies

Index Medicus, which began in 1879, represented new methods of dealing with information and addressed the problem of updating indices. In 1874 John **Billings** began indexing the journals of the Surgeon General's Library in Washington, DC. By 1875 he had accumulated tens of thousands of cards. Those from 'Aabec' to 'Air' were published by the Government Printing Office. The object of the publication, Billings wrote, was

Index Medicus

> to show the character and scope of the collection, to obtain criticisms and suggestions as to the form of catalogue which will be most acceptable and useful, and to furnish data for the decision as to whether it is desirable that such a work should be printed and distributed.

The implications of the last phrase become apparent from the letter that accompanied sample copies sent to prominent physicians around the United States. As Billings hoped, these physicians used their lobbying skills to help persuade Congress to appropriate the necessary funds to publish a full catalog (Blake, 1980). When the first *Index Catalogue* was complete in 1895 it took 16 volumes. It listed some 170000 books and pamphlets under both author and subject and over 500000 journal articles under subject alone. *Index*

Medicus was devised as a monthly periodical supplement to the *Index Catalogue*, listing current books and journal articles in classified subject arrangement. The publication of *Index Medicus* continues unabated today. One of the keys to the success of Billings' approach was to obtain government sponsorship for the maintenance of the index.

3.1.2 Memex

1930s

The notion of a computerized macrotext system begins in the 1930s, when **Vannevar Bush** started to argue the importance of applying modern technology to the production of information tools that would turn text into something like **macrotext**. Bush was imagining a scenario in which one individual dealt with the text of many other individuals by placing connections among the text items.

national science adviser

Bush's hypertext machine, called memex, was conceived in the 1930s but not publicized until the end of the Second World War (Nyce and Kahn, 1989). Bush was President Roosevelt's science adviser and overseer of all wartime research in the United States, including the nuclear bomb project. Memex was intended as a major new direction for technological investment in a **peaceful society**. At the end of the Second World War, Bush published several essays about memex, one of which appeared in the *Atlantic Monthly*, raising so much interest that it was republished in revised form in *Life*.

vital information is lost

Bush firmly believed in the power of tools to facilitate **information sharing**. In a letter to a funding agency, he outlined how monies should best be spent to support **research**:

> I would not be surprised if developments of new methods ... and new ways of making ... material for research workers readily available, would have more effect on ultimate process ... than many a direct effort. In fact, I would go much further. Unless we find better ways of handling new knowledge generally as it is developed, we are going to be bogged down ... I suspect we now have reincarnations of Mendel all about us, to be discovered a generation hence if at all.

Mendel's famous work in genetics was lost for generations because it was not published in a generally available source. The discoveries of other researchers were often wasted because of inadequate dissemination of results. Bush said that more research value would be obtained from an improved method to share research progress than would be obtained by any single research result.

microfiche automated

Bush's memex machine, which was designed but never built, was meant to personalize libraries. Physically, the device looked like a work desk with viewing screens, a keyboard, sets of buttons and levers (see Fig. 3.3). Storage of printed materials of all kinds was accomplished using **microfiche**. Pages of books were selected for viewing by typing an index code to control a mechanical selection device or by moving levers to turn page images of the selected item. Any two items in the memex could be coded for permanent association. Bush called this coded association a trail, analogous to the trail of mental associations in the user's mind.

analog device

While the digital computer was being developed in the 1940s, and Bush was

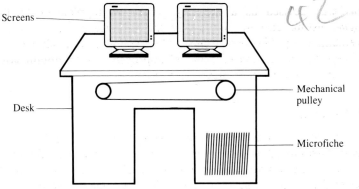

Screens

Desk

Mechanical pulley

Microfiche

Figure 3.3 Memex. A rough depiction of some of the features of the memex, as envisioned by Vannevar Bush. Documents were stored on microfiche which had to be brought into position mechanically to be viewed on a screen. On one screen the user could view documents and on another screen make annotations on the same document. Alfred D. Crimi was hired by *Life* magazine to make the illustration of Bush's memex which is partially captured here (Nyce and Kahn, 1989).

aware of those developments, he did not wish to incorporate digital features into his memex system. He felt that **analog** features were somehow critical to the success of memex. Recent advances in computer systems, such as the mouse, make some analog capabilities available and are related to the revived interest in memex-type devices. A practical memex needs high-resolution, large graphical screens and massive, inexpensive memory. Both of these features were better seen as analog in the 1940s but have proven to be more readily available digitally in the 1990s.

3.1.3 On-Line bibliographies

The **National Library of Medicine** built the first macrotext computer system, drawing up specifications for a computerized retrieval system in the 1950s. Originally, the Library planned to graft the retrieval system onto its typesetting system for *Index Medicus*, but after repeated setbacks realized that priorities would have to be reversed so that the typesetting system became secondary to the retrieval system. The retrieval system was called the Medical Literature Analysis and Retrieval System (MEDLARS) and first operated successfully in the mid-1960s. It began with about 100000 journal articles and in its first year processed thousands of queries. To obtain citations a health professional first conveyed an information need to a search intermediary at the National Library of Medicine. The search intermediary then formulated an on-line query, and a list of relevant citations was then printed and mailed to the health professional. The turn-around time was one month.

MEDLARS

The **1970s** witnessed the advent of inexpensive, long-distance communications networks, inexpensive fast terminals, and inexpensive large storage devices. These three factors combined so that users could operate on a terminal in their office and get citations instantly in response to their queries. There were over 300 bibliographic retrieval systems by the late 1970s, storing tens of **millions of citations** and receiving millions of queries each year. Access to these databases was made available in the United States largely through commercial suppliers. The growth in the number of bibliographic citations available on-line and in the number of queries to these on-line systems has been remarkable (see Fig. 3.4). The literature in these on-line systems is predominantly scientific and most of the queries are for scientific material (Hall and Brown, 1983).

1970s growth in on-line bibliographies

Number of references and queries on-line			
Category	1970	1975	1980
References	1 million	20 million	60 million
Queries	100 thousand	1 million	5 million

Figure 3.4 Growth of on-line bibliographies. The numbers are order of magnitude estimates.

1980s optical disks

In the 1980s **optical disks** became available. An optical disk is a few inches in diameter and the thickness of cardboard, yet one such disk can hold a thousand million bytes of information. Large document databases can be carried on a single optical disk. The cost of reproducing an optical disk is hardly more than the cost of reproducing a regular disk. Furthermore, personal computers can be equipped with an optical disk drive for about the same cost as any other disk drive. These characteristics of optical disks suggest that they will become the medium of the future for delivering macrotext. Many modern libraries have document databases available on optical disks, and these media are frequently and heavily used in those libraries.

popularity of database on optical disk

The University of Liverpool Library has maintained for decades an on-line service to MEDLARS, the medical literature database. To access the database, patrons of the library must make an appointment with a librarian, usually days in advance of gaining access, and provide money to pay for the access. In the late 1980s the library acquired an optical disk version of the database. On each optical disk about one hundred thousand citations from the database can be stored. Since this equals about four months of citations, a new optical disk is shipped to the library each four months. Now patrons can go to a personal computer in the library and directly search the database (see Fig. 3.5); no librarian is needed. However, the system has proved so popular that queues of

Figure 3.5 Optical disk. The library patron is accessing the MEDLARS database on a personal computer with an attached optical disk. To the right is a printer so that the user can get paper copy of selected citations. To the immediate left of the patron is a rack of optical disks covering several years of citations. Further to the left is the optical disk device and a stack of *Index Medicus* books. One optical disk itself, which is smaller than a person's hand, can hold more information than is contained in the stack of books.

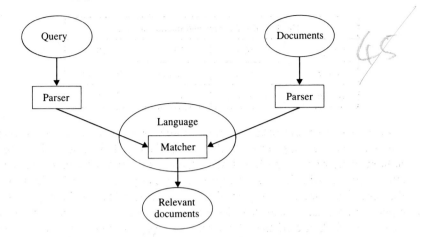

Figure 3.6 Query and document model.

people form to use it. The patrons use the optical disk free of charge, and while the library must pay for the disks, a better service is provided at a lower cost.

3.2 Principles

Macrotext systems are often constructed as database systems for which queries and documents enter the system and documents return to the searcher (Stonebraker *et al.*, 1983). If the language of **queries** and **documents** is not unified at some point, a match cannot be made between queries and documents (see Fig. 3.6). Document indexing and retrieval can be seen as a combination of parsing and matching. Parsing moves a document or a query into another representation. In matching, the parsed form of a query is compared to the parsed form of documents.

parsing and matching

3.2.1 Word-based principles

The **parsing** of documents and matching of documents to queries can be based on the **words** in the documents and queries. In the simplest case the documents are unchanged in parsing, and the query is one string of characters which is directly matched against strings in documents. A more sophisticated process represents a document by the words with a certain frequency in the document. Queries are likewise represented as words which are then matched against the frequent words in each document.

strings versus word frequencies

3.2.1.1 String methods

A string-searching, document retrieval system is one which allows the searcher to type an **arbitrary string** of characters and which returns the documents that contain that string. String-searching retrieval is on its surface disarmingly simple. It means storing the documents on a computer so that every string can be located. This approach is attractive because it takes advantage of massive digital technology and reduces the load on human indexers of documents.

arbitrary strings

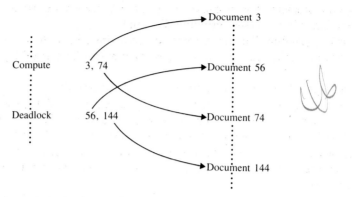

Figure 3.7 Inverted index. The list on the left contains the words of the inverted index. The numbers in the middle are adjacent to the index of words and point to documents. The list on the right contains the documents themselves.

INDICES

document representation

Computationally, string-search across a large document database can be very costly. The method of **inverted indices** captures much of the meaningfulness of the string approach, but more efficiently (the term 'inverted index' is commonly used, although 'index' alone would seem to do). A list of words is created, and adjacent to each word in the list is another list of pointers to documents that indicate which documents contain that word (see Fig. 3.7). While there is overhead to creating and maintaining this list, given that the user specifies a word from the list, the documents in which that word occurs can be quickly retrieved.

Boolean queries

Inverted indices support queries with set operators. If the user specifies 'word$_x$ INTERSECT word$_y$', then all the documents which have both word$_x$ and word$_y$ in them will be returned. This can be extended into arbitrary queries of words with UNION, INTERSECTION, and COMPLEMENT operators between the words. Given that only the lists of pointers need to be manipulated, simple set operations on the lists can very quickly produce retrieval results (see Exercise 3.1). A **Boolean** query is a parenthesized logical expression composed of index terms and the logical operators OR, AND, and NOT. The effect of these Boolean operators is the same as the corresponding set operations UNION, INTERSECTION, and COMPLEMENT.

adjacencies

Given that the pointers to documents indicate at what word position in the document the word occurs, queries about specific **adjacencies** can be posed. One can ask for all documents in which 'word$_x$ is within n words of word$_y$'. If one wanted documents on the President's position on taxes, one might ask for 'President within 4 words of taxes'.

STRING AMBIGUITY

synonym problem

If one allows free-form English (or whatever the natural language of the users is) to be entered for queries, several problems can occur (Sudarshan, 1979).

1. The **synonym problem**: A searcher and a document author may use different terms to characterize the same concept. For example, 'acoustic' and 'sound' mean the same thing.
2. The **homonym problem**: There are some words which look identical but have entirely different meanings. The word 'tank', for instance, can mean either a container or an armored vehicle.

3. The **syntax problem**: This is caused by using improper word order, such as 'diamond grinding' versus 'grinding diamond'.
4. The **spelling problem**: The same word will sometimes be spelled in different ways. For example, 'gauges' and 'gages' may mean the same thing.

The **synonym** problem is the most serious of these in practice.

In an early assessment of full-text, string-search on a database of 750 documents, such searching by computer was significantly better than conventional retrieval using human subject indexing (Swanson, 1960). More recent evidence, however, suggests that string-searching is only effective on small textual databases. **String-search** behaves poorly when the document space is of substantial size.

> string search effective only on small databases

In one famous, large-scale study, a string-search system was loaded with 40000 documents totaling about 350000 pages of hard-copy text. The content of the documents concerned a large corporate law suit. Several lawyers and para-legals worked with the information retrieval system over many months and their satisfaction with the performance of the system was assessed. It was determined that the searchers expected to get about 75 per cent of the **relevant documents** which the system contained. Searching was continued until the searchers said they were satisfied. Subsequent analysis showed that only 20 per cent of the relevant documents had been obtained (Blair and Maron, 1985).

> a large experiment: only 20 per cent retrieved

Why did the **searchers** believe they were getting 75 per cent of what they needed to recall, when in fact they obtained only 20 per cent? For example, one query concerned an accident that had occurred and had become the subject of litigation (Blair and Maron, 1985). The lawyers wanted all the documents pertaining to this accident and posed queries that contained the word 'accident' in combination with a wide variety of other relevant terms. Subsequent study of the database found that many relevant documents did not refer to the event as an accident. Instead, those who had written documents arguing against a guilty charge on the accident tended to refer to an 'unfortunate situation' or 'event'. Sometimes relevant documents dealt with technical aspects of the accident without mentioning it directly. Depending on the perspective of the author, references to the accident took far different forms than the searchers had anticipated.

> the synonym problem again

String-search is difficult to use to retrieve documents by subject because its design is based on the assumption that it is a simple matter for users to foresee the exact words and phrases that will be used by authors. One needs to find the **phrases** that **characterize exactly** the documents one wants. This has never been shown to be possible on large textual databases. It is very difficult for users to predict the exact words that are used in relevant documents.

> explanation for result

3.2.1.2 Word frequency

A document may be perceived as concerning the subject symbolized by a certain word within its content if that word occurs more frequently than could be expected in any randomly-chosen document. In this manner, words may convey information as to what a document contains. In a set of documents, each of which contains a certain word to the same extent, one expects that the

> frequency times rank equals constant

occurrences of that word would be as though random within that set. If all words were to occur with equal frequency, the main concepts of a document could not be distinguished from the frequency of word occurrence. In fact, words occur in text **unevenly**. In general,

$$\text{frequency} \times \text{rank} \approx \text{constant}$$

where the rank of the most frequent word is one (Zipf, 1949).

INDEXING

mid-frequency

The strategy for indexing a document by word frequency is to determine first the frequency with which each word in the document collection occurs. In one approach:

1. the **low-frequency** words are then excluded as being not much on the writer's mind, and
2. the **high-frequency** words are discarded on the grounds that they are likely overly general as indicators of document content.

This leaves the **mid-frequency** words to characterize documents.

high-frequency words in a document

To improve the value of word-frequency assessments of content, many techniques have been elaborated. For instance, one technique generates mid-frequency phrases based on the adjacency of **high-frequency** words. For instance, the words 'word' and 'frequency' occur with high frequency in this book but do not significantly characterize the book's content. However, the term 'word frequency' occurs with mid-frequency and is a significant indicator of content. For another example, consider a library of documents on the topic of aerodynamics. Though the three words 'boundary', 'layer', and 'flow' occur with high frequency in these aerodynamic documents, the term 'boundary layer flow' occurs with mid-frequency in the collection. 'Boundary layer flow' is an important index term for some documents, while the word 'boundary' does not meaningfully characterize any of the documents.

low-frequency words

Another technique maps **low-frequency** words into synonym classes. Words which occur with low frequency in a document may either indicate that the document is not about the topic which that word symbolizes or may indicate a synonym group which is important to the meaning of the document. For instance, the word 'querist' may only be used once in a document about about searching the literature, but as a synonym to the frequently used word 'searcher', 'querist' is significant.

algorithm

One algorithm for **word-frequency indexing** follows:

1. Identify all the unique words in the document set.
2. Remove all common function words included in a 'stop' list. This stop list includes articles, such as 'the', prepositions, such as 'of', and conjunctions, such as 'and'.
3. Remove all suffixes and combine identical stems. For instance, the words 'searcher', 'searching', and 'searches' would be represented by the single stem 'search' after the removal of the suffixes 'er', 'ing', and 'es'.

4. Determine sequences of words that form frequent terms.
5. Determine synonyms for low frequency terms.
6. Give a range of frequencies for terms to be considered for indexing. All terms that are within the range are index terms.

Words are the basis of the indexing, but in some cases they are combined into meaningful terms based on word frequency and co-occurrence. Since a word is a term, the algorithm concludes in step 6 by referring to terms only (see Exercise 3.2).

Imagine that a searcher wants a book from the library about microcomputers. If every book that contains the word microcomputer is given to the searcher, then ideally all those documents would be relevant and no other documents would be relevant. The relevant documents that contain the term 'microcomputer' are **true positives**, and the irrelevant documents without the term are **true negatives**. An ideal retrieval produces no **false positives** or **false negatives** (see Fig. 3.8). In reality, however, a search such as the above would produce many false positives and false negatives.

positives and negatives

One method of reducing the false negatives or false positives is to **weight terms** based on their frequency of occurrence in each document relative to their total frequency in the document collection. For instance, if the document collection contains 10 documents, document$_A$ contains the term 'microcomputer' 20 times, document$_B$, document$_C$, and document$_D$ each contain the term 10 times, and the other 6 documents do not contain the term, then the weight on the term 'microcomputer' for document$_A$ is 2/5, for document$_B$, document$_C$, and document$_D$ the weight is 1/5, and for the other 6 documents the weight is 0. If retrieval for the query 'microcomputer' requires a document to contain the term microcomputer with a weight greater than 1/5, then false positives are likely to be lower than if the weight has to be simply greater than 0.

effect of weights on retrieval

To exploit the good features of very frequent and infrequent terms, while minimizing their bad ones, a weighting scheme can be used. Assume that all the terms in a set of documents are stored in a **vector**. Any document might be represented by this vector where each term is replaced by a number between 0 and 1. Each number testifies to the extent to which the corresponding term characterizes the document at issue.

weights on terms

Discrimination analysis ranks terms in accordance with how well they are able to discriminate the documents of a collection from each other (Salton *et al.*, 1975). The best terms are those which achieve the greatest separation. If each document is described as a weighted vector of terms, one can define a distance between two documents as the distance between the vectors. A number of document retrieval studies indicate that in a good set of document vectors the average distance between pairs of documents is maximized. The highest weight

discrimination analysis

	Document relevant	Document NOT relevant
Term present	true positive	false negative
Term absent	false positive	true negative

Figure 3.8 Positives and negatives.

is assigned to those terms in a vector which cause the maximum separation among the document vectors.

RETRIEVAL

relevance and distance

Human information processing involves conceptual matching, for which relevance is an important aspect. The more relevant two concepts are, the smaller the **conceptual distance** between them. When concepts are represented by vectors, conceptual distance can be measured by the distance between the vectors. When a document and a query are each represented by a vector, the distance between the two vectors can be used in determining whether or not the document is relevant to the query (see Exercise 3.3). In other words, for a document retrieval system, distance can be used to determine which documents should be retrieved in response to a query.

example computation

In an information retrieval system a document is returned to a query when the distance between the document and query is under some threshold. One example of a distance between a **weighted document vector** and a **weighted query vector** subtracts corresponding weights and then adds the absolute values of those differences. Thus if

$$document_1 = (0.1, 0.7, 0.3),$$
$$document_2 = (0.2, 0.5, 0.1), \text{ and}$$
$$query = (0.1, 0.6, 0.4), \text{ then}$$

the distance between document and query is given by

$$distance(query, document_1) = 0.0 + 0.1 + 0.1 = 0.2$$
$$distance(query, document_2) = 0.1 + 0.1 + 0.3 = 0.5$$

In this case the query is closer to $document_1$ than to $document_2$. If the retrieval system returned documents which were within a distance of 0.3 from the query, then $document_1$ would be returned and $document_2$ would not be returned.

better than manual indexing

Some evidence indicates that **word-frequency text analysis** is as effective as manual indexing. A simple indexing process based on the assignment of weighted terms to documents and queries has, at times, produced better retrieval results than a more sophisticated manual document analysis (Salton and McGill, 1983). Furthermore, in many cases manual indexing is not feasible.

DOCUMENT CLUSTERS

reduction in search time

The cost to determine the distance between document vectors and a query vector is prohibitive for large document collections. Each time a query is posed, the retrieval system would have to compute the distance from the query to each document. The cost of search for close documents can be reduced by **clustering documents** into classes, where the elements of each class are within a prescribed distance of one another. Each cluster is described by one vector. The search strategy simply finds the cluster vector which is closest to the query and then returns the documents in the cluster.

example computation of cluster

One way to build clusters is to determine first the distance between all pairs of document vectors in the document collection. Then, any two document vectors whose distance is below some threshold are included in a cluster. Next, a **cluster centroid** is defined as a vector that is an average of the other vectors in the cluster (see Exercise 3.4). For instance, if document$_1$ and document$_2$ are the only two documents in a cluster, document$_1$ = (0.1, 0.7, 0.3), and document$_2$ = (0.2, 0.5, 0.1), then the centroid for that cluster is (0.15, 0.6, 0.2).

Clustering reduces **search time**. If a document collection has one million documents and two equal-sized clusters are made, then after the search has found the closest cluster to a query, there still remain 500 000 documents to filter. On the other hand, if the collection is divided into 100 000 clusters, then retrieving the cluster closest to a query requires 100 000 computations. By defining the centers of clusters it is possible to assess the similarity among clusters and to add another level of organization to the classification of sets of documents (Salton and McGill, 1983). For example, given the 100 000 clusters, grouping them into tens, and repeating this process, one gets a hierarchy of clusters in which the top level has 10 clusters, the second level has 100 clusters, and so on. In retrieval one would never need to do more than a few computations of distance between the query vector and the centroid of a cluster in order to find a small cluster of documents which was close to the query.

example benefit in search cost

Cluster-based strategies need substantial **initial investment** of computer time to construct the hierarchy of document clusters. This initial investment pays dividends in reducing the effort involved at search time in retrieving documents in response to each request (see Exercise 3.5). For a fixed document collection which is frequently accessed, the benefits of clustering are substantial.

initial cost versus subsequent benefit

3.2.2 Indexing language principles

The effectiveness of a retrieval system is largely dependent upon the document classes in it. These classes may be based on terms from an indexing language which semantically relates terms, is used to index documents, and supports queries (Lancaster, 1972). An indexing language is an **ordering system** which is 'any instrument for the organization, description, and retrieval of knowledge that consists of verbal or notational expressions for concepts and their relationships and which displays these elements in an ordered way' (Dahlberg, 1983).

role of indexing language as ordering system

In a string-search system the searcher who wants to find documents about a complex multi-word concept, like 'on-line bibliographic system', could request all documents that contain the words 'on-line', 'bibliographic', and 'system'. Each retrieved document contains the three words, which the search has **post-coordinated**. A paper index does not, however, readily support such post-coordination. If the user were to search in the paper catalog under the term 'on-line', make a list of the documents, then search under the term 'bibliographic', make another list of the documents, and determine the documents which both lists have in common before continuing with the term 'system', the user would be tired. Accordingly, for paper indices concepts are **pre-coordinated**, and a concept like 'on-line bibliographic system' is directly represented with a single term.

pre- and post-coordination

Specificity in indexing refers to a semantic property of **index terms**: a term is more or less specific as its meaning is more or less detailed and precise. Index term specificity must also be considered from the view of what happens when

specificity

a given index vocabulary is actually used. As a document collection grows, the descriptions of some documents may not be sufficiently distinguished because some terms are frequently used. Thus it may be the case that a particular term becomes less effective as a means of retrieval, whatever its actual meaning. A frequently-used term may thus function in retrieval as a non-specific term, even though its meaning may be quite specific in the ordinary sense (Jones, 1972).

query

A **query** to a macrotext system whose documents have been indexed with terms from an indexing language naturally supports retrieval with queries expressed in the terms of that indexing language. In the simplest case, the user presents a single term to the system, and the system returns those documents which have been indexed with that term. More generally, index terms are combined with set or Boolean operators.

3.2.2.1 Indexing

personnel costs in
indexing

When maximum specificity is sought in the indexing procedure, the **index terms** representing a document often represent significantly distinct concepts. To use an indexing language in the indexing of documents typically requires a large investment of intellectual effort. At the National Library of Medicine, which indexes about 300 000 documents per year, about 100 people are devoted to indexing. About a dozen index terms are assigned to each document, but an indexer is expected to spend only 15 minutes on each document. The **indexing staff** includes a quality control unit. Similar situations apply at other large information services which index documents.

term matching

Aids to indexing have been developed. In one strategy, an index term from a thesaurus is suggested for a document, if it is in the title of the document (Rada and Evans, 1979). While this approach seems overly simple, it can provide a guide to human indexing, when the thesaurus has been developed to coincide with terms in titles of documents. Other strategies extend the **term matching**, so that the occurrence of parts of an index term in the abstract of a document suggests that index term be applied to the document.

3.2.2.2 Thesaurus

definition of thesaurus

One of the most popular forms for an indexing language is a thesaurus. While a thesaurus in the lay use of the word usually suggests an alphabetically sorted list of terms with attached synonyms, in the library science field this is often expanded. A thesaurus is a set of **concepts** in which each concept is represented with at least synonymous terms, broader concepts, narrower concepts, and related concepts (National Library and Information Associations Council, 1980). A term is a word or sequence of words that refers to a concept. For instance, 'shortness of breath' may be considered a term when discussing symptoms of patients. Each concept may be associated with one term that serves as the name of that concept.

example thesauri

Popular thesauri for classification of library books are the Dewey Decimal System and the Library of Congress Subject Headings. A popular thesaurus for general use is *Roget's Thesaurus* (Roget, 1977). *Roget's Thesaurus* has several hierarchical levels so that, for instance, 'general form' is narrower than 'form' which is, in turn, narrower than 'space', but synonyms are only given for the narrowest terms.

The relations or links **broader**, **narrower**, **related**, and **synonymous** have been defined for thesauri (National Library and Information Associations Council, 1980). link types

1. The relation 'broader' can mean:
   (a) Class inclusion, such as neoplasm is a disease.
   (b) Whole-part, such as hand is a part of arm.
   (c) Other connected concepts, such as 'electron tube' is broader than 'characteristic curve of an electron tube'.
2. The relation 'narrower' includes the reverse relations of those listed for 'broader'.
3. Two terms are considered to be 'related', if they are related but neither is 'broader' than the other. 'Related' may be used to identify terms that are related to each other from a certain point of view, such as usage, action, or process.
4. The 'synonymous' relation points to terms that mean the same thing.

The standards for thesauri restrict the relations to little more than the above.

From a computer scientist's perspective 'thesaurus' and 'classification structure' might mean the same thing, but from a librarian's view they have traditionally had different meanings. To a librarian a **classification structure** is a listing of terms that depicts **hierarchical structure** (Litoukhin, 1980). For instance, a classification structure would show the terms 'disease', 'joint disease', and 'arthritis' one after the other on the page with indentations and numberings to indicate 'narrower' relationships (see Fig. 3.9). The terms in a thesaurus are alphabetically, rather than hierarchically, sorted. classification structure

As computers become more common in library work, the difference between an alphabetically sorted list (thesaurus) and a list sorted by hierarchical position (classification structure) becomes less critical, and each is more likely to be viewed as a different representation of the same information (Dahlberg, 1980). From a **thesaurus**, where each term points to its conceptual parents and children, a computer program can readily generate a **classification structure**. Furthermore, a classification structure could incorporate with each entry a list of synonyms and related terms, and in that case a computer could generate a thesaurus from a classification structure. converting between thesaurus and classification structure

1. Disease

    1.1. Joint disease

        1.1.1. Arthritis

Figure 3.9 Classification structure.

3.2.2.3 Thesaurus construction

how to build a
thesaurus

The thesauri for large on-line bibliographies are massive—they may contain over 100 000 concepts. How are these thesauri **constructed** and **maintained**? What is the relationship between indexing and thesaurus maintenance? Can word frequency information be useful in thesaurus maintenance?

THESAURUS CONSTRUCTION GROUP

thesaurus and index
experts

An institution which indexes many documents and maintains a large thesaurus may have an indexing staff of 100 people and a thesaurus staff of 10 people. The **thesaurus group** consists of experts in the domain of the literature to be processed. These experts have a grasp of the terminology and semantic subtleties of the subject field. The thesaurus group is responsible for collecting index terms, and making the thesaurus as up-to-date as possible for the index group. The index group then indexes the documents according to the latest version of the thesaurus and suggests new index terms to the thesaurus group.

index first or construct
thesaurus first?

In the development of a macrotext system, one dilemma is whether to **build a thesaurus** first and then use it for indexing the documents or to **index the documents** by free terms and then construct the thesaurus after accumulating a good number of these free terms. As is often true in life, the middle ground is particularly attractive, and that means in this case building a thesaurus and indexing documents hand in hand.

how to add terms to a
thesaurus

To build a thesaurus and index documents simultaneously requires both selecting a set of documents and creating a thesaurus around which to begin. Then an indexer scans a document and chooses in a free-form fashion a set of terms to characterize that document. In case a term is not available in the thesaurus, one of the following three approaches may be taken (Sudarshan, 1979):

1. If a synonymous term is available in the thesaurus, then the thesaurus experts should be asked to include this **synonym** in the thesaurus. For example, if the term 'lathe' is available in the thesaurus but the indexer has chosen the synonym 'turning machine', then 'turning machine' should be added as a synonym to 'lathe'.
2. If the indexable concept can be broken into parts which are in the thesaurus, then this breakdown should be made and the thesaurus might be augmented to indicate the relation which exists between the component terms. For instance, if 'hydrostatic thrust bearings' is initially chosen to describe the document but the index only has 'hydrostatic bearings' and 'thrust bearings', then the document is indexed under both terms and the thesaurus might be augmented to indicate that these two types of bearings are related.
3. If steps 1 and 2 do not produce index terms from the thesaurus, then a check is made for terms in the thesaurus which are **broader** than the one chosen by the indexer. If the initial thesaurus is well-designed, then any new term must, at least, be able to fit under some pre-existing broader term. So the indexer next asks the thesaurus group whether the indexer's term should be added to the thesaurus as a 'narrower' term or whether the existing 'broader' term itself should be used.

This hybrid method of free-text and controlled vocabulary for thesaurus construction depends on both the thesaurus group and the index group. Purely intellectual attempts to produce perfect thesauri do not work. Feedback from indexers must guide the development of a thesaurus (Wessel, 1979).

WORD FREQUENCY

Terms that frequently occur in a document collection are candidates for inclusion in the thesaurus for that collection. Conversely, a term which rarely occurs in the collection is unlikely to make a good thesaurus term. The **frequency of usage** of thesaurus terms by indexers can itself serve as a guide to thesaurus maintenance. If a term is frequently chosen by indexers, then terms more specific than it should be added to the thesaurus. A thesaurus term which is never used by indexers is a candidate for removal from the thesaurus.

frequency implies value

Determining the relations among thesaurus terms is particularly difficult. Association by **frequency of co-occurrence** between two terms, x and y, suggests relationships, such as (Jones, 1971):

suggest thesaurus relations

(a) x and y are synonymous,
(b) x is narrower than y, and
(c) x and y are members of a compound term, like 'flip flop'.

For instance, x may be narrower than y, if the number of documents containing y is much larger than the number containing x. Word-frequency thesaurus building is not feasible by itself. The identification of terms and relationships by word-frequency methods may be useful as pre-processing that results in a list of important terms and potential relationships between them. These relationships can then be combed by people to establish which relationships are cognitively meaningful.

3.2.3 Retrieval interface

The interface to a retrieval system must make apparent all the relevant options to a **user** (Mittman and Borman, 1975). For instance, since a retrieval system must allow documents to be retrieved based on author or date, one option on the interface should lead to an alphabetically sorted list of author names. The interface should make it easy for searchers to request documents written across some period of time; for instance, one might ask for all documents published between January and July of 1985. However, the most complex part of the retrieval interface must support access by content descriptions. How can the searcher be guided into ways of requesting documents on an arbitrary topic?

requirements for retrieval interface

When a very large thesaurus is accessed via a computer screen, the user may need to change the contents of the screen many times to find the terms for a query. This difficulty has been substantiated in experiments on the impact of depth of **menu** on performance. Those results indicated that performance time and errors increased as the hierarchical levels of the data in the menus increased (Seppala and Salvendy, 1985). Thus the user should be allowed parallel modes of presentation of data and not just one menu.

menu depth

A new generation of systems depends on **graphical interfaces**, menus, and

graphical screen

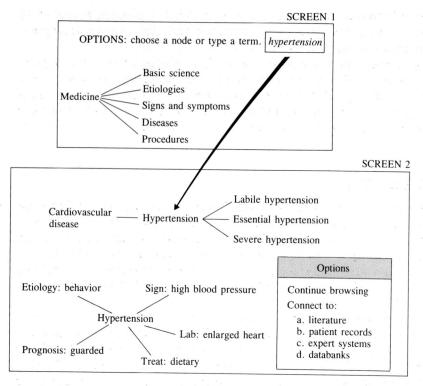

Figure 3.10 Retrieval interface for a richly-connected term. In screen 1, the user requested information about 'hypertension'. In screen 2, the user sees the hierarchy of terms around 'hypertension' and also the attributes of 'hypertension' relative to etiology, prognosis, treatment, signs, and laboratory values.

natural language processing to help end-users exploit the access points of the macrotext system. A fictitious screen is presented in which a user is looking for articles about hypertension and its genetic etiology. The user first has the choice of browsing the thesaurus or entering a term directly. Say the user enters the term 'hypertension'. Next, the conceptual neighborhood around hypertension appears on the screen. That neighborhood includes both the 'broader' and

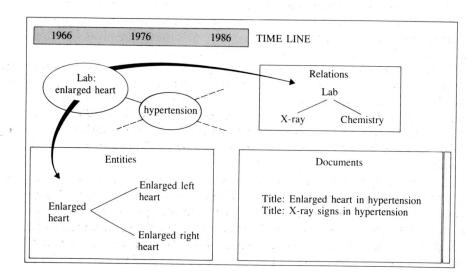

Figure 3.11 Expansion of relations.

'narrower' terms for hypertension and a constellation of terms connected by 'etiology', 'prognosis', 'treatment', and other such links that are appropriate for the disease hypertension (see Fig. 3.10).

If the user now chooses to pursue the 'lab link' of hypertension, there appears another screen which shows both specific 'lab links', namely 'X-rays' and 'chemistry', and specific 'enlarged heart' terms (see Fig. 3.11). Simultaneously there appears: (a) a **time line** and (b) the titles of the documents. Users can interact with the time line to specify the dates of publication for retrieved articles.

further graphical views

3.2.4 Usability

A common **querying strategy** is to submit first a broad request and then refine the request by adding conditions, until a reasonably small set of relevant documents is returned (Fidel, 1984). This trial-and-error process can be very tedious when performed by a novice who is not familiar with the way documents are indexed. Further, when no document matches all the conditions of a query, there is no knowledgeable way of telling which documents might be close to the query.

querying strategy

Many interfaces to information systems attempt to be all things to all people. They have not been designed with a specific **target audience** or **user model** in mind. Human factors research has shown the importance of iterative design with a group of subjects drawn from the intended population of users. When an interface is tailored to one narrow population, that population can accomplish a search with relatively little training (Case *et al.*, 1986). The user who can understand the principles of the system is better able to present complex queries effectively. Conversely, for simple queries a more mechanistic view of the system seems to be adequate for successful searching.

need for user models

Pursuant to psychological testing, people can be categorized as 'accommodators' or 'assimilators'. **Accommodators** solve problems in intuitive, trial-and-error ways, while **assimilators** prefer to reason and reflect. In one study of novice MEDLINE searchers, assimilators were consistently more successful than accommodators (Logan, 1990). Distinct training programs and interface styles could be designed for these different types of users.

accommodators versus assimilators

Novice users often pose natural language queries in writing to professional search intermediaries. The search intermediary then accesses the document database and generates queries. While novices often have difficulty with the mechanical and conceptual aspects of searching, **search intermediaries** are experts and use such systems easily (Borgman, 1986). These differences in behavior might be due to effects of training, experience, frequency of use, and knowledge about information structures.

role of search intermediary

If macrotext systems are to be widely used, then many users must be able to search satisfactorily without the intervention of a search intermediary. Users may, however, be expected to undergo a brief training period. In one study, novice users were given four hours of training, and then their performance was compared to that of search intermediaries. These '**trained novices**' obtained results similar to those of the search intermediaries (Sullivan *et al.*, 1990).

role of training

Furthermore, the novices felt more committed to reading the relevant literature, because they had done the search themselves.

3.2.5 Evaluation methods

evaluating several
aspects

Evaluation takes several forms for a macrotext system. What is put into the system has enormous impact on both the creators and accessors of the documents. The indexing and indexing language should also be evaluated. Most carefully studied has been the quality of **retrieval** from a given system. Recall and precision are the popular devices for evaluating retrieval from a macrotext system.

3.2.5.1 Document acquisition

the dead document

The decision about what documents to include in an information retrieval system is crucial to the perceived utility of the system. There are major practical, often financial but sometimes also technical, limits to what documents any given information system can hold (Kraft and Hill, 1973). Including a document in a macrotext system means that a link exists between that document and the users of the macrotext system. A document lives to the extent that it is somehow used. In this sense, the decision not to place a document into a macrotext system is to hurt the document. If the document is also not available anywhere else, it is effectively **dead**.

heuristics for
acquisition

The acquisition of documents for a macrotext system seems to be largely controlled by rules of thumb. Clearly, customers should be satisfied, and the budget should be balanced, but how these goals should be obtained is less clear. Methods for selecting documents to include in an information retrieval system may be scientific, political, or economic in orientation. Within the life sciences alone there are several information systems, and each has its own method of selecting journals (Garfield, 1985). One of the criteria for a journal to be indexed is that it has significant **circulation**, though given that a significant circulation may be difficult to achieve before the journal is indexed, a kind of vicious circle is created.

citation analysis

A variety of quantitative tools has been used in the determination of journal quality. **Citation analysis** has been repeatedly recommended as a tool for journal selection (Dhawan *et al.*, 1980), and has also been applied to the elucidation of specific features of a document, such as its methodological rigor. One analysis of documents notes that the appearance of a colon ':' in the title of a document suggests scholarly content (Perry, 1985).

publish or perish

The popular dictum in academia is **publish or perish**. By implication the authors best fit to survive in academia are those who publish the most. Extending this notion to the assessment of journals, one might expect that the more important a journal the more frequently the authors in it publish. Various experiments do not, however, confirm this hypothesis but rather indicate that the papers in good journals are written by authors who publish in other good journals (Rada *et al.*, 1987). This suggests that the 'publish or perish' mandate

---

1. Sponsorship of the journal by a professional organization of recognized status in a given discipline or subject area.
2. Sponsorship by a national academy or national institute.
3. Existence of an active editorial board consisting of knowledgeable and critical referees with high professional standing.
4. Regular contributions to the journal by leaders in the subject.
5. Strict adherence to an established format in presentation of methodology, tables, graphs, references and other data.
6. Publication policy that appears in the journal.

Figure 3.12 Journal selection criteria developed by experts in the 1960s.

is sound only when qualified as 'publish in good places or perish' (see Exercise 3.6).

There are about 20000 biomedical journals in existence. Of these, about 3000 are indexed in *Index Medicus*. When a medical library tries to decide what journals to purchase, the library typically refers to *Index Medicus* and will avoid subscribing to a journal which is not **indexed**. Circulation is thus related to indexing. When authors write good papers, they often prefer to publish them in journals which are indexed. In the medical field, a scholarly paper which appears in a non-*Index Medicus* journal is much less likely to reach its audience than if it appeared in an *Index Medicus* journal, so publishers and editors of a new journal go to great lengths to attain a position in *Index Medicus*. Membership in the index may be necessary for membership in other critical groupings, such as the high-circulation grouping, the quality-papers grouping, and the often-read grouping (Rada, 1990).

journal acquisition for Index Medicus

Until 1964, journal selection decisions at *Index Medicus* were made by the Head of the Indexing Section. However, efforts were continually made to provide some rationale for the inclusion or exclusion of articles. These attempts usually reiterated a concern with the inclusion of 'quality' articles (without defining quality) and admonishments as to what should not be indexed (Karel, 1967). In 1964, due to the recognized impact of *Index Medicus* on the selection of journals for acquisition by libraries, a panel of experts was constituted and given the task of deciding which journals should or should not be indexed. The panel produced six general **criteria** (Bachrach and Charen, 1978), which stressed that the people associated with the journal are reputable and that norms of publishing are obeyed (see Fig. 3.12).

criteria include quality

3.2.5.2 Indexing and thesaurus evaluation

When human indexers assign index terms to a document, how consistent, accurate, or thorough are they? If the best experts can perform an indexing which is considered ideal, then how will one test any other indexing against the ideal? The **validity of indexing** is not simply the exact matches between an ideal and a test indexing. When a thesaurus is used, terms from the test indexing which are close in the thesaurus to terms from the ideal set should be considered more correct than terms which are not close (see Exercise 3.7).

indexing evaluation

thesaurus evaluation

One can axiomatize the desirable properties of a good thesaurus based on psychological rules. A standard method of portraying the hierarchy in a thesaurus to a user is for any concept to list all the 'narrower' concepts in a menu. As a novice searcher traverses a thesaurus in search of appropriate query terms, the searcher's short-term memory limitations make it desirable that each concept should have a handful of narrower concepts so that the menu display is neither too sparse nor too cluttered (Lee and MacGregor, 1985). The number in a handful varies with the application and user, but as a rule of thumb falls roughly between 4 and 18 with the ideal being 7. The number of narrower terms from any given term is called the **branching factor** for that given term. A quantitative assessment of a thesaurus can be made of the extent to which the thesaurus maintains a good branching factor. Thus thesaurus T_2 is better than thesaurus T_1, if T_2's branching factor is more consistently about 7 than is T_1's branching factor.

3.2.5.3 Retrieval evaluation

cognitive model

Searchers on a macrotext system may have many different notions of what constitutes a relevant document. One person may want the most recently published document. Another may want a document that is frequently cited by other people. The **cognitive model** of a searcher is necessarily complex. Given some way to measure relevance (and this measure is the hard one), retrieval performance can be easily assessed with recall and precision measures.

recall and precision

If the document collection is separated into **retrieved** and **not-retrieved** sets and if procedures are available for separating **relevant** items from **nonrelevant** ones, then **Recall** and **Precision** are defined as:

$$\text{Recall} = \frac{\text{number of items retrieved and relevant}}{\text{total relevant}}$$

$$\text{Precision} = \frac{\text{number of items retrieved and relevant}}{\text{total retrieved}}$$

Recall measures the ability of a system to retrieve relevant documents, while conversely, precision measures the ability to reject nonrelevant materials. Everything else being equal, a good system is one which exhibits both a high recall and a high precision.

relevance is subjective

Measures like recall are based on a person's assessment of relevant and nonrelevant documents. Some people consider these **subjective assessments** unreliable. Among other things, a document may be relevant by content, by timeliness, by cost, or many other factors. However, in one well-controlled comparison of the ability of humans to judge consistently the relevance of documents, humans were able to make such judgements consistently (Resnick and Savage, 1964). While the internal decision-making apparatus is clearly complex, humans are able to produce **consistent** decisions about document relevance under certain circumstances.

single value based on correlating rankings

One measure of effectiveness of a document retrieval system assigns a single number to the value of retrieval (Swets, 1969). This contrasts with the popular covarying pair of measures of recall and precision. A computer system can assign values or scores to documents, the scores attesting to the closeness between a document and a query. Likewise, people can be asked to make the same assessments. From these scores can be derived **rankings**, and the rankings may be compared with a correlation coefficient. The assumption here as for recall is that human experts are the gold-standard of performance. The evaluation of a system's retrieval ability compares the system's ranking with the ranking of human experts. The higher the **correlation**, the better the system is performing.

3.3 Systems

Many organizations maintain **macrotext systems**, as do in fact some individuals. Effective and efficient document indexing and retrieval may be critical to a company's success. Often the documents are classified simply by author, date, and title. Retrieval by more specific content is typically difficult, unless indexing by word patterns or an indexing language has been done.

companies need macrotext systems

3.3.1 Text databases

Text is unlike other types of data in the complexity of its structure. For the purposes of storage, a text may be regarded as a very long string. For retrieval purposes, however, substrings of the text must be identified. Although the data structuring capabilities of **relational database** systems are well adapted to support complex structures, they provide few built-in tools for the analysis of text strings. Furthermore, the modeling process appropriate for building a relational database is not necessarily appropriate for building a text database. A text system must concern itself with the document, the part of a document which is to be searched, and the set of documents which are to be returned to a searcher. A text database must support definition of text structures, retrieval of document sets, formatting of retrieved documents, control of document terminology, and addition of documents.

special needs of text

STAIRS is a storage and information retrieval system marketed by IBM. IBM sells the software separately from any document database to go with STAIRS. The system includes utility programs for database maintenance and a retrieval system. The **database** structure includes a dictionary, an inverted file, a text index, and text files (see Fig. 3.13). The text files are the actual documents which users want. The dictionary contains all words that are in the document set. The inverted file says for each occurrence of each word exactly where it occurs relative to paragraph, sentence, and word number. The text index allows some documents to be marked private.

STAIRS structure

Search statements in STAIRS may include logical and proximity operations among words. For instance, the logical command 'Computer OR Machine' would retrieve pointers to documents that contained the word Computer or the word Machine. The **proximity** operator ADJ means that two words must be adjacent in the document, while the operator WITH means that the two words

STAIRS search

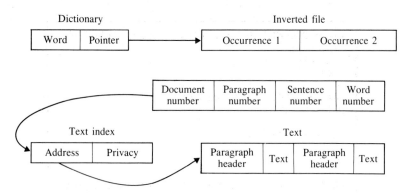

Figure 3.13 STAIRS
structure.

are in the same sentence. Specific fields within the database can be defined, and the user can search on these in traditional database query ways.

evaluation of systems

Dozens of major, commercial text database systems are available. An extensive evaluation was recently performed on three of these systems: BASIS, BRS, and STATUS (Bain *et al.*, 1989). Each of these provides all the basic functions required of large text database systems. On the majority of tests the performance of the three systems was essentially identical, though, in comparing one system to another, the evaluators did criticize the BASIS interface, the BRS recovery facilities, and the STATUS retrieval techniques.

3.3.2 An on-line session

DIALOG

Bibliographic systems typically contain citations to documents. A citation to a journal paper, for instance, may include the paper's title, journal name, journal pages, date of publication, authors, abstract, and index terms. **DIALOG** is an on-line bibliographic system with approximately 300 different document or citation databases. The system is based on an inverted file design. In response to a search statement, the system first returns sets of document pointers. The user can operate on these sets and at any point ask to see the citations associated with the reference numbers. The following is a sample of an interaction on DIALOG. Notice that the system returns all data in upper case.

initiation

The first step for a DIALOG user is to gain access to the system (see Fig. 3.14). One way to begin is to **telephone** a computer network (TELENET in this example) and then specify a code number (202 13E in this example). DIALOG then prompts the user with a question mark after a logon and welcome message. If the user types 'begin number', the system enters the database identified with 'number'. In this example the database number 202 is entered which refers to 'Information Science Abstracts'.

search

The **search strategy** for a DIALOG session involves Boolean queries over terms in the database. A search statement begins with an 's'. In the example (see Fig. 3.15) the first search statement is 's information and systems'. DIALOG responds with a list of how many citations contain each of the terms in the search and the result of the Boolean operation. In this example, the database has 94090 citations with the term 'information' in them, 34978 with the term 'systems' in them, and 34359 citations that have both terms. The query

```
Dialing TELENET: .9 429 7800 Carrier Detected ..Online!

TELENET
202 13E

DIALOG INFORMATION SERVICES
PLEASE LOGON:

Welcome to DIALOG

?b202

File 202:INFORMATION SCIENCE ABSTRACTS 66-86/MAY
(C. IFI/PLENUM DATA CO. 1986)
```

Figure 3.14 DIALOG startup.

```
?s information and systems
      Set Items  Description
           94090 INFORMATION
           34978 SYSTEMS
      S1    34359 INFORMATION AND SYSTEMS
?s information(1w)systems
           94090 INFORMATION
           34978 SYSTEMS
      S5    13584 INFORMATION(1W)SYSTEMS
?e information

Ref  Items   Index-term
E1     3     INFORMATIOIN
E2     3     INFORMATIOM
E3   94090   *INFORMATION
E4     1     INFORMATION ABOUT EUROPEAN COMMUNITIES SOURCES
E5     1     INFORMATION ABOUT PRODUCTIVITY
E6     1     INFORMATION ABSTRACTING DOSE-RESPONSE
E7     3     INFORMATION ACCESS
```

Figure 3.15 DIALOG search. The 's' command returns pointers to citations. The 'e' command shows the index. As the index is generated automatically from document citations, if those citations contain misspellings, then the index also contains those misspellings.

'information(1w)systems' asks for the citations which have the term 'information' within one word of the term 'systems' in the citation. While 34359 citations contained both terms, only 13584 had the two words adjacent. The expand command (abbreviated 'e') asks for a listing of the terms in the index dictionary in alphabetical order around the term given in the expand command. For instance, 'e information' returns the list shown in Fig. 3.15. These terms have been used to index documents in the 'Information Science Abstracts' database.

In order to retrieve specific citations, users enter print requests. Each request **retrieved citations** may have several options. The parameters '6/4/1' request data for search statement 6, with printing format 4, and for the first citation retrieved (see Fig. 3.16). Information **retrieved** includes the title (TI), the authors (AU), the source (SO) which in this example is the journal *Scientometrics*, the abstract (AB), and the descriptors (DE) used to describe the contents of the article. The FN field notes the particular database from which the article has come. The full abstract in English is available for many articles.

To use a system like DIALOG one must have an account with DIALOG. The **billing**

```
6/4/1
0047229
FN-  INFORMATION SCIENCE ABSTRACTS
TI-  ON SCIENTOMETRICAL CHARACTERISTICS ON INFORMATION ACTIVITIES OF
     LEADING SCIENTISTS.
AU-  GRANOVSKY, YU.V.; MULCHENKO, Z.M.; STRAKHOV, A.B.
SO-  SCIENTOMETRICS 1(4), 307-325 (1979 MAY). 9 ILLUS. 8 TAB. 4 REF.
AB-  A COMPARATIVE ANALYSIS OF THE INFORMATION ACTIVITIES OF LEADING
     SCIENTISTS HAS BEEN CARRIED OUT, INCLUDING 5 SOVIET CHEMISTS AND
     5 FOREIGN ONES . . . CITATION RATE (NUMBER OF REFERENCES PER NUMBER OF
     PAPERS) IS A CRITERION FOR SEPARATING THE PUBLICATIONS OF THE
     'INTELLECTUAL INDUSTRY' FROM THE PILOT STUDIES FULL OF NOVEL IDEAS.
DE-  UTILIZATION OF INFORMATION, USER STUDIES
```

Figure 3.16 DIALOG retrieval. The abstract has been substantially shortened for this example.

```
?b 13
      28jan87 13:24:45 User020257

29.19  0.417 Hrs File202
 4.58  Telenet
33.77  Estimated cost this file
34.87  Estimated total session cost 0.444 Hrs.
```

Figure 3.17 DIALOG costs.

costs of these accounts are substantial; one can expect to pay about 100 dollars per hour for on-line access to the database, the charge depending on the particular database. As one leaves a database and enters another database still within DIALOG, one gets a summary **cost statement** for the exited database (see Fig. 3.17). In the example, the command 'b 13' signals a move to another database. What is first returned is a billing statement. The interaction with 'Information Sciences Abstract' through DIALOG ended at 13:24:45 on the 28th of January 1987. For 0.417 hours of access time the charge was 29.19 dollars. The separate charge due to TELENET was 4.58 dollars.

summary of features

The DIALOG system supports searches of many kinds. Various fields, such as date, author, and title, have been pre-defined, and a searcher can request documents which satisfy some condition on a particular field. Every document is **indexed** not only by **every word** in the document, but if index terms have been assigned to a document, then the document can be found via those index terms as well. Word frequency indexing or retrieval techniques are not, however, supported by DIALOG.

3.3.3 Word-based systems

humans not needed

For **string-search** and **word-frequency** systems humans are no longer needed to index documents. The computer does the work. What kinds of systems exploit these methodologies and do not get overwhelmed by the computational costs?

3.3.3.1 String-search

cost

The **computational feasibility** of 'pure' string-search is limited to small textual databases on conventional computers. The cost in computer time of searching character by character across the text database is high. Commercial systems do, however, offer a partial string-search capability. Users may find documents containing any particular word but not necessarily any string.

To do string-search, the computer must load into its memory the document content before the search is performed. For a large system like MEDLARS one may be advised to do a retrieval through the word index. If one gets no more than about 300 documents in return, then one may do string-search on those 300 documents. In other words, string-search is best reserved for a **small document set**.

string-search on small document set

The decreasing cost of processors is stimulating the search for efficient uses of **parallel computers**. Work on very-large, textual databases is turning to parallel machines to deal with the need for reasonable response times when string searches are performed. The Connection Machine is commercially used for parallel string searching (Stanfill and Kahle, 1986). The machine has 65 536 processors (2^{16}). When scanning thousands of articles for a single string, a conventional machine would go through them one by one. The **Connection Machine** can read all of the articles at once, because each article, in effect, is assigned to an individual processor, with each processor executing the same 'scan' instruction. The process can be metaphorically described as follows: 'Each of 65 000 people in a stadium has a different document. A word is announced over the public address system, and all the people scan their article to see whether it contains that word.' This approach makes 'pure' string-search computationally feasible.

parallelism

3.3.3.2 Word frequency

Many word-frequency based document retrieval systems have been built in academia and extensively tested. One of the most famous is the **SMART macrotext system** developed by Gerard Salton's group at Cornell University (Salton and McGill, 1983). The system supports **automated indexing**, **clustered documents**, and **interactive search** procedures. Documents are basically represented as vectors of weighted words, and retrieval relies on similarity between document vectors and query vectors.

methods

The **STAIRS macrotext system** supports ranking by word frequency. From a retrieved set of documents, a user can request a ranking based on word frequency. For instance, the user may specify that the more frequent a word in a document the more relevant that document is. This ranking facility is, however, invoked only after other search strategies have yielded a **small document set**.

STAIRS ranking

The macrotext system **Personal Librarian** supports word-frequency indexing and retrieval. Given a query of terms, the system can rank the relevance of documents to a query according to four principles:

Personal Librarian

- If one search term occurs rarely and another occurs commonly, documents with the rare term are considered more relevant than documents with the common term.
- The larger the number of different search terms occurring in a document, the more relevant the document will be.

- The higher the frequency of a given search term in a document, the more relevant the document will be.
- The fewer the number of words between occurrences of terms in a document, the more relevant the document will be.

Queries can be posed as **natural language** and the system will extract search terms from the query. The user can specify a topic search in three ways:

- expanding a term (e.g., expand computer) returns terms statistically related to the first term (see Exercise 3.8);
- expanding a document (e.g., expand document34) returns terms statistically related to the document;
- matching a document (e.g., match document34) returns statistically related documents.

Personal Librarian works on personal computers or mainframes and various operating systems. The personal computer version operates with a windowing system that facilitates use by novices.

printed indices
      While some document retrieval systems offer word-frequency tools, these are not commonly used, partly because organizations which maintain document databases often want to produce **printed indices**. To structure printed indices properly, human indexing of the documents has been seen as critical. Once this human indexing has been done, it also supports computer retrieval.

3.3.4 Indexing language systems

standards needed
When an individual has a small library, he develops an indexing language which may be highly **idiosyncratic**. For instance, material of recent interest may be in a stack on the table; one file drawer may hold proposals sorted by topic; and one bookshelf may hold books of a certain size. As the number of people who use a library grows, the need for **standard indexing languages** grows. Many types of indexing language exist; one unusual type is based on 'keyword in context' principles.

3.3.4.1 Preserved Context Index System

PRECIS
One method of automatically generating a simple kind of index for a set of documents is to list each word followed by a few of the words that occur in that word's immediate context. Such an index is called a key-word-in-context (KWIC) index. A substantial extension of the **KWIC** approach has been taken in the Preserved Context Index System (**PRECIS**) whose name conveys the idea of context dependency as well as the fact that a précis of the subject is provided.

relations among index terms
      To index with the PRECIS method, indexers scan a document looking for those terms which they regard as essential to a verbal expression of the document's subject content. They next consider the role which each of these terms plays in the subject as a whole. The relation between terms in the classification of the document is restricted to a handful of relations, including (Austin, 1984): (0) Key system, (1) Active concept, and (3) Study region. If one were indexing a document about 'The management of railways in France', one

railways, management, France
management, railways, France
France, management, railways

Figure 3.18 PRECIS published index.

would begin by breaking the subject into 'management', 'railways', and 'France'. One then checks each of these terms against the set of relationships and decides under what relations to place each of the three terms. In this example 'management' is recognized as the **active concept**. 'Railways' would be stored under **key system**, and 'France' would be under 'study region'.

The published version of the indexing shows an entry for each term of the index. The indexing of 'The management of railways in France', might appear as in Fig. 3.18, with each term associated with all the other terms in the index in a systematic way.

PRECIS is used by parts of the British Library for the classification of books. It was designed with the computer in mind but is largely a manual system both for indexing and retrieval. The **British Library** publishes the results of the PRECIS indexing in a document which is then used by searchers. A number of other PRECIS-like systems have been implemented (Farradane, 1977).

Retrieval has been compared for documents indexed with the Library of Congress Subject Headings (LCSH) and for documents indexed with the British Library's PRECIS scheme (Schabas, 1982). Queries were about **social science** topics and about **pure science**. The users seemed equally satisfied with LCSH and PRECIS for queries in the pure sciences but felt that PRECIS allowed substantially more good documents to be retrieved in the social sciences than did LCSH. The explanation for the difference between the social and pure sciences may rest on the 'soft' versus 'hard' nature, respectively, of the vocabularies. In the social sciences, more so than in the pure sciences, terms tend to be used less precisely, new terms keep emerging, and several terms often overlap in meaning.

published index

implementation

evaluation

3.3.4.2 Thesaurus system

Thesauri are common in both specialized and general macrotext systems. The phone book illustrates a simple index which is meant to be understandable to all. A medical thesaurus shows the great detail which has evolved over time for a medical community.

thesauri are common

ELECTRONIC YELLOW PAGES

The *Yellow Pages* is a phone directory which provides product and service information to an enormous audience. An *Electronic Yellow Pages* (EYP) has the ability to provide many additional features that a paper *Yellow Pages* can not. Each entry in the EYP can be viewed as a small document which may include pictures of products, photos of salesman, sentences describing the product, addresses, hours of operation, and maps (see Fig. 3.19). To properly

definition and example entry

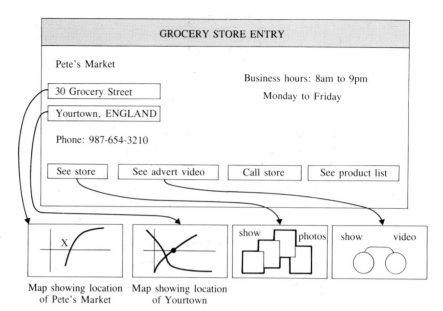

Figure 3.19 Electronic Yellow Pages. Information within a grocery store entry may include pointers to other information that may contain graphics, sound, or video.

Map showing location of Pete's Market

Map showing location of Yourtown

convert the *Yellow Pages* into macrotext an augmented indexing scheme is needed (see Exercise 3.9).

indexing

Yellow Pages tend to have short indices. The directory for a city of millions of people may have an index of only a few pages. This **index** is usually presented as an alphabetically-sorted list of terms, with an occasional level of indentation (see Fig. 3.20). The popular advertising slogan 'Let Your Fingers Do the Walking Through the *Yellow Pages*' implies that the user knows the routes to follow through the index.

Figure 3.20 Yellow Pages index. An actual *Yellow Pages* is in the background, while a sample of 5 terms from the index has been reproduced and enlarged, and placed on the right.

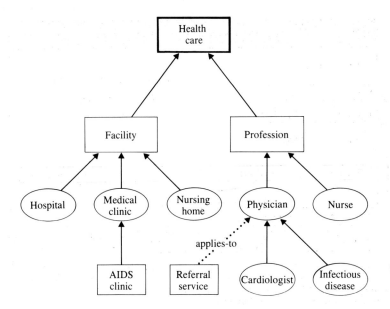

Figure 3.21 Electronic
Yellow Pages index. The
concepts in ellipses were
present in the original Yellow
Pages. The concepts in boxes
have been added as a result
of the effort to build a more
useful index. All the links are
'is-a' links, such as 'Hospital
is-a facility', except that from
'Referral service' to
'Physician'.

An extended indexing language for the *Yellow Pages* would have several more **levels** than the current indexing languages for *Yellow Pages*. For paper, a small index is in some ways more manageable than a large index. For an electronic index, the index size is less a factor than is its organization and presentation. Figure 3.21 illustrates an augmentation of the index in Fig. 3.20. New levels have been introduced into the hierarchy; now a user can find the concept 'Health care' and proceed from there to a breakdown of concepts into 'Facility' and 'Profession'. These three new terms also introduce two new levels in the hierarchy. 'AIDS clinic' has been added as a new leaf in the tree. Figure 3.21 also illustrates another augmentation which could be made to the index. **Non-hierarchical** relations might be useful. For instance, a 'referral service' to direct patients to appropriate physicians would be important for some users of the *Yellow Pages*. 'Referral service' could be explicitly connected to the term 'physicians' via the non-hierarchical link 'applies-to'.

extended index
language

MEDLARS

The MEDLARS bibliographic citation system at the National Library of Medicine uses thesaurus terms in representing queries and documents. Originally, retrieval was performed by a **librarian** in interaction with a user (McCarn, 1980). Now, simple interfaces and compact disks have frequently allowed **end-users** to access directly the MEDLARS databases.

trends with MEDLARS

A flowchart of the MEDLARS system emphasizes that **documents** and **queries** are encoded into terms from a medical thesaurus (see Fig. 3.22). A trained indexer scans a journal article and assigns it indexing terms from the **Medical Subject Headings** (MeSH). Searchers generate queries as Boolean combinations of terms from MeSH and are then shown the citations which were indexed with those terms.

flowchart

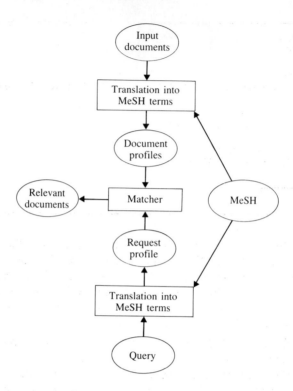

Figure 3.22 MEDLARS. Translation is done by people; profiles include MeSH terms.

deep hierarchy

MeSH includes about 100 000 terms in an 11-level hierarchy. A handful of terms are immediate descendants of the root node and include 'Anatomy', 'Disease', and 'Chemicals'. The major classes of disease, such as 'Neoplasm' and 'Immune disease', are the immediate descendants of the 'Disease' term (see Fig. 3.23).

MeSH database structure

MeSH is so large that it needs its own sophisticated **database structure**. The record for a term in MeSH includes fields for 'On-Line Note', 'MeSH Tree Numbers', 'Backward Cross-References', and 'MED66 Postings' (see Fig. 3.24). For the MeSH term 'EGO' the 'On-Line Note' says that 'EGO' is

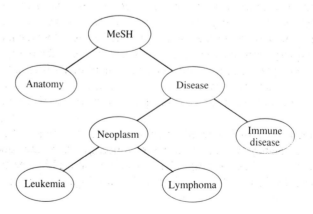

Figure 3.23 MeSH Tree. Sample from hierarchy in MeSH; the root node has several other descendants, as do each of the nodes indicated here.

```
 ┌──────────────────────────────────────────────────────┐
 │  MeSH Term                                           │
 │      EGO                                             │
 │                                                      │
 │  On-line Note                                        │
 │      to search SELF use EGO back thru 1975 & SELF CONCEPT 1966-68 │
 │                                                      │
 │  MeSH Tree Numbers                                   │
 │      F1.752.747.189, F2.739.794.206                 │
 │                                                      │
 │  Backward Cross-References                           │
 │      SELF, REALITY TESTING                           │
 │                                                      │
 │  MED66 Postings                                      │
 │      618                                             │
 └──────────────────────────────────────────────────────┘
```

Figure 3.24 Example of a record for MeSH term. There are several other categories of information in the thesaurus which are not presented here.

synonymous with 'SELF', and the 'MeSH Tree Numbers' field says that 'EGO' occurs in the hierarchy at F1.752.747.189 and F2.739.794.206 (National Library of Medicine, 1986). One knows that 'EGO' is non-hierarchically related to 'Reality Testing' since it occurs in the 'Backward Cross-References' field. From the 'MED66 Postings' field one can recognize that 'EGO' was used 618 times to index documents on MEDLARS prior to 1966.

At Harvard Medical School the **students** are introduced to an educational method that uses tutoring, self-pacing, and computers. Each student is provided with a personal workstation that facilitates communication with other students, with faculty, and with databases. The students are expected to take advantage of the computer to help themselves organize their classroom information. MeSH is being explored as a tool to help in the organization of information. Students may explore the MeSH vocabulary by browsing its hierarchical structure, and terms have been added to MeSH to make it more useful to students who want to learn about medical care and to organize their own library.

MeSH for medical students

GRAPHICAL TRAVERSAL

One retrieval system is designed principally to help a **novice user** with a **graphical display** of a thesaurus (McMath *et al.*, 1989). The user can move about the hierarchy by pointing and clicking with the mouse. Queries using thesaurus terms can be formulated by pointing to terms. Documents can be retrieved by the query, and the quality of the match between the query and the documents is also displayed graphically. The process of query formulation and document retrieval can be repeated often, and the system supports the comparison of the results of one retrieval against the results of the preceding retrieval.

selecting query terms with the mouse

Multiple windows are implemented so that the user can see simultaneously the thesaurus, a histogram of document rankings, and the document descriptions themselves. The ranking of documents produced by the system is presented graphically in a histogram. From the rankings one can go via the mouse to each document.

document ranking

satisfaction depended
on user background

A survey of users of this system and a more traditional system revealed that the **user background** was a critical factor in determining the user satisfaction. The lack of experience of the users with mouse-driven interfaces interfered with their appreciation of the graphical, multi-window system, but they agreed that the graphical concept should be a better way to handle an information retrieval interface.

3.3.5 Searching and browsing systems

historical example

Microtext is linked text within a single document. Macrotext, on the other hand, is a large collection of documents with links among the documents. A microtext system is used by one person on a personal computer, while a macrotext system typically runs on a large computer and is accessed by many people. In many situations, however, the distinction between microtext and macrotext is blurred. For instance, thousands of note cards with text about the shipping activities in the Liverpool harbor during the 18th century are being organized in the Liverpool University Archives (see Fig. 3.25). Is this microtext or macrotext? The cards are connected for browsing and indexed for searching.

motivation

When a **searcher** finds a citation through a macrotext system, their next likely requirement is the entire cited document. If this is available on-line, then the user would want facilities for **browsing** or **reading** the document. This browsing and reading functionality are the strengths of microtext, and systems are being marketed which combine the strengths of microtext and macrotext in what might be called 'large-volume microtext'.

full text

Since many documents are currently prepared on the computer, at least, the alphanumeric parts are easily made available. Some database vendors now

Figure 3.25 Liverpool archives. Thousands of cards with text about the Liverpool shipping activities of the 18th century are being organized by the two library assistants. While this work is being done by hand, hypertext techniques are relevant.

provide on-line the alphanumeric **full text** of major journals (Humphrey and Melloni, 1986). Subscribers to such a database service may see the latest copy of the text of the journal on-line, before they get the paper copy in the mail. Encyclopedias, dictionaries, and textbooks are also increasingly available as full text on-line.

Furthermore, the availability of large amounts of cheap storage in the form of **optical disks** or **videodisks** is supporting the delivery of on-line documents with images. Photographs of journals from cover-to-cover can be economically stored on videodisk. In this way over 200 journals are distributed in the ADONIS system (Campbell and Stern, 1987). The videodisk is indexed by typical bibliographic citation information, and a user of ADONIS can request an exact copy of a document as photographs of every page.

videodisk for storing exact image

3.3.5.1 IDEX

In experiments in the mid-1980s a document retrieval system was combined with the **Guide** microtext system to create a new type of macrotext. The microtext interface was augmented to allow options to generate Boolean queries (Bovey and Brown, 1987). Pointers to retrieved documents were given in one window, and queries were developed in another window. Within the retrieved window the user could explore further details of each document by using microtext buttons to 'unfold' a document. The method of browsing an individual document involved the same interface as that for generating queries.

development history

Now, the commercial version of Guide has evolved and extensions of it for large volume work have been implemented for such diverse applications as:

applications

- manuals for automotive repair and catalogs of spare automotive parts,
- standards documents for design engineering in the aviation industry,
- user documentation for a computer manufacturer, and
- maintenance manuals for power generation facilities.

These applications may easily require more than a gigabyte of memory and include thousands of complete documents. The new system, called IDEX, allows users to **search** large document databases and to **browse** individual documents (Ritchie, 1989).

The large-volume component of IDEX uses a catalog card to represent the indexing of a document and supports a query language. Each document is represented by a **catalog card** that includes Document Type, Date, Author, and Keywords. The indexer can also determine that some documents will be accessible to certain users and not others and can elect to organize certain terms as a hierarchy. The hierarchies are then included on special catalog cards which searchers can exploit to find documents.

catalog cards

IDEX can automatically convert **text to microtext** or **microtext to text**. Given that a document has been prepared with a standard markup language, the system can automatically translate the document into a Guide form which users can browse. Furthermore, the system can print a document by traversing the Guide hierarchical representation in a depth-first fashion and printing the

converting between text and hypertext

sections as it visits them. The user can request to have a paper copy or a screen copy.

combining micro and macro

What is particularly intriguing about IDEX is that once a text has been converted into microtext, it also becomes integrated into macrotext. IDEX maintains a document database which can be searched—thus forming macrotext. Once a pointer to a document is found, the document can be browsed in detail—the browse facility indicates microtext. This integration of **microtext** and **macrotext** exemplifies the spirit of hypertext.

3.3.5.2 Reference book searching

advantages of electronic form

When a large reference book is to be browsed with microtext techniques, the question may arise as to where the reader should start. The reader may have some specific topic in mind and want to browse only in the areas closely connected with that topic. Research with **SuperBook** has shown that a macrotext search facility can significantly help users to get information from a book. Some users were given a paper copy of the book and asked to answer a set of questions, while other users were given the book in SuperBook (electronic) form and asked to answer the same questions. The SuperBook users answered more questions correctly and took less time than did the users of the paper copy (Egan *et al.*, 1989).

first search, then browse

Word-frequency approaches can be used to index automatically the paragraphs of a reference book. Then the reader can generate search statements as with a regular macrotext system and be given relevant paragraphs. Once the searcher has retrieved a relevant paragraph, then the microtext links from that paragraph may be followed by browsing.

intrinsic and extrinsic weights

If a **hierarchically structured** hypertext contains several blocks of text with the term x, in response to a query for x the system could emphasize the blocks whose children in the hierarchy also contain term x. The utility of a block of text relative to a query can be approximated by a numeric weight consisting of two components. The intrinsic component is computed from the number and identity of the query terms contained within the block. The extrinsic component is computed from the weight of immediate **descendants**. The optimal starting point for browsing is the block with the highest weight, and this block is found through a macrotext search technique.

application to medical reference book

For a hypertext medical reference book, word-frequency techniques were used to connect terms to blocks of text (Frisse, 1988). The reference book was first converted into a microtext by exploiting the markup language of the handbook. Then **word-frequency** indexing techniques were combined with information about the microtext structure to facilitate initial entry into the text via a query (see Exercise 3.10).

3.4 Hypertext to hypertext

dream of connectivity

One of the dreams of hypertext users is to connect documents easily. Vannevar Bush had said that the user would be able to find documents which otherwise would be lost (Bush, 1945). Some have spoken of the 'universe of connected documents'. Behind these dreams is a dilemma. If the connections between documents are idiosyncratic and thus **intuitively** clear to one individual, then those same connections may be unclear to another individual. The links and nodes of hypertext constitute a language. Different hypertexts have different languages. To connect the languages is to connect the hypertexts.

In the 1960s, a **connection** between the Universal Decimal Classification and other **classification systems** was established (Dahlberg, 1983). The United Nations has funded the construction of unified languages for the classification of documents in a number of fields, including in particular the social sciences. In 1977, the United Nations undertook the ambitious project of collecting, identifying, clarifying, representing, and delivering data on concepts in the social sciences on an international level. During the course of the project, they discovered the need to define clearer criteria for identifying the concepts and for preparing operative definitions. The Armed Services Technical Information Agency and the Atomic Energy Commission have each linked their indexing languages (Svenonius, 1983), while the National Library of Medicine has developed the Unified Medical Language System which connects many of the indexing languages of biomedicine.

recent history of institutional commitment

3.4.1 Translating meta-languages

Translation schemes that take a meta-language or indexing language from one group and make it compatible with a meta-language from another group have been devised. The problem is to formulate translation schemes that preserve the original meaning as much as possible, while allowing different groups to create or change their languages with as much autonomy as possible. The objectives include maximizing **expressive adequacy**, minimizing the need for **consensus**, and minimizing the need for propagation of changes (Lee and Malone, 1990).

goals

A common language for a set of groups is the language that all the groups use to communicate with one another. So to communicate using the common language, each group must either use the common language itself or be able to translate between the **common language** and the **group language** (see Exercise 3.11). For the case where all the group languages have the same relationship to the common language, then general solutions to the translation problem

translation schemes

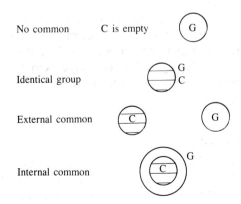

Figure 3.26 Group versus common language. G is one of the group languages; C is the common language.

include: no common language, identical group language, external common language, and internal common language (see Fig. 3.26).

When no common language is shared by groups that wish to communicate, each pair of groups must be able to have **pairwise translations** made into and out of each other's languages. This corresponds to the real-world situation with languages like **English**, **French**, and **Japanese**. Such a scheme can provide case-specific translations in fine-grained detail. The scheme also supports autonomous evolution. It is, however, only applicable when the effort to build the translation rules and dictionaries can be justified.

When the common language is the same as all group languages, the need for consensus is large. Since all groups have to agree on changes, the only changes that are easy for a group to make will be those that do not affect other groups or those that are valuable to all groups. The **Dewey Decimal Classification Scheme** is such a common language or **standard** and is used in the classification of books in libraries.

With an **external common language**, a group communicates with another by first translating its language into the common language, and then having the receiving group translate the common language into its own group language. This approach is applicable when groups have well-established group languages and cannot afford pairwise translations with all other group languages. Languages like **Esperanto** were designed to serve as external common languages.

The internal common language approach has special appeal when each group language is a **hierarchy**. If, for instance, the common language is the root and top levels of the hierarchy, then when highly specific, idiosyncratic terms from one group language need to be translated into the common language, the translation procedure need simply move up the hierarchy until the common term is reached. This scheme is useful when

1. there do not already exist numerous well-established and incompatible language groups,
2. there are important commonalities across groups, and
3. there are also significant local variations among groups.

3.4.2 Mapping

One way to begin translating from one meta-language to another is to **map** the terms of one meta-language to the terms in the other meta-language. How can this mapping be done? How far can one get with direct lexical matching of terms? What role might knowledge about the components of terms play?

A variety of rearrangements of terms can be performed to determine whether a kind of **syntactic match** exists between two terms (Niehoff and Mack, 1985). Two examples illustrate the type of rewriting that can facilitate connecting two main terms (Klingbeil, 1985):

- x of $y \equiv y\, x$
  (as in shortness of breath $\equiv$ breath shortness).
- $x, y \equiv y\, x$
  (as in cancer, lung $\equiv$ lung cancer).

Here '$u \equiv v$' means that u is the nearest concept for v.

After **decomposing** two terms into their components, one can match the terms word decomposition
based on these components. Such matching may succeed where direct matching
fails. For instance, start with the two terms 'hypertension' and 'high pressure'.
If the term 'hypertension' has been decomposed into the components 'hyper'
and 'tension' and those components have been equated with 'high' and
'pressure', then 'hypertension' would map to 'high pressure' (Wingert, 1986).

The **synonym** relation can assist in mapping. Assume that one language synonyms
includes a term called x which has a synonymous term called y. The other
language includes a term called z which has a synonymous term called y. By
going through the synonymous term y, an algorithm can connect x and z
(Soergel, 1974).

The **Vocabulary Switching System** (VSS) contains the subject descriptors from Vocabulary Switching
15 indexing languages in the areas of physical science, life science, social science, System
and business. With it, a user is able to generate automatically document
requests in 15 indexing languages based on a request in just one (Niehoff and
Mack, 1985). VSS utilizes five file types: term file, word file, stem file, stem
phrase file, and concept file. The first four are inverted files, and these provide
access to the fifth file.

- The term file contains all terms in all indexing languages. Each term is assigned
  a pointer to a concept, which is used to retrieve data from the concept
  file.
- The word file contains a record for each component word in the term file. This
  file is useful for retrieval of parts of multi-word phrases.
- The **stem file**, like the term file, contains an inverted list of all terms. However,
  each term is processed by a stemming algorithm to create a root or stem.
  User input is stemmed via an identical algorithm when a stem search is
  specified.
- The stem phrase file contains stem strings, formed by the stem of each of the
  unique words in a term. This file is useful for retrieving terms in which the user
  query differs from the term only in word endings.

VSS has been shown to reduce search preparation time, improve search
strategies and retrieval, and increase usage of existing databases.

3.4.3 Merging languages

The indexing languages of hypertext may be viewed as semantic nets. mapping and nearest
Connecting two semantic nets allows access directly or indirectly to the
contents of two semantic nets or the documents to which the semantic nets point
while only requiring mastery of one semantic net. Methods for connecting two
semantic nets may depend on mapping or on merging. Assume that the
semantic net includes relations of the following types: synonymous, broader,
narrower, and related. In mapping two semantic nets SN_1 and SN_2 a new slot
has to be entered for each concept in SN_1 which slot can be called the **nearest**
slot. In merging SN_1 with SN_2 the nearest slot is not needed but changes may
be made to the values for the synonym, broader, narrower, and related slots for
all concepts.

While **database management systems** often deal with numbers, such as objectives like database management systems

salaries, and **hypertext systems** deal with text, each system has common objectives. Three primary objectives of database management systems are:

1. making an **integrated collection** of data available to a wide variety of users;
2. providing for quality and **integrity** of the data; and
3. allowing centralized control of data.

These goals can be related to the goals and problems of merging languages:

1. the objective of merging languages which index documents is to make data available to a wide number of users;
2. one of the difficulties in this merge is to resolve the conflicts which can occur when two different systems disagree on the relationship which should exist between two terms;
3. the merged languages can be controlled from a centralized site.

As database work becomes more complex, more sophisticated methods for ensuring integrity and maintaining central control are needed. For instance, in the modeling of time in databases it becomes important to decide when two versions of data from different times are equivalent. This problem is connected to that of determining when two concepts in different languages are equivalent.

theory

One can **prove** that retrieval through two merged semantic nets may lead to better information retrieval than retrieval through each semantic net separately (Mazur, 1986).

Given that:

1. Semantic net A has the term a_1 with children a_2 and a_3.
2. Semantic net B has the term b_1 with children b_2 and b_3.
3. A search on a_1 in the document space indexed by semantic net A retrieves all documents that contain the terms a_1, a_2, or a_3.
4. A search on b_1 in the document space indexed by semantic net B retrieves all documents that contain the terms b_1, b_2, or b_3.
5. $a_2 = b_1$ and a merge of semantic net A and semantic net B reproduces semantic net A but adds b_2 and b_3 as children of a_2 (see Fig. 3.27).

Then:

A search on a_1 in the document space indexed by semantic net A after the merging of semantic nets A and B retrieves all documents that contain the terms a_1, a_2, a_3, b_2, or b_3.

Since more relevant documents should be retrieved with the search $\{a_1, a_2, a_3, b_2, b_3\}$ than with the search $\{a_1, a_2, a_3\}$, the merge of semantic nets A and B has improved **retrieval**. A retrieval that knew a_2 equaled b_1, but did not know that b_2 and b_3 were more specific than a_2 would miss relevant documents. Thus a merge of two semantic nets may lead to a more powerful semantic net for information retrieval purposes.

similarities and differences

The process of merging semantic nets involves two crucial steps: finding similarities and exploiting differences. Finding similarities involves steps like those in mapping. Terms in SN_1 are mapped to terms in SN_2. Exploiting differences can involve a number of principles, but two which are most germane could be called **hierarchical transitivity** and **analogy**.

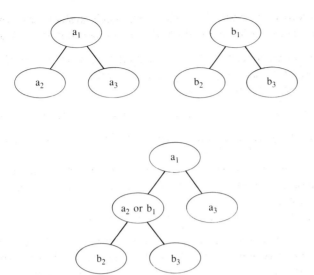

Figure 3.27 Merging semantic nets. Upper—Semantic nets A and B. Lower—merged semantic net formed by joining A and B at the common nodes a_2 and b_1.

- Merging by hierarchical transitivities involves grafting a subtree from one semantic net into another semantic net.
- Merging by analogy involves determining that terms are related in one thesaurus but not in the other and then copying the relationship into the semantic net that was lacking it.

For a merging by analogy example, if in SN_1 concept 'a' has a relationship to concept 'b' but the same concepts in SN_2 have no direct connection, then SN_2 can be augmented by copying the relation between concepts 'a' and 'b' from SN_1 into SN_2.

One merge played a key role in the construction of a semantic net for the field of medical information science (Mili and Rada, 1988). However, various **conflict resolution** strategies had to be introduced when the information in one semantic net was not consistent with that in the other semantic net (see Exercise 3.12). For instance, in one semantic net 'pattern recognition' was broader than 'artificial intelligence', while in the other semantic net 'artificial intelligence' was broader than 'pattern recognition'.

conflict resolution

3.5 Epilogue

In the **1950s**, there were significant advances in the theory of indexing documents, and the use of Boolean expressions to indicate index term relationships was elaborated. Also in the 1950s precision and recall were defined as criteria of retrieval effectiveness. In the early **1960s** the first large-scale macrotext system, MEDLARS, became available, with documents being manually indexed into terms from an index language. In the **1970s** methods of classifying documents by word-frequency were established. Many current macrotext systems maintain indices of all the words in the document collection. Queries are posed as words which are matched against words in documents. One ironic feature of this history is that, while the technology has advanced, the

history of technology

conceptual sophistication of the indexing and retrieval strategy has not. What has gone forward with the technology is the amount of literature that can be stored and accessed.

macrotext system advantages

The speed of the computer, its ability to store vast amounts of information, and its ability to manipulate information all contribute to the special features of computerized macrotext. A computer macrotext system offers many advantages over a paper system:

- The search is **faster**.
- Queries can be readily reformulated and a new search executed.
- From any one place more literature is available on-line than on paper.
- More **access points** exist for each document.

One way to search in a macrotext system is to specify an item, like an author name, after which a list of citations which contain that item are returned. Alternatively, one can search by content labels or a combination of content labels and author names. Many other types of queries can be generated and each should be able to operate on large document sets quickly.

strings and words

The methods for retrieving documents which exploit the simplest patterns are the string and word-frequency methods. In the string method, documents are found by locating **strings of characters** in the documents. In the **word-frequency** method, patterns of co-occurrence of words support indexing and retrieval.

word patterns in microtext and macrotext

Word-frequency tools can generate characterizations of blocks of text, which on the one end might be large documents and at the other end might be short paragraphs. With queries that perform matching based on word-frequency one could thus get not only a pointer to a document within a large set of documents but also continue the search to locate smaller text blocks within a single document. Within one large document, the paragraphs may be considered mini-documents to which macrotext methods may be applicable. Macrotext methods facilitate searching and users may want to do searching to put themselves in a neighborhood from which reading or browsing may proceed. Macrotext differs from microtext in that its emphasis is on searching, in contrast to microtext, which emphasizes browsing. Together, **macrotext** and **microtext** form a foundation for hypertext.

indexing language

A thesaurus or indexing language assists indexers and searchers in the choice of appropriate terms and facilitates inclusive searches. If term x has y as a narrower term, then an **inclusive search** with x automatically includes y. But the theory and practice of indexing languages needs to be further elaborated. The **structure** of current indexing languages is often idiosyncratic, and the better languages show regular patterns. As the structure becomes more regular, the opportunity to exploit that structure for indexing and retrieval improves.

indexing language versus outline

Indexing languages constitute a semantic net which is usually hierarchical. The question remains as to what relationship should exist between **indexing languages** and **outlines** for individual documents. An outline may also be viewed as a semantic net. Typically, indexing languages resemble taxonomies and have information like 'bacteria are microorganisms are organisms'. The outline of a typical scientific paper is '1. Introduction', '2. Method', '3. Result', and '4. Discussion', but the outline of a large textbook may be more taxonomic in character (see, for instance, the outline of this book). Creators and accessors of hypertext should be able to connect the semantic nets of macrotext and microtext (indexing languages and outlines, respectively). The insights about search interfaces, including giving users alphabetical and hierarchical views of the indexing language, should also apply to the outlines of microtext.

A dominant problem in macrotext systems is connecting across document systems which use different indexing languages. The same problem exists at the microtext level, in that a document by one author may well have a semantic net which has nothing in common with the semantic net by another author for a document which is otherwise similar. The hypertext system should facilitate the **connections** among these semantic nets. One simple way is to map the terms from one semantic net into those of another and merge the semantic nets at those points of commonality.

connecting indexing languages

3.6 Exercises

3.1 In document systems the representations for documents and queries usually simplify the document or query. A document might be characterized by a set of words, and queries might be words connected by the set operators **intersection** ∩, **union** ∪, and **complement** ¬. Imagine three documents indexed, respectively, as {boy, dog}, {dog, football}, and {boy, football}. Give examples of queries and the documents which they should retrieve. How do these set operators relate to Boolean logic operations? (30 minutes)

set and logical operators in queries

3.2 Develop an algorithm which will identify the terms in a document whose **frequency** makes them significant. (45 minutes)

word frequency

3.3 Assume that a document is represented as a weighted vector of m terms $(doc_1, \ldots, doc_m)$ and that queries are similarly represented as $(qu_1, \ldots, qu_m)$, where doc_k refers to the weight on the kth term of the vector for this document and qu_k has the corresponding meaning for the query. Define a measure of **relevance** between the document and query. (25 minutes)

a relevance formula

3.4 Given a set of n document vectors over a vocabulary of k terms, the vector for document$_j$ may be of the form $(w_{1,j}, w_{2,j}, \ldots, w_{k,j})$, where $w_{i,j}$ is the weight of term$_i$ for document$_j$. A **centroid** C of the set of document vectors may be defined with its ith term c_i defined as follows:

discrimination analysis

$$c_i = \frac{1}{n} \sum_{j=1}^{n} w_{ij}$$

How might the centroid be used in assigning weights to terms so that the vectors are best separated? (30 minutes)

3.5 If one is searching for documents, a hierarchical organization can reduce the **cost of search**. Present an analysis of the search cost in a hierarchy as contrasted to the search cost when no organization exists. The advantage is similar to that of ordering a list in order to reduce the cost of search on the list. (30 minutes—assumes background in analysis of algorithms)

hierarchy search benefit

3.6 To test the hypothesis that the 'more important a journal, the more frequently its authors publish' both the notions

publish

1. of importance for a journal and
2. of **author publication frequency**

term$_m$	no	yes	. . .	no
. . .	yes	no	. . .	no
term$_2$	no	no	. . .	no
term$_1$	no	no	. . .	yes
	document$_1$	document$_2$	. . .	document$_n$

Figure 3.28 Term-document matrix

need to be defined. Suggest such definitions. Go to the library or a macrotext system and collect information to test the hypothesis. (2 hours)

validity of indexing

3.7   How does the performance of an average indexer compare to that of an expert indexer? The evaluation should consider that some index terms may be close to the expert's choice but not correct. Suggest a method for evaluating indexing that exploits the relationships in the thesaurus from which the indexing terms are chosen. (45 minutes)

network

3.8   Develop an algorithm which will take as input a set of documents, each of which has been indexed into a set of terms, and output a network of index terms. A **term-document matrix** may be imagined in which a yes entry in the term$_i$, document$_j$ cell of the matrix means that term$_i$ was used in the indexing of document$_j$ (see Fig. 3.28). Two terms have the same distribution across documents, if they are used in indexing exactly the same documents. If two terms have similar distributions across the documents, then those two terms should be connected in the graph. While complex definitions of similarity have been produced (Mili and Rada, 1985), a simple one is good enough for this exercise. Define a simple measure of similarity and build a small network of terms by connecting terms that have similar distributions across a few short documents. (2 hours)

Yellow Pages

3.9   Why should someone want an *Electronic Yellow Pages* when a paper *Yellow Pages* is free, is delivered to the door, and is adequate for many needs? How big should an index be in order to be most useful on paper versus computer? (30 minutes)

searching for paragraphs

3.10   To search for a block of text from which browsing may ensue, an intrinsic **block weight** may be useful which satisfies the following conditions:

- The intrinsic block weight is proportional to the number of times each query term occurs in the block and is inversely proportional to the number of blocks that contain each query term.
- A block with many immediate descendants, but only one query term in an immediate descendant, has a lower extrinsic block weight than does a block with fewer immediate descendants but also one query term on one immediate descendant

Suggest a formula for the intrinsic block weight of block$_i$ due to term$_j$. The intrinsic block weight component may be combined with the extrinsic component due to weights of immediate descendants, to determine the total weight for block$_i$. Also suggest a formula for the total weight for block$_i$. (45 minutes)

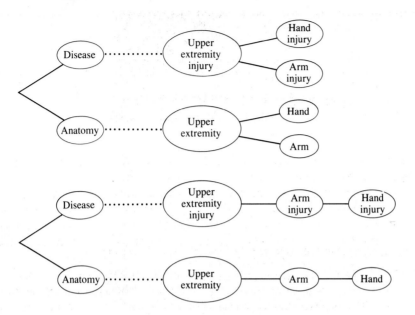

Figure 3.29 Inconsistency in merge. Upper semantic net which shows upper extremity as having two immediate descendants, hand and arm; lower semantic net in which hand is shown as part of arm.

3.11 **Group languages** and **common languages** may be related in several ways, such as: no common language, identical group language, external common language, and internal common language. What are two other relationships between common and group language? (25 minutes) — translations

3.12 Merging two medical semantic nets illustrates the role of consistency (see Fig. 3.29). In one 'arm injury' is broader than 'hand injury'. In the other 'arm injury' and 'hand injury' are both narrower than the same concept. How might one resolve this **inconsistency**? Might any secondary problems ensue? (45 minutes) — inconsistency

4

Collaborative hypertext

Figure 4.1 Group. People are discussing and taking notes about a document which they need to prepare.

synonyms of grouptext

Collaborative hypertext is created or accessed by a group of people and may be called 'grouptext'. **Groupware** is a popular new term that refers to software which supports group activity. A grouptext system is groupware for text. Another popular new term is **computer-supported collaborative work** (CSCW). Collaborative hypertext is **CSCW** on text. Whereas a microtext system supports one document for one user, a grouptext system supports a few related documents for a few collaborating users.

discussion, authoring, and annotation

Grouptext systems help groups of people create and access text in three phases.

1. The **discussion** phase occurs first as people brainstorm and formulate plans as to how the writing should proceed.
2. In the **authoring** phase, blocks of text are attached to a network of ideas and the network is traversed to generate a document.
3. The analog of reading in the collaborative sense is the making of notes by a group of people on a document. This **annotative** phase may also lead to a

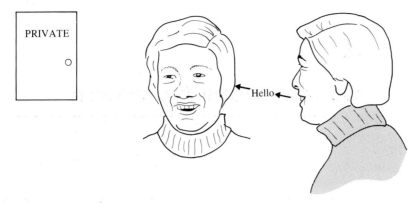

Figure 4.2 Privacy. The door with the private sign on it indicates that at times a participant in a grouptext event may want privacy.

Figure 4.3 The 'hello' message going from one person to another indicates the role of communication.

revised document as the annotators incorporate their comments into the original document.

A grouptext system may allow people to create information which is private or public—i.e., not accessible to others or accessible to all (see Fig. 4.2). The system should support messaging—a person may send a message directly to another person (see Fig. 4.3). **Collaborators** may also want to communicate face-to-face with audio-video support from the grouptext system.

features of grouptext

The single, most compelling argument for collaborative writing is based on the simple observation that the purpose of writing is to communicate. The Ancient Greeks emphasized the importance of organizing material so that it was persuasive to the intended **audience** (Magill and McGreal, 1961), stressing that a persuasive speaker or writer must thoroughly know himself and his audience. Collaborative writing brings together creators and accessors of text so that the final text will be persuasive—so that authors have feedback from readers before the text is finished.

connects reader and writer

A collaborative writer plays a special role because he can contribute directly to the co-author's writing process and reader model. Studies of the differences between **expert** and **novice** writers show that experts use reader models, and novices do not (Scardamalia and Bereiter, 1987). The model of the expert writer includes a reader model against which the writer tests prose before it is shared with actual readers (see Fig. 4.4). Better writers also go through greater effort to refine versions of their text iteratively (Neuwirth and Kaufer, 1989).

reader model

Group creation and access of texts has a history as old as that of text itself. Before text, town criers announced local news, while balladeers conveyed stories in song from one generation to the next. History was an **oral tradition**. As the

town criers

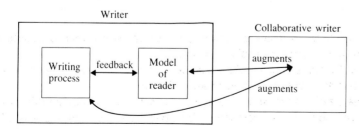

Figure 4.4 Writer–reader model.

ability to read and write appeared, the stories were transcribed onto clay or papyrus. This transcription process constituted a kind of collaboration in that the writer collaborated with the balladeer or town crier.

New Testament

The **New Testament** is one of many historic examples of a document whose parts were written by different people. For instance, the sections of the *New Testament* entitled 'John', 'Jude', and 'Luke' were written by the apostles John, Jude, and Luke, respectively. They may not have directly interacted with one another, but in some sense the combined text is grouptext. About 380 years ago the book was revised by a team of 50 scholars under the commission of King James I of England, and their effort illustrates the annotative phase of grouptext.

Augmentation System

The first grouptext computer system was the **Augmentation System** of the 1960s (see Sec. 2.3.2.1). To quote the creator of the Augmentation System (Engelbart and English, 1968):

> We are trying to maximize the coverage of our documentation, using it as a dynamic and plastic structure that we continually develop and alter to represent the current state of our evolving goals, plans, progress, knowledge, designs, procedures, and data.

They placed all the work of a group of people on the computer—including computer programs, memos, and reports. The system augmented the documentation capabilities of the group by facilitating communication.

1970s student experiment

The interest in computer-supported collaborative writing and reading continued in the **1970s**. In one authoring and reading experiment with an English poetry class a hypertext was available on a multi-terminal computer. For three hours a week students had to read the text and comment on it through the computer. Students enjoyed reading the text on-line but had difficulty making comments. Some students who were very articulate in a classroom were silent on the screen and conversely. In general, one can expect that technology to support collaboration will help some people and not others.

developing infrastructure

The **1980s** witnessed a burgeoning use of electronic mail and bulletin boards. Greater bandwidth in communication channels and more powerful workstations led to developments in synchronous communication that would have been awkward without the new technology. These tools formed a stimulating infrastructure for grouptext.

4.1 Principles

technology and people

Some of the principles of grouptext are extensions of those for microtext. But when people collaboratively create a document, they have discussions before writing. When they collaboratively read a document, they make annotations on the document. On the **technology** side, grouptext systems must address database and interface issues that are unique to the group context. On the **people** side, the principles of human–human interaction are critical to grouptext but not to microtext or macrotext.

4.1.1 Technology principles

The grouptext **database** must provide information about the authorship and date of each block of text. Depending on the author, the date, and other information, different versions of a document are defined. The **interface** must support people in a way that helps them to communicate and share information.

database and interface

4.1.1.1 Grouptext links

When groups of people are asked to build documents with semantic nets as integral parts of the document, they typically do not know what types of nodes or links would be meaningful. As one person adds nodes and links to the semantic network the **ambiguity** of these additions make it difficult for another person to know the overlap between what had been done and what might be done next. For this and other reasons each collaborator should be asked to include with each node a definition and an example of that node's use (see Exercise 4.1). In independent assessments of the 'goodness' of additions to a hypertext semantic net, it was the step of including definitions and examples that made the biggest, positive difference in the quality of the semantic net.

semantic net

In addition to writing the document itself, people engage in other activities relevant to writing. Initially, a **discussion** occurs to determine the general goals. After the first draft of the document is prepared, **annotations** are collected to guide revision of the document.

discussion and annotation

DISCUSSION LINKS

The discussion phase of grouptext occurs early in document construction. The discussion will include blocks of text or notes which are connected by links. A discussion may begin with someone posting an **Issue**. Another person may post a Position in response to this Issue. The goal of the discussion is for each of the participants to try to understand the whole problem better, to exchange viewpoints, and to persuade others of one's own point of view.

first phase: discussion

This model of a discussion supports three types of **nodes**—issue, position, and argument (Rada *et al.*, 1990b). An issue represents a problem, concern, or question which needs discussion. Each issue is a root for a subtree and can have one or more positions linked to it. A position is a statement or assertion which attempts to resolve an issue. It can have one or more arguments, but not more than one issue, linked to it. An argument responds to a position through either a support or refute link (see Fig. 4.5).

model of nodes and links in discussion

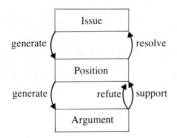

Figure 4.5 Node and link types in a discussion.

Text block	Author	Date
23	John Smith	June 13
107	Sue Jones	June 11

Figure 4.6 Date and author.

ANNOTATIVE LINKS

comment link

A colleague may write a comment on some part of an evolving document. Grouptext must support this annotative activity. The link in this case is initially just a **comment link** from the comment to the relevant portion of the document. What more can one say about the links for annotations? For annotations the semantic net approach to hypertext seems less germane. The commenters are not building a complex web of concepts and relations but are making a single point about a single portion of the document. Rather than terms pointing to terms with semantic links, the basic structure might more usefully be a block of text connected to another block of text.

an experiment

The label on the link from an annotation to the source document might simply be 'Comment'. Might, however, the link from the annotation to the document be usefully given other labels? In one experiment, half the users of an annotation system were asked to indicate five paragraphs in an evolving book that they did not like by pointing to a paragraph and simply typing 'bad' as the comment. The other half were asked to choose one paragraph which they did not like and explain why. Analysis of the results of this experiment showed that the simple 'bad' **votes** were not as helpful as the **detailed comments**. Furthermore, almost all the detailed comments addressed either the paragraph style or its content.

style and content

Comments should be more specific than good or bad. A breakdown of comments into the types good or bad **content** and good or bad **style** might be important for an annotation system. This information would help authors focus on the types of changes that were needed. A poorly written paragraph could be, of course, reworded. After identifying a conceptually flawed paragraph one may want to delete it and to modify the adjacent paragraphs.

date and author

When reviewing the contributions made by colleagues, one may want to know who has made what contribution when—to have a history. This applies whether discussing, writing, or annotating text is at issue. Accordingly, the recording of **author** and **date** for each contribution is important (see Fig. 4.6). A good grouptext system should allow a user to see all contributions made by a person over a period of time.

4.1.1.2 Data sharing

data sharing issues

As a group manipulates text, various data sharing issues become prominent. How can information be stored so that users can both quickly get what they need and yet rest assured that information is **safe** and widely accessible? If two people try to modify simultaneously the same block of text, are they allowed to do so, and if yes, how are conflicting changes resolved? Social mediation may be the best approach to **resolving conflict**.

SHARING CONTROL

Grouptext systems are composed of a large number of interacting components (people, workstations, documents) and must process information concurrently (Hewitt, 1986). The conventional approach to ensuring database **consistency** in the face of concurrent access is to ensure that each transaction on its own preserves consistency. The effect of running multiple transactions must be the same as if they had been executed one at a time. An underlying premise is that transactions will be short and conflicts resolved quickly. If **long interactions** are managed in the same way, they can impose severe limits on concurrency. Manipulating text files requires long interactions. It may, however, be acceptable to present users with data that is not guaranteed to be up-to-date. This relaxation of consistency reduces conflicts among activities that read and update the same item and is particularly appropriate for grouptext (Greif and Sarin, 1987).

consistency

Of the various database models, a **cooperative database** model is one of the best for the needs of grouptext (Stefik *et al.*, 1987). To support a collaboration

database models

- the delay in getting information should be short,
- the delay in changing information should be short,
- the database should converge quickly to a consistent state, and
- the database should not be vulnerable to the accidental actions of participants or their machines.

In a centralized database approach the data is in one central place, and retrieval time is too slow for synchronous, collaborative work. In the centralized-lock database model, each workstation has a copy of the database but cannot make changes to an item until it obtains ownership of that item. To secure ownership of data means obtaining a lock from a centralized lock server. In the cooperative database model, each machine has a copy of the database, and changes are installed by broadcasting the change without any synchronization. While this approach allows inconsistencies to occur, social factors in the collaborative setting may mitigate against the likelihood of these inconsistencies (see Exercise 4.3).

To implement a cooperative database, one may unfortunately also have to create one's own operating system. In many operating systems, the right of users to perform a read or write operation on a file depends on how attributes of the user match the access rights associated with the file. This is, however, not sufficient for an application that has a more abstract model than reading and writing files (Greif and Sarin, 1987). This limitation implies that the cooperative database's **access control** must be implemented by the cooperative database itself. If the operating system is not changed, files must be left unprotected at the **operating system** level and are vulnerable to accidental or malicious modification by users who bypass the cooperative database program.

access control

SOCIAL MEDIATION

In the 'optimistic' approach to managing text for groups, text blocks are not **locked**. Optimistic concurrency control assumes that since text blocks greatly

optimistic concurrency

outnumber users, a conflict between users editing the same text block is rare (Akscyn *et al.*, 1988). When a user tries to save changes to a text block when someone else has just saved changes to that same text block, the system saves a backup copy of the latest changes and notifies the user. The users must decide how to resolve the conflict. Optimistic concurrency control relies on social mediation.

group editing of a semantic net

A handful of users may be simultaneously changing a large semantic net for a document. In one approach to this problem each user has a full copy of the semantic net, and each is connected to a central server (Lenat and Guha, 1990). Each user views and modifies a personal copy of the semantic net. Each editing change is checked locally, to see if any constraints are violated, and then the change is **broadcast** to the central server. At the central server, checks are again made because now the interaction with the changes of other users can be determined. If, once more, no constraints are violated, the update is broadcast to all users. The constraints might include that a link type be defined before it can be used or that two nodes may not be given the same name.

detecting contradictory statements

A grouptext system may also check for contradictory statements. By example, two **contradictory** statements are 'x is part of y' and 'y is part of x'. Due to the time-consuming nature of error checks, a background process runs these checks, while a foreground process keeps a fast response interaction with the user. If an error is detected by the central server, then a dialogue is initiated to resolve it. While waiting for the conflict to be resolved, the system may make an arbitrary decision in favor of one of the statements. In the case of collaborative authoring of semantic nets experience suggests that such contradictory statements are seldom simultaneously asserted (Lenat and Guha, 1990). In those rare cases where it does happen, one of the two participants will temporarily win, and the loser will have a chance to change the decision later.

VERSION HISTORY

definition of version management

A text block can undergo a number of changes in its lifetime. The contents may be totally changed, or one word may be spelled differently. Each time a text block is **revised**, a new version of the text block is created. A **version management** tool provides a useful means for distinguishing between versions of a text block and facilitates the retrieval of different versions (see Exercise 4.2).

saving space by storing editing commands

In one version management model, revisions are traced in a **tree structure**. The method saves space because, instead of storing copies of files, the differences between files are stored (Tichy, 1982). Only the original version has the full contents of the file. Each revision is stored as the **editing commands** which caused the change. To go from the original to a first revision, the editing commands are applied to the 'full file'. For example, if one had a file called 'A', which had the contents [a b c] and after revision became [a b c d], the method would hold the revision as 'add [d]' and the original as [a b c].

choosing a revision

Given that a group of people may create many revisions, how does the group finally decide which revisions to incorporate in the **final version**? For instance, Pete may have changed a paragraph by adding a sentence to it, while Susan may have deleted a sentence. If one version must now be defined as authoritative, should Pete's or Susan's change be accepted? One method for answering this

Figure 4.7 Several hands cannot easily work on one piece of paper.

question is to have a discussion and then vote. An alternative method is to accept as authoritative the latest revision.

4.1.1.3 Interface

A computer grouptext system offers opportunities which paper cannot. A group of people cannot simultaneously write and read from the same piece of paper but *can* simultaneously write and read the same page of text on the computer (see Fig. 4.7). The **constraints of paper** are overcome in the electronic world, and people can interact in novel ways. Annotations may be made on the computer in ways that simulate the ways of paper, except that with the computer authors have the additional option of automatically incorporating any annotations into the final document.

special opportunities for interactions

SHARED SCREEN

'What You See Is What I See' (WYSIWIS) environments allow multiple authors to type simultaneously into the same screen image. All users have their own physical screen, but the users share the screen image. **WYSIWIS** refers to the presentation of consistent images of shared information to all participants. It recognizes the importance of being able to see work in progress (Stefik *et al.*, 1987). In the alternative of relaxed-WYSIWIS, a change on one workstation, such as adding an entry, is not immediately broadcast to all others. Instead, new information is automatically retrieved and the screen updated on the next user action.

WYSIWIS

Allowing private windows and control of placement of windows on an individual screen seems advantageous for the **flexibility** it gives the user. Yet, in practice the users may be frustrated by not being able to see what others are doing in their private windows and needing to manage screen layout options. In

flexibility versus simplicity

trials of one WYSIWIS system, the researchers who developed the system liked its flexibility, but other users thought the technology was too complicated (Stefik *et al.*, 1987). The proper trade-off between simplicity and flexibility depends in part on the class of users.

ANNOTATIVE INTERFACE ALTERNATIVES

approaches

Computer annotation facilities may vary radically in the interface style. In one simple approach, the original document is in one file and all comments are in a separate **file**. In another approach each comment is a separate file and may be directly linked to that part of the original document to which it most pertains. In viewing such annotations, **windows** are appropriate, and each comment appears in its own window with an explicit link to another window that contains the relevant portion of the original document.

acetate mode

Isolated annotative windows do not simulate the normal mode of annotation, which is to mark a piece of paper with red ink. The **acetate-overlay** approach provides this natural facility (Catlin *et al.*, 1989). The idea is that a sheet of transparent acetate is laid over a sheet of the document to be annotated. Annotations can be made on the acetate which seem to be directly made on the document but by removing the acetate one separates the annotations from the original, unchanged document (see Exercise 4.4).

extended version management

A relatively straightforward alternative to annotative windows involves allowing an annotator to work with a copy of the document and make changes to it with the same tools that an author uses to make changes. However, all changes are recorded so that either the original document or any of the changes can be recovered (Catlin *et al.*, 1989). The system records the activities of the annotator and separately maintains an unmolested version of the original document. After the annotator has finished, the original author may browse the annotations and choose which amendments to have incorporated into the document. This annotative method may be viewed as **extended version management**.

AUDIO-VIDEO PRINCIPLES

communication media

One dimension of grouptext is communication between people. The telephone, which was developed in 1876, is an early example of an electrical aid to communication. The use of telephone connections between computers supports electronic mail. The combination of **telephone** links with **television** links allows people to hear and see one another at the same time. However, the combination of technologies to support electronic communication does not always lead to the beneficial effects that might be predicted.

audio-visual links

The first commercial application of the telephone plus television was called the **PicturePhone**. When AT&T introduced the PicturePhone at the 1964 World's Fair the product was expected to sell very well. Julius Molnar, executive vice-president of Bell Laboratories wrote in the *Bell Laboratories Record* in 1969:

> Rarely does an individual or an organization have an opportunity to
> create something of broad utility that will enrich the daily lives of

everybody. Alexander Graham Bell with his invention of the telephone in 1876, and the various people who subsequently developed it for general use, perceived such an opportunity and exploited it for the great benefit of society. Today there stands before us an opportunity of equal magnitude—PicturePhone service.

Regular users of PicturePhone over the network between Bell Laboratories and AT&T's headquarters agreed that conversations over PicturePhone conveyed important information over and above that carried by voice alone.

The enthusiasm for PicturePhone from its creators at AT&T was not, however, shared by other users. These new users felt self-conscious about being on television and did not feel that the value gained by the extra information outweighed the equipment or social costs. In one assessment use of the PicturePhone was described as 'talking to a mentally defective foreigner' (Egido, 1988). The PicturePhone was a **commercial failure** and highlights the difficulty of predicting how high technology will work. PicturePhone failure

The history of videoconferencing provides a good lesson for developers of grouptext systems (similar to the lessons from the PicturePhone). By the 1970s the enthusiasm misplaced for the PicturePhone had been replaced by a somewhat similar enthusiasm for **videoconferencing**, which was to allow groups of people to see and hear each other through electronic media and thus avoid large travel costs. Videoconferencing has not become as popular as many predicted it would become. The reason for this is partly that people prefer the informal, face-to-face contact that meetings in person support. In two studies of the early 1970s, it was concluded that 85 per cent of physical meetings could be replaced with videoconferencing, while a very similar study concluded that only 20 per cent of the meetings could be thus substituted. The latter study had taken the extra step of asking people whether they would choose to use videoconferencing as a substitute for a face-to-face meeting (Egido, 1988). failure of videoconferencing

How do different combinations of audio and video affect collaborative work? In one experiment, the only communication between individuals was through workstations in **WYSIWIS** mode. In another experiment, each workstation included broadcast-quality **microphones** and speakers. In yet another experiment, the workstations were further augmented with a **camera** and television monitors. The users finished their tasks the most quickly in the 'WYSIWIS plus audio' condition. The presence of the video channel affected the performance of the group by increasing, not decreasing as had been expected, the time to perform the task. Thus one cannot a priori conclude that adding bandwidth to a communication will improve the speed at which collaborative work can be done with that communication (Gale, 1990). no advantage to audio or video

Methods of evaluating groups must consider variables which are not usually considered in evaluating computer systems. How does one evaluate the impact of computers on **human–human communication**? Assessing group work as impacted by new technologies is challenging. Laboratory studies typically are performed over short time periods on contrived tasks. Yet, the real value of group work may only be evident over long periods of time and for real tasks. need to evaluate human–human communication

4.1.2 People principles

sociology and
administration

What kinds of people collaborate well together under what circumstances? **Sociology** and **administrative science** are among the disciplines relevant to a study of grouptext. The principles of group organization and management must be appreciated for collaborative work with text to succeed.

4.1.2.1 Organization principles

collaboration in many
environments

Grouptext requires a group of people to organize themselves (see Exercise 4.5). The **classroom** is one site of collaborative discussion, authoring, and annotation where organizational principles must be appreciated. **Software teams** have been carefully studied so as to better understand the factors which contribute to effective organization for the collaborative production of software documents. In the **scientific community** the role of co-authorship has grown dramatically, and since that community uses literature as a kind of life-line, interest is high in knowing the characteristics of successful collaborative organization.

CLASSROOM ORGANIZATION

solo writing problem

When class teachers introduce collaborative writing, they are in fact working against a **tradition of writing** in English lessons, where the emphasis has been on personal expression and individual performance. Most children have come to regard writing in English as a kind of test, even when writing creatively. It is a test in the sense that it has no specific purpose beyond that of a pupil demonstrating an ability to a teacher, and has no audience other than the teacher.

collaborative solution

Traditionally, writing has been viewed as a solo operation, and children were told that collaboration was cheating. The student was expected to struggle with formulating ideas, organizing them on paper, and then await a few written criticisms from the teacher. The contemporary view is that writing should be done collaboratively. By collaborating, each child in a classroom can get more **feedback** than from a single teacher, and, more importantly, the feedback of peers has a relevance to the child's perceptions of the world that the teacher misses.

one set of experiences
with children

Several projects have focused on principles of collaborative writing for **children**. One English teacher's experience with collaborative writing in two secondary school classes (ages 11 and 12) illustrates the value of collaboration (Rada *et al.*, 1989a). Students were asked to produce a guidebook to their town. At first the students' main purpose lay in making the information as comprehensive as possible for their own satisfaction, but pupils soon became aware that with organization the guide would be useful to others.

psychological support

When given the opportunity, pupils can be very supportive of each other in a way that is both critical and constructive. One girl originally described a tourist attraction as follows (uncorrected quote):

> Albert Dock a different kind of shopping center. See the shops with most of the things man-made. After you have finished your shopping

you can have something to eat and drink in our cafe so why not come
and visit.

She had only seen the shops on her initial visit and was unaware of the Museum
of Emigration and other maritime displays and entertainments at Albert Dock.
Her group, convinced that there was more than her description suggested,
advised her how she might phone Albert Dock with a list of questions, the
answers to which could be incorporated into her description. A friend offered
to help her to find the telephone number and stayed with her during the call.
This is just one of many interactive situations in which conversation and
consultation provided the kind of **psychological support** that apprentice writers
need.

During the collaborative writing exercises, notions of audience, purpose, and   audience
appropriate format began to develop in the students. Pupils came to perceive
that writers go through various stages as they proceed from original idea to
finished product. At one stage, a writer must discover a theme; at another stage,
organize notes; at another stage, format pages of text. The experience of
collaborative writing for the group dramatized these stages. However, the factor
which seemed to motivate and enhance collaboration most strongly was a
growing awareness of the needs of a real **audience**. Collaboration was teaching
the students to write with readers in mind (see Exercise 4.6).

SOFTWARE TEAM ORGANIZATION

Developing large software systems must be treated, at least in part, as a   communication
communication process (Curtis *et al.*, 1988). In the early phases of a project,
much of the effort must go into communicating with end users about their
needs. Although a circumscribed requirements phase can be identified in most
software process models, requirements processes occur throughout the
development cycle. Decisions on new requirements must be carefully
communicated to all concerned.

The normal hierarchical structure of an organization is not necessarily   chief programmer
suitable to programmers. One organizational structure for programmers utilizes
an experienced chief programmer and provides him with substantial support
(Baker, 1972). The members of the team might include a backup programmer,
a librarian, a toolsmith, a documentation editor, a project administrator, and a
language expert (see Fig. 4.8):

- The backup programmer provides general support as well as developing test
  cases.
- The librarian does all clerical work associated with the project and is assisted
  by a computerized document management system.
- The toolsmith produces software tools.
- The documentation editor revises and publishes the documentation that the
  programmers draft.
- The project administrator performs administrative tasks for the chief
  programmer.
- The language expert is familiar with the idiosyncrasies of the language and
  helps the chief programmer to take advantage of those idiosyncrasies.

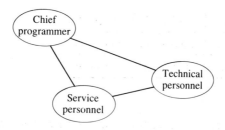

Figure 4.8 The chief programmer paradigm allows the expert programmer to take advantage of the resources of a team of assistants. The technical personnel includes the backup programmer, the toolsmith, and the language expert. The service personnel include the librarian, the documentation editor, and the project administrator.

The chief programmer concept allows **decentralization** relative to the traditional approach where a programmer is at the bottom of a large hierarchy of administrators. This decentralization helps motivate programmers (Shneiderman, 1980).

programmers do not work alone

The popular image of programmers is that they work alone—this image is held both by the programmers themselves and others. In fact, a great deal of programming is **cooperative**. In one major study, 50 per cent of a typical programmer's time was spent interacting with other team members, 30 per cent working alone, and 20 per cent in not directly productive activities (McCue, 1978). Clearly, the interactions within the group are critical to success.

mixture of individual types needed

Individuals can be classified into types based on psychological tests. One classification of programmers notes three types according to the degree of task-orientation, interaction-orientation, or self-orientation.

1. **Task-oriented** individuals prefer to focus on the task.
2. **Interaction-oriented** individuals enjoy the presence of co-workers.
3. **Self-oriented** workers are motivated by personal success.

In practice, group members often play complementary roles. A task-oriented person is good at recognizing the parts of a job and allocating resources to tasks. An interaction-oriented person helps maintain the social equilibrium of the group (Weinberg, 1971). The most successful groups are made of individuals from each class with the leader being task-oriented. Since the majority of those involved in computer programming work are task-oriented, care must be paid to the selection of members of a group to assure that successful social interaction can occur.

male versus female

Some studies have shown that many programmers are task-oriented and **male**. Conversely, **females** are often interaction-oriented. Given that a programming team should have an equal mix of task- and interaction-oriented individuals, one might argue for an equal mix of male and female programmers on a team. Of course, such arguments must respect that for any individual programmer the characteristics must be ascertained independently of any bias by sex.

SCIENTIST ORGANIZATION

increasing collaboration

Collaborative research is increasing in many scientific disciplines. For instance, more papers are now **co-authored**. Furthermore, in engineering and natural science disciplines, the research projects are now often so complex that only teams can handle them.

	Initiation	Execution	Presentation
Relationship	share assumptions	maintain trust	divide credit
Task	generate ideas	coordinate work	write document

Figure 4.9 Research collaboration model.

An investigation into the character of collaboration in science has produced a model which shows that research collaboration progresses in three stages (Kraut *et al.*, 1988): initiation, execution, and presentation. Furthermore, at each stage or phase, activity takes place on two levels: a **relationship level** and a **task level** (see Fig. 4.9). The relationship level refers to how the people relate to one another. Factors considered at the task level are relevant only to the task itself, regardless of how many people are involved or who the people are.

phases of collaboration

- In the **initiation phase** people meet and agree on basic styles and objectives.
- In the **execution phase** the research is performed as labor is shared and subtle supervision of a peer occurs.
- In the **presentation phase** the collaborators must evaluate what they have done and distribute credit.

Typically about two years are required for a pair of researchers to move through these three phases of collaboration.

In the initiation stage of collaborative research, physical proximity is very important. Potential collaborators must have opportunities to assess informally one another's abilities and styles before committing to work together. People believe that they make better judgements about another person when they can physically see that person. This effect of **physical proximity** should be given serious consideration when designing research facilities; if people are physically proximal and have frequent opportunities to meet informally, they are more likely to develop productive research relationships (Allen, 1980).

initiation and physical proximity

In the execution phase, collaboration tends to be less prominent than one might expect. Instead, the collaborators try to divide the task so that the work can be done independently and so that the need for communication and coordination is minimized. Often the researcher who has primary responsibility for a part of a project presents his partner with a completed subunit, but does not communicate the details of how the subunit was produced.

execution

At the presentation phase the research is presented to those outside the research team. As this presentation is normally in the form of reports and the authors of the report are given credit for the work, deciding who the authors should be is important. If a member of the team was ill for most of the project and could barely contribute, should that person be listed as an author? The order in which authors are presented implies the importance of the authors to the project. The first author is considered to have done the most work. Accordingly, deciding the ordering of authorship is a major challenge. While various conventions may exist for determining this ordering, the implicit assumptions which different collaborators may have been making about the ordering during the work often do not come to light until the final report is

presentation

prepared. At that juncture, the authors may unfortunately worry less about the content of the report than about the **ordering of authorship**.

social circle

Informal and unplanned communication plays a crucial role in communication networks of scientists (Menzel, 1980). The organization of scientists is largely not hierarchical. Instead patterns of communication are more like those in a **social circle**, where certain individuals have more importance because they are local centers of communication. In one study of scientists, the most respected scientists proved to be those who could easily contact the other respected scientists in their disciplines (Crane, 1980). The average scientist often struggles to maintain a communication link with an important scientist (see Exercise 4.7).

4.1.2.2 Management principles

management steps

The **management** of collaborative writing requires several steps and several types of expertise. Before collaborative writing begins, an initial meeting can establish the desired content of the final document. The workload is then divided, and each section is allocated to an appropriate individual. A task specialist can set, allocate, and coordinate the work of the group. Reviews should be held regularly throughout the writing process in which discussions take place to summarize progress. An independent reviewer should periodically inspect the document to highlight problems which may have been overlooked by those familiar with it.

individuals

In studying the behavior of authors as an aggregate and then as **individuals**, one notices over and over again a wide variability of skills and tendencies. A particular author might be very good at making graphics but weak at writing prose, while another would be just the opposite. One would be good at coordinating the behavior of others, while another was better at getting work done alone. These wide variabilities in abilities or preferences suggest that any given group should be either balanced in its constituency from the beginning or should be re-aligned through time so as to bring people with varied strengths to the group. Since the members of the group constitute a kind of review panel for themselves, this revolving character of the group membership means that the group has no chance to stagnate and the review can cover all the important areas.

individual versus group tensions

If a team leader allocates work fairly and ensures that it is completed within a specified time, then the leader's authority is an added incentive to produce a high standard of work. Friendly **competition** among team members may also be conducive to a high level of productivity. On the other hand, if the size of the team is large, it may be possible for an individual to take advantage of the fact that the team leader cannot easily check the work of each team member. The temptation to leave work to others in such a situation is great.

4.1.2.3 Efficiency

circumstances for efficiency

How can one assess the value of a collaboration? In some cases, one person cannot do what two people can do—consider the extreme case of sexual reproduction. In some cases, one person can do the job, but two people can do it significantly more quickly (see Exercise 4.8). In yet other cases, two people may interfere with one another and take longer to finish a job than either of them alone would take. In what circumstances is collaboration **efficient**?

Collaborative work is such a complex phenomenon that sociologists, psychologists, systems scientists, engineers, and mathematicians have different but valid views of what it entails. The efficiency of collaboration can be compared to the efficiency of parallel computing. As **communication costs** rise disproportionately to productivity, efficiency declines. The notion of the 'mythical man-month' is that assigning more people to work on a task will get the task finished more quickly. This notion is a myth because the costs of communication may detract from productivity rather than add to it (Brooks, 1975).

A key issue in the design of collaborative systems is **decomposition** for parallel action. For parallel action, a task must be broken into appropriately sized operations that can be executed independently by different members of the group. If the operations are too small, they will be too interdependent and interference will preclude any substantial parallelism. For example, in creating a shared text, operations at the level of individual sentences may be too small, while operations of writing many pages may be too large.

No matter how fast a computer control processor is, it must wait for the transfer of data from **memory** to processor. In applications which need to access large amounts of information, not all information can be stored in primary memory. Accordingly, the processor must query secondary devices to find some information. Such queries take more time than a query to primary memory.

The cost of **memory access** is what often makes a human–human collaboration particularly effective. If one person is an expert radiologist and the other is an expert surgeon, they may work efficiently as a team because they do not have to sort through large amounts of information to rediscover what is relevant to the problem at hand. The radiologist knows that a certain density on an X-ray means broken bone. The surgeon knows what procedure is needed to treat a broken bone. Each has the necessary knowledge readily available, and they share a vocabulary; thus they collaborate effectively.

Margin notes: mythical man-month; decomposition; memory access cost; example with people

4.2 Systems

Grouptext systems may support discussion, authoring, and annotation. These phases of collaborative work with text follow a natural progression: one cannot annotate a text that has not been written, nor readily author one without some discussion or plan. But a grouptext system should allow users to go from one phase to any other phase—a user may want to make annotations and then enter into a discussion before authoring further. Few of the existing systems support such free movement of users.

Margin note: movement among phases

4.2.1 Authoring

variety of experimental
systems

Collaborative authoring systems may be extensions to single author systems (this happened with NoteCards). Alternatively, they may be specifically built with collaborative authoring in mind (as with the Augmentation System). Some systems focus on the facilities for physical sharing of information, while others focus on the logical structure of the information. The systems are varied, but none have established themselves in the marketplace—they remain **experimental**.

Augmentation System

Already by the 1960s, the **Augmentation System** (see Sec. 2.3.2.1) had supported collaborative work. A conferencing room was equipped with six displays for on-line conferencing. Twenty participants sat around a large table which contained the six displays so that each could work with the display (Engelbart and English, 1968). One participant controlled the system, and all displays showed the same view. The other participants had mice that controlled a large arrow on the screen.

television

To facilitate collaboration between two people not in the same geographical area, the Augmentation System used **television cameras**. A television display allowed the user's computer-generated video display to be mixed with the image from a camera focused on a distant collaborator at another terminal. Each user saw the other's face superimposed on the display of data.

commercial difficulty

The Augmentation System was used successfully by the group that created it for several years. Commercially, however, the success of the system has never been outstanding. The high cost of computer equipment in the 1960s may explain why the system did not have much commercial success.

NoteCards

NoteCards was developed as a single-user hypertext system but has been extended to deal with collaborative authoring (Irish and Trigg, 1989). Early collaborative use of the single-user NoteCards occurred despite the lack of explicit support for such use. In NoteCards a block of text is stored in a card that may be arbitrarily linked to other cards. In collaborating, authors took advantage of many links among cards. To support collaboration more specifically, the developers of NoteCards created a 'Collaborator Card'. A card of this type is created for each participant in a group writing project; it identifies preferences of the author and helps trace which cards in a document have been produced by which author.

4.2.1.1 MUCH

semantic net and
functions

The **Multiple User's Creating Hypertext** (MUCH) system was developed at George Washington University and Liverpool University to support collaborative authoring by students and staff (Rada and Barlow, 1989). With the MUCH system, multiple authors collaborate to create text by creating a semantic net and attaching paragraphs to it. The semantic net is decomposed into frames where each frame corresponds to a node of the semantic net and the links emanating from it. Users can view individual frames or can see outlines that are automatically generated by traversals of the semantic net. After selecting terms in the 'Frames' or 'Outline' windows, the user is shown associated text in the

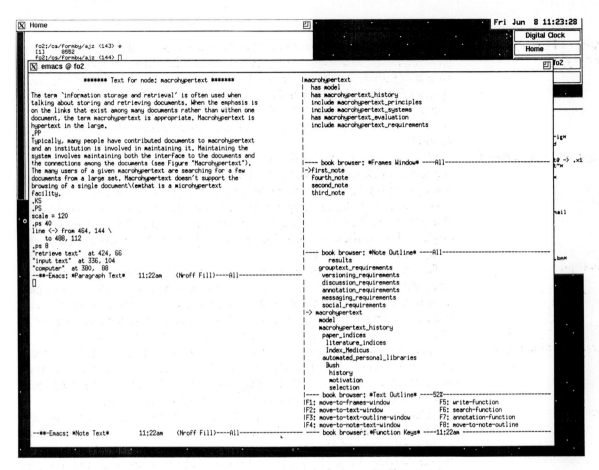

Figure 4.10 MUCH system. The screen contains several labeled windows: the 'frames window' shows one one frame; the 'text outline' window shows the outline of the document. The 'paragraph text' window displays a paragraph of text that also contains formatting commands. When the user points to a term in the 'outline' or 'frames' window and hits carriage return, then the corresponding paragraph appears in the 'paragraph text' window. The 'function keys' window describes options of the user.

'Paragraph' window (see Fig. 4.10). The 'Function' window supports access and creation functions in hierarchies of menus. Functions exist to translate documents into MUCH and to take documents from MUCH and print them. All information in the database is tagged with the name of the person who created the information and the time of creation. System functions support retrieval by author or date of creation.

The MUCH system has been developed by four graduate students at the University of Liverpool (Mhashi *et al.*, 1991). Each student has a graphics **workstation** that is networked to a file server. While the students work in one large room, the system supports collaboration across any workstations on the network throughout the building (see Fig. 4.11). A relational database management system runs on the file server and stores the hypertext. The

environment: tools and space

Figure 4.11 Students using the MUCH system. The graphic workstations are networked to a file server, and each student has his own workstation.

workstations run the Emacs extensible editor which has been tailored to support collaborative creation and access of hypertext.

application to this book

This **book** was written on predecessors of the MUCH system. A book written previously by this author was loaded into the relational database format in order that parts could be reused in this book. Students commented on the new draft via the database. One version of the book required about 500 frames in the semantic net and about 1000 paragraphs.

4.2.1.2 Collaborative Editing System

document structure

In the **Collaborative Editing System** a document contains a hierarchy of sections in which each section has a caption and a body. Each section is assigned a numeric label in accordance with its position in the hierarchy (see Fig. 4.12). A user edits one section of a document (in window 'Document Node') at a time but can see a view ('Text Image') of the entire document and its structure ('Outline'). The document structure can also be edited to add and remove sections or to rearrange the order and hierarchical position of sections.

locks and updates

The Collaborative Editing System supports a set of coauthors with read or write access to the document outline and sections. Authors may work independently on separate sections of the document. If two or more authors try to write in the same section at the same time, one of them will be granted a **lock** and the others will be informed of who holds the lock. The lock is obtained implicitly when an author starts editing. A user may read text that is being modified. If someone else is writing a section, the reader's view will be refreshed periodically as the section is **updated**. Although the system does not explicitly support real-time conferencing, a degraded form of real-time interaction (with

```
Outline
1. Collaborative Editing System
     1.1.  One installation
     1.2.  Simultaneous views
     1.3.  Real-time screen editor

Document Node
1.1.  One installation
One Collaborative Editing System installation can support
an unrestricted number of editing sessions on documents.

Text Image
1. Collaborative Editing System
1.1.  One installation
One Collaborative Editing System installation can support
an unrestricted number of editing sessions on documents.
1.2.  Simultaneous views
Each author participating in a Collaborative Editing System
session can simultaneously view a shared document while
```

Figure 4.12 Document screen for collaboration. The top section is the outline only. The Document Node gives one portion of the document. The Text Image is the entire document (Greif and Sarin, 1987).

longer delays in propagating changes) is achieved by having multiple users view the same section and taking turns updating.

4.2.2 Discussion

While discussion is an intrinsically human-to-human activity, computer support may be helpful, so long as **social factors** are carefully considered. What are the phases of discussion? What types of links are useful in a discussion? Maintaining a focus in a discussion on the computer may be difficult. Discussions based on issues are particularly suited to computer support (see Exercise 4.9).

social factors

4.2.2.1 Discussion phases

Each type of discussion may require its own computer system. The **Colab** system is an experimental meeting room designed for use by about five people who want a discussion supported by a network of workstations (Stefik *et al.*, 1987). Besides the workstations, the room is equipped with a touch-sensitive computer screen that is several meters wide (see Fig. 4.13).

Colab

One subsystem of the Colab system helps users to organize ideas and plan a presentation. The output of this 'idea organizing' mode is an annotated outline of ideas. Outline generators have similar output but Colab supports collective use. The Colab 'idea organizer' divides a meeting into three phases: brainstorming, organizing, and evaluating, among which users may move in any order they like:

idea organizing

- In the **brainstorming** phase a participant selects a free space in a public window and types a phrase.
- In the **organizing** phase the group attempts to establish an order for the ideas generated in the brainstorming phase. The basic operation is to assert that

Figure 4.13 Colab system. The three people in chairs are before their workstations, while the man at the podium has been using the large screen on the wall.

one idea comes before another and to indicate this visually by directed links between ideas.

- In the **evaluating** phase, participants review the structure of the linked ideas and eliminate peripheral ideas.

The system prepares an outline by traversing the idea graph.

design

Colab also has a subsystem to support the design and evaluation of proposals. The Colab 'proposal evaluator' has three phases: the proposing, arguing, and evaluating phases:

- In the **proposing** phase, a set of connected windows is created to describe a proposal.
- In the **arguing** phase, reasons for choosing or rejecting a proposal are written on the screen.
- In the **evaluating** phase, an argumentation spreadsheet is created to help organize belief sets.

The system differentiates between proposals, arguments, assumptions, and belief sets, and computes the relevant logical support relationships.

intermediate organizing

In sessions with a prototype 'idea organizer', even before moving to the organizing phase, members began using **spatial groupings**. Even after items were explicitly linked, the spatial cues helped to display the relationships. The creators of Colab assumed that the outliner would be used after the evaluation phase. In practice, participants found the outlining tool useful for displaying intermediate states of the emerging structure.

The premise behind a discussion system is that serial access to problem-solving technology obstructs the kind of equal participation that ideally characterizes collaboration. However, experience demonstrates that the constraints imposed by current technologies are not just a limitation on collaboration, but in some ways a resource as well. When a writing technology allows only one person to enter text at a time, a kind of **shared focus** is enforced. Users tend to agree socially on what the focus of activity needs to be each step of the way.

focus caused by technology

4.2.2.2 Issue network

In an issue-based discussion, issues and arguments are represented as nodes with links between them. An **Issue-Based Information System** (IBIS) supports an issue-based discussion. In one implementation of an IBIS there are four windows in the interface (Conklin and Begeman, 1989):

graphical issue discussion

1. a graphical browser to provide a visual presentation of the IBIS graph structure;
2. a node index window to provide an ordered, hierarchical view of the nodes;
3. a control panel which is composed of a set of buttons which extend the tool's functionality beyond simple node and link creation; and
4. an inspection window in which the attributes and contents of nodes and links can be viewed.

This IBIS has been used for several applications, and the role of red color in helping delineate meaningful nodes and relations was particularly remarkable.

An IBIS developed at the University of Liverpool has been used for developing **software requirements** documents and for recording various types of discussion (Rada *et al.*, 1990b). The user may create a node as an issue, argument, or position and must connect this node to an existing node. Through a menu the user may choose among three listings of node attributes:

applied to software requirements document

1. the author and date (see Fig. 4.14),
2. the title, or
3. the text.

The system has been used successfully for creating a requirements document.

In another IBIS, conclusions are explicitly justified or negated by individual items of **evidence**. The participants have to assess items of evidence as to their validity and relevance, in addition to posting their issues and arguments. If a participant posts an issue and someone responds with an argument, then each person scores the argument. As each score is attached to the argument, the system computes a new average score. The average score tells whether or not the group believes in the argument (Lowe, 1985).

scores on items

Yet another IBIS imposes a **hierarchical structure** on issues (Fischer *et al.*, 1989). In this IBIS, issue A is hierarchically subordinate to issue B if the arguments to A influence the arguments given to B. This system has been applied to the architectural design problem and works as long as designers are actually decomposing issues. While working in this predominantly verbal mode,

hierarchy of issues

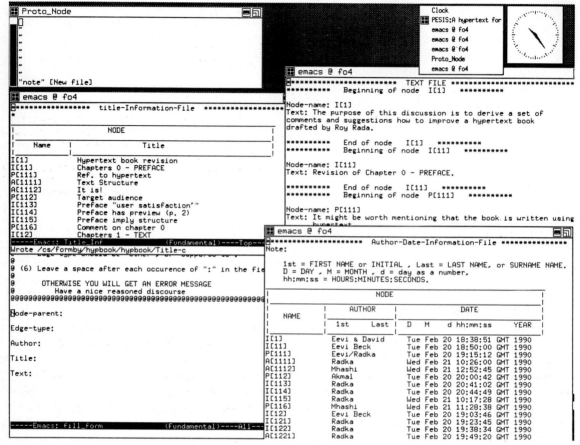

Figure 4.14 Example discussion screen. This screen image shows the multiple windows which a user may generate by selecting various menu options.

the designer wants all information relevant to an issue, but the users consistently proved unable to do construction within the IBIS itself.

construction versus discussion

The inability to perform construction in the hierarchical IBIS was true when students used the method without the computer. Thus the difficulty with the system was not an artifact of the implementation (Fischer *et al.*, 1989). This was surprising, as video-taped protocols revealed hand-drawn construction to involve continual decomposition of issues. The explanation for this apparent paradox is that the **discussion** about **construction** is not the same as construction. Discussion and construction are distinct modes of creativity; both may be required for creating a good document, but they tend not to be performed simultaneously.

4.2.3 Annotation

annotations and computers

The computer can facilitate the collection of information from users as to what they think of the various parts of a document. Existing annotation systems emphasize the placement of **annotations** in a separate record that points to the

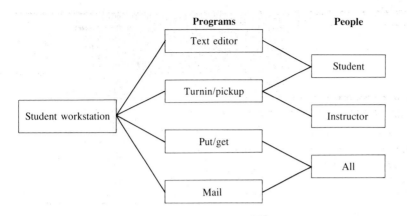

Figure 4.15 Education On-Line System. The instructor and student have a privileged communication link through the turnin/pickup programs; everyone has access to mail and put/get programs.

original document, but more intimate placement of an annotation to a document can also be supported. Educational applications are prominent because students need to read and annotate documents.

4.2.3.1 Education example

One way to implement collaborative annotation is to have files stored and shared which constitute comments by one person on another's work. A basic computer network is adequate to support such a system, and several such annotative file-sharing systems are being used at universities. The **Education On-Line System** at the Massachusetts Institute of Technology runs on 1500 workstations connected campus-wide over an electronic network. Access to workstations and network software is available to any user, anywhere at any time. The network file system provides abundant on-line storage for all user files.

networked workstations

The Education On-Line System consists of a suite of programs which support **conferencing** and **instructional processes** (see Fig. 4.15). A turnin/pickup program allows exchange of text between student and instructor. A put/get program permits files to be exchanged from one person to all others. A user puts a file into a pickup bin and then whoever wants may access it. A grade program permits storage, classification, and annotation of versions of documents. The grade program allows an instructor to survey an individual student's work over any period of time. With an annotation program the instructor places comments directly into a student file.

suite of programs

The Education On-Line System was used to teach scientific writing to **students** (Barrett and Paradis, 1988). In a typical meeting, an iterative process of studying documents, preparing drafts, and criticizing those drafts occurred. For instance, in one class, three sample documents were listed in each student's directory. Each document in turn was viewed on the overhead projector, while an instructor analyzed it for style and structure. Students also had these files displayed on their monitors. This presentation was followed by a short in-class writing exercise to practice key points from the discussion. Students were instructed to get an assignment from the put/get bin. In an adjacent editing

usage in class

window the students were then to write an essay quickly. The instructors then chose some essays for immediate display in class. The students and instructors then criticized the essays. This cycle of lecture, in-class exercise, review, and feedback was much more immediate than in a conventional class.

dissatisfaction with interface

In assessing their course, the students emphasized the value of the rapid feedback which the course provided. The ability to store files was also appreciated. On the other hand, students were either indifferent or actively opposed to on-line annotation. All students missed the bold symbolism of **red marks** to assess an instructor's reaction. Comments were hard to read because they were not easily demarcated from the original. More generally, the students thought that the user interface needed substantial improvement so that they would not have to worry about information handling processes.

4.2.3.2 Annotative windows

windows

An annotation system may use window management so that an annotation becomes a new window but points to the part of the document which is being criticized. To implement such systems one needs at least a **windowing environment**. The system may support the processing of annotations in the same way as it supports the processing of the rest of the grouptext and in this way maintain a modeless environment.

ORGANIZING ANNOTATIONS

organizing notes

The **Notes** system supports the 'annotative writing process' by giving authors a text to criticize (Neuwirth *et al.*, 1987). The authors make notes about that text and try to organize these notes into a coherent comment on the source text. To take a **note** the user selects a region in the source text and chooses Take Note from a menu. The system automatically creates a link between the region and the note. An icon is placed in the region so that subsequently a reader can invoke the note by pointing to its icon in the region. The user can easily copy material from the source as well as do general writing. The user must title each note, can view a list of all current titles, and after pointing to a title, is shown the text of the relevant note. Searching can be done on the basis of titles, authors, and dates of notes. Since users were expected to organize their notes into a report, they were given features for organizing notes into sublists. Each sublist might correspond to a section of the report.

users want more representational flexibility

Notes has been used in **writing classes** at Carnegie Mellon University. Interviews with students suggests that they want more representations, with each representation matching a particular sub-task. For example, some students would like to cluster their notes in a graphical network before deciding on any linear order for them. Some students would like their notes to represent a path through an issue.

MODELESS ANNOTATIONS

graceful environment

A major prerequisite of a 'friendly' system is that its users can gracefully move from one action to its natural successor. This capability in a system merits it the qualifier of modeless. For instance, a **modeless system** will allow a user to

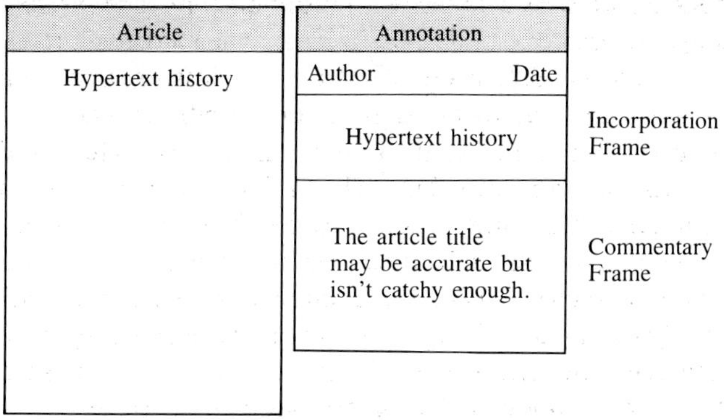

Article	Annotation	
Hypertext history	Author Date Hypertext history	Incorporation Frame
	The article title may be accurate but isn't catchy enough.	Commentary Frame

Figure 4.16 InterNote screen. Depiction of InterNote annotation structure. The original text is on the left, with the annotation on the right.

switch between editing and reading a block of text without having to issue multiple commands before each switch. The **Intermedia** system is one of the most sophisticated and modeless hypertext systems and includes an annotation system, called **InterNote**, that tries to minimize the awkwardness for users going from one type of operation to another.

InterNote helps groups of coworkers comment on each other's documents and satisfies the following requirements (Catlin *et al.*, 1989):

system features

- Annotations can be created with any available editing tools, including those for creating text, graphics, and animation.
- Multiple interfaces are available for viewing annotations. For instance, the user may see simultaneously the source document and the annotation.
- Annotations may be added to annotations.
- Any number of annotators may simultaneously add annotations to a given document.

The author may easily incorporate an annotation into the document. The author may also merge or sort annotations and assign them statuses.

When annotating a document with InterNote, one links a Note to any selection in a document by using the 'Create Annotation' command. A Note consists of two frames: the Incorporation Frame fills the top portion of the Note window and the Commentary Frame fills the bottom portion of the Note window (see Fig. 4.16). When a Note is first created, the Incorporation Frame initially contains an exact copy of the material from the article which one has elected to annotate. The **annotator** may edit the contents of the Incorporation Frame and in the Commentary Frame may include general suggestions for revising the document.

method of use

In InterMedia, links are made between document objects, called the local anchor and the remote anchor. To traverse a link, a user selects a link and picks the 'Follow' command. To deal with annotations, a new type of link has been created. To transfer data across this link, a user selects the link and issues the **Push** or **Pull** command (see Fig. 4.17). The Push command copies the contents of the local anchor and pastes it at the other end of the link, replacing the contents of the remote link anchor. Pull has the opposite effect and copies the content of the remote anchor over the local anchor.

push and pull

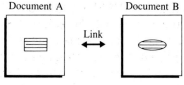

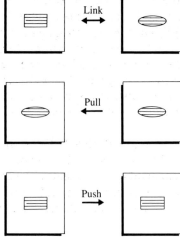

Figure 4.17 Push or Pull. In the top diagram, the rectangle in document A is linked to the ellipse in document B. Document A contains the 'local anchor' and a pull will move the ellipse from document B to document A. Conversely, a push will move the rectangle from document A to document B.

4.2.4 Publishing

authors and publishers collaborate

Publishing means to make generally known or to disseminate. Successful publishing typically requires collaborative work on a large scale. Not only might a group of editors collaborate on a large project, but, more generally, the authors, editors, and distributors must collaborate.

4.2.4.1 Electronic journals

use electronic and paper forms

Electronic journals have advantages over **paper journals**. The time between the acceptance of a document into an electronic journal and its reaching an audience may be substantially reduced over that required to produce and distribute paper copy. Additionally, the user can compactly store and quickly retrieve electronic forms. On the other hand, people are comfortable with paper forms; they can read the paper form while they travel or readily annotate it with red ink. The ideal situation might be one in which journals are delivered electronically but printed by the recipients.

electronic research journal

From 1980 till 1984 the British Library funded an electronic journal. The journal was occasionally published in paper form, with about 100 papers of varying length and quality appearing in the journal. The journal 'died' in 1984, because the readers preferred **paper copy**. Papers in academic journals benefit from graphics but these graphics were difficult to exchange electronically. Readers concluded that a traditional paper copy of the journal was necessary (Brailsford and Beach, 1989).

USENET Cookbook

The USENET Cookbook is an electronic journal which has appeared in over one hundred weekly issues (Reid, 1988). It is centrally published and is distributed free of charge via **USENET**, a world-wide bulletin board system built on many electronic networks and accessed by hundreds of thousands of people.

The only member of the **editorial staff** of 'The USENET Cookbook' is Brian Reid, who has highly modularized and automated the editorial functions. Submitted articles arrive by electronic mail to the internet address Recipes@decwrl.DEC.COM. Articles arrive in different formats, although it is the goal of the editor for the submitted articles to have a consistent format. An acquisitions-editor program reads the incoming mailbox and sends an acknowledgement to the author. A mailer program files each submission chronologically. The copy-editor program processes the submissions by placing them in standard form. Internationalizing units of measure and other terminology is particularly difficult.

programs for editors

The publishing process itself is completely **automated**. If the queues of publishable articles are full enough, The USENET Cookbook can run completely unattended for weeks. The circulation department of the cookbook is handled by an automated mail-response server. When people mail requests for back issues, the server locates their requests in its database and mails the back issues to the requester.

automated publishing

4.2.4.2 Book publishing

Many publishing houses are extensively automated. Documents are created, stored, printed, and communicated electronically. One publishing system, called **Shared Books**, explicitly supports collaboration and is modeled on the **folders** view of publishing (Lewis and Hodges, 1988). Folders contain the items needed to produce a publication, such as drafts of text and production schedules, and are passed from one worker to another as each job step is finished. An icon on the Shared Books screen represents a folder. Upon opening the icon, the user sees a window that displays the status of all items. Operations such as Open, Copy, and Paginate may be applied to items in the folder.

folders approach

A test of Shared Books was performed with a group of technical writers who were writing and updating a large document. The document consisted of 1800 printed pages in six volumes. The users found the folders valuable, but used them in a different way than had been expected. Instead of dividing the document into six folders based on the six volumes, the writers divided the document into four folders entitled: Chapters, Quick Reference Guides, Glossary Submissions, and Release Deliverables. This reflected the way the writers normally worked with a document collection. Shared Books was **adaptable** to the style of its users.

adapted by users

4.3 Epilogue

Grouptext systems allow users to share a rich set of linked information. The **links** among text blocks which are particularly relevant to grouptext include those which support versioning, discussion, annotation, and messaging. These links, along with the conceptual links in a semantic abstraction of the document, help writers to share reader models and thus develop a more effective document.

links

Each block of text should have attributes which note who created it and

versions

when. As text is changed, a history of the changes should be retained. To facilitate access to the various **versions**, a revision tree may be maintained whose root is the original version. Each collaborator has an option as to which part of the revision tree to extend, but at some point agreement must be reached as to which versions to print. The system should support simple heuristics, such as the last changed version is the current version, but also allow the users to override the heuristics.

link types for discussion phase

The **discussion phase** of collaborative work may be supported by special systems. The links might be of the type Support or Refute among nodes of type Issue and Argument, but users should be allowed to enlarge or constrain the set of node and link types. The discussion system should be able to collect votes from users to support decision-making.

annotation features

Annotation occurs after a draft of a document has been prepared. In the traditional database approach to annotation, each annotation is a new record which points to the record which is being annotated. The author and date of the annotator are recorded. Furthermore, the annotator can specify action which must be taken, and the system can monitor that the action is taken. An annotator should be able to circle arbitrary material in the document and comment on it in a separate text block. Filters should be available so that annotations can be viewed according to who wrote them, and when. People are familiar with paper copy on which red marks are rendered, and the annotation system supports this style by placing a transparent sheet over the text. Writing on the transparent sheet both preserves the original document, while creating a copy with red marks.

space and time dimensions

Collaboration occurs in space and time. Collaborators can be in the same place or distant, and they can respond to a communication instantly or after a long delay (see Fig. 4.18). Being in the same place does not have significance unless it also includes being there at the same time. The 'same-time' communication is **synchronous**: one person must be responsive to another person in real time. 'What You See Is What I See' (WYSIWIS) environments support synchronous communication, while responding after an arbitrary delay is **asynchronous**. A salient example of a collaborative environment that supports people in the same place at the same time is the Colab system. The MUCH system is a kind of 'same-space' system because it requires the users to be on the local network of workstations connected to a certain file server, but it does not support synchronous communication. Videoconferencing is an example of synchronous, distant collaboration. Electronic mail provides a 'different-place, different-time' connection.

Figure 4.18 Ways of collaborating. The Colab and MUCH systems are examples of collaborative systems which have been developed in particular laboratories as exploratory systems. The 'distant-places' systems are general purpose, and exist in multiple commercial versions.

	Synchronous	*Asynchronous*
Same place	Colab	MUCH
Distant places	video-conferencing	electronic mail

In a WYSIWIS environment, while many decisions must be made by the system designer, some should be reserved for the user. For instance, a window on the screen could be private in that other users would not be able to see what happens in that window. Whether or not any given window should be **private** or **public** could be determined by the user who invokes the window. Distant collaborators can share computer databases or could also share audio and video messages. In such 'distant' settings, users could have the option of seeing collaborators in video windows and of activating audio channels so as to talk with other people.

decisions about what to share

A meeting with data, audio, and video might produce a decision to which people were more committed or might lead to increased team spirit. Working in teams is essentially a social process and is very important to a company's success. The growth in personal computers has emphasized individuals but emphasis might beneficially shift to groups. The analysis would then need to be of **human–human interaction** rather than of human–computer interaction. Current software systems are designed to support only one form of interaction —between the user and the computer. Group interfaces are different—they are designed to support groups and may be simultaneously controlled by multiple users.

benefit to team work

In order that people successfully collaborate, they must share a goal. Second, they must have complementary skills and personalities. Third, the collaborators must agree on the sharing of resources. These three factors together create a '**social glue**'. The computer can support collaboration in ways which other technologies could not, but the people must initiate and maintain the social glue.

social glue

As the overwhelming factor in determining collaborative success is social glue, problems in collaboration are usually of the sort that a colleague was irresponsible or seized too much **credit** for the work. Rarely are difficulties in the collaborative work process itself cited as hindering a collaboration. These observations make a sharp comment on the character of technology to support collaboration—most of which has been task-oriented but which needs to consider personal relationships.

credit

4.4 Exercises

4.1 The common wisdom is that **node names** can be anything, but link types should be constrained. The common character of this wisdom does not necessarily attest to its insightfulness. Suggest guidelines that could be given to a collaborating group of authors for the construction of node names. (20 minutes)

node names

4.2 Providing a branched version history for entities in a hypertext network raises difficult issues regarding the **semantics of references** between entities (Halasz, 1988). Illustrate this difficulty. (30 minutes)

versions

4.3 A **cooperative database** management system suits certain situations where transactions are long-lived and many items exist in the database. Sketch the operations of this cooperative database relative to users. (1.5 hours)

cooperative database

4.4 In one approach to the acetate mode of annotations, users have to **freeze**

acetate mode

the underlying document and turn it into a bitmap before annotations can be added. There is a dissonance between the annotation mode and the authoring mode. A document frozen in authoring mode cannot be later changed in authoring mode without losing alterations that may have been introduced in the annotation mode. Why might such freezing be used and how could one avoid it? (25 minutes)

capitalist versus communist

4.5 What are the advantages and disadvantages from an 'economic perspective' of a competitive versus a cooperative approach to writing (loosely speaking one might refer to the **capitalist** and the **communist** approach)? (30 minutes)

student collaboration

4.6 Describe some advantages and disadvantages of **collaborative writing** in the school environment. (25 minutes)

scientist evaluation

4.7 Published papers constitute a kind of society. One practical reflection of this is seen in **promotion policies**. A Dean in a university must decide whom to promote among a group of academics whose success is measured by the impact of their writings on the academic community. Assume the Dean has access to a full-text document database which includes all the literature related to the work of his academics. Suggest how the Dean should use full-text document databases to evaluate the research effectiveness of his staff. (45 minutes)

efficiency exceeds one

4.8 Traditionally, when all n processors of an n-processor machine are active, an optimal efficiency of 1 has been obtained. On the other hand, the definition of **efficiency** does not preclude efficiency exceeding 1. The time for a 1-processor machine to solve a class C of problems is $T_1(C)$, and for an n-processor, is $T_n(C)$. The speedup $S_n(C)$ of a n-processor machine on C is defined as:

$$S_n(C) = \frac{T_1(C)}{T_n(C)}$$

The efficiency $E_n(C)$ of a n-processor on C is defined as:

$$E_n(C) = \frac{S_n(C)}{n}$$

Define a task, memory access costs, and communication costs such that collaborative efficiency on the tasks exceeds one. (2 hours)

wicked problem for discussion

4.9 Discussion facilitates systems analysis in the face of **wicked problems**. Wicked problems cannot be solved by the traditional systems analysis approach of define the problem, collect data, analyze the data, and construct the solution. Choose a small, wicked problem and create a short discussion to solve it. (1 hour)

5

Intelligent hypertext

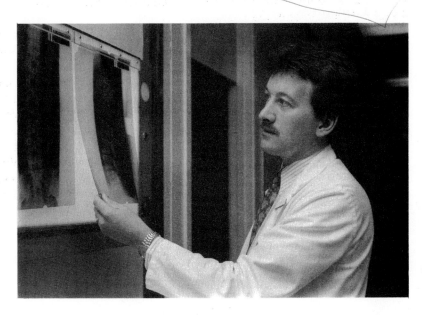

Figure 5.1 Expert. The physician is an acknowledged expert who deals with images and documents as a routine part of his effort to interpret patients' problems. Intelligent hypertext can incorporate some of this expertise.

While links within and among documents are critical to hypertext, the future of hypertext may depend on the addition of artificial intelligence capabilities to hypertext systems. One way to do this is to embed knowledge in links and to allow these **links** to precipitate arbitrary computations. With intelligent hypertext some of the **expertise** of people which is otherwise outside the computer system is moved into the computer (see Fig. 5.2).

expertise

Hypertext systems of the 1970s already faced challenges of how to incorporate more flexibility or intelligence into the computer. The Dynabook system included navigation aids that introduced the possibility of the hypertext system

hypertext history

Figure 5.2 Intelligent hypertext. The outer box represents the computer system. In an expertext system a human's expertise is partially incorporated into the system.

143

responding dynamically to the user. Miniature page icons stamped with **time** and **date** could be selected. This not only took one to a page previously visited, but also to its status at that time. The model for Dynabook supported dynamic and not just static hypertext. The reader could cause different information to appear on the same page as a function of the traversal. Thus on two successive accesses a page might appear different through either hiding information or showing new information. The creators of Dynabook concluded that to use such dynamic facilities to help the user in the best way, knowledge must be incorporated into the computer.

5.1 Principles

definitions

Expert systems are built by knowledge engineers and experts who together translate expertise into a knowledge base plus inferencing mechanism (see Fig. 5.3). While the **expert system** may directly solve problems, it also communicates knowledge from an expert to a user (Hayes-Roth *et al.*, 1983). Similarly with a **hypertext system** a writer communicates with a reader (see Fig. 5.4). These parallels suggest improvements to both expert systems and hypertext systems.

MYCIN

The development of hypertext systems has parallels with that of expert systems. One of the first expert systems, MYCIN, was developed in the mid-1970s. MYCIN employed a few hundred if-then rules about meningitis and bacteremia in order to deduce the proper treatment for a patient who presented with signs of either of those diseases. MYCIN, while provably expert within its

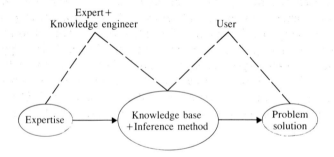

Figure 5.3 An expert system contains a knowledge base and inference method which a knowledge engineer and expert have built to solve problems of users.

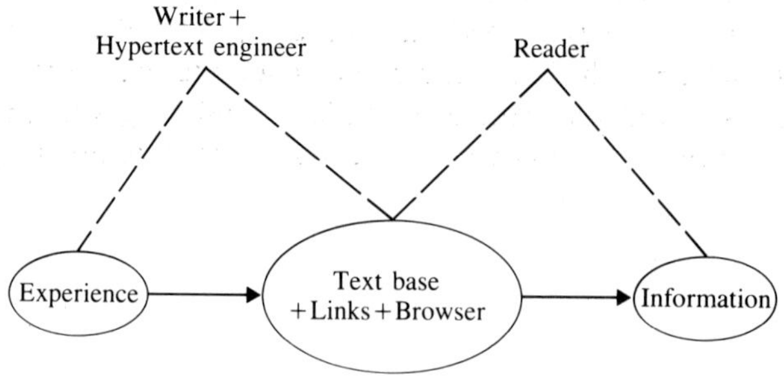

Figure 5.4 A hypertext system contains a text base, links, and a browser which a hypertext engineer and writer have developed to present information to readers.

domains of bacteremia and meningitis, did not cover enough of the information which physicians routinely need for them to spend valuable time accessing MYCIN. The developers of MYCIN have partly shifted their attention to the development of user-friendly or hypertext information systems that incorporate expert systems but primarily handle the day-to-day **work flow** of a physician in a hospital ward (Shortliffe *et al.*, 1981). The need to incorporate expert systems into the work flow has been a stimulus to the development of expertext. Other medical expert systems are following the hypertext paradigm in order that the computer's services may be more attractive to the health-care professional (Timpka, 1986).

INTERNIST

The INTERNIST expert system which was developed in the mid-1970s was the first expert system to handle a wide range of internal medicine problems. Over 4000 signs and symptoms were connected with over 1000 diseases for diagnosis and treatment purposes. Unfortunately, the user had to know how to phrase his patient's problem in the exact terms that the developers of the expert system had chosen—this discouraged the user. Alternatives are being pursued which take advantage of hypertext strategies. For instance, INTERNIST has been converted into a **teaching** tool which allows the user to browse through the knowledge in INTERNIST in a hypertext fashion (First *et al.*, 1985). The options of what to pursue at each point are made clear, as the user browses the options. The user does not have to guess at the phraseology of one expert. The expert system, modified for medical teaching, is expected to fit more easily into the work flow of students than it did into the work flow of physicians.

synergism

The rules on which an expert system is based often seem inadequate when the expert system attempts to explain its decisions to users. Hypertext can be integrated with an expert system so that the expert system can (synergistically) better explain its decisions. Textbook information can be offered to the user when the expert system is questioned. From the other side, the links in hypertext may be difficult to follow. Hypertext systems can include expert system features that help the user find relevant information. The combination of expert system and hypertext system is called an **expertext system** (Rada *et al.*, 1990a). More generally, the terms intelligent hypertext and expertext may be used interchangeably in this book.

5.1.1 Links

dynamic links

The links in hypertext can be exploited or extended so that the user can appreciate a dynamic, intelligent text. In one case, the links are not more complicated but **patterns** of links are exploited. In another case, the graph has predicates at the nodes and implications on the links, and the graph can support **inferencing**. Procedures can be added to the links and support all kinds of computation.

5.1.1.1 Semantic net patterns

semantic patterns

The computer can exploit the pattern of links in a hypertext and give the user different perspectives on the hypertext. For instance, the user may express an interest in 'causes', and the system could organize information so as to emphasize the causal links. The nodes and links of hypertext may be viewed as a semantic net. A link attributes meaning to the pair of nodes it connects, and a node may have more than one meaning, when it participates in relations of different types (Carlson and Ram, 1990). Inheritance of properties along hierarchical links in a **semantic net** and spreading activation in a semantic net both take advantage of the patterns therein.

SPREADING ACTIVATION

Electronic Yellow Pages

When submitting a query to an *Electronic Yellow Pages*, the consumer wants a certain type of product or service, a phone number, and a location. The consumer is constrained by nearby location, degree of specificity in product-service hierarchy, time available for search, and amount of information wanted. Responding to a consumer's **query** with a list of hundreds of businesses would not be reasonable. At the other extreme, returning without the name of at least one business which could satisfy the consumer's needs would not be very helpful. In each case, whether reducing the solution space to present the consumer with a manageable set of alternatives or enlarging the solution space to present the user with at least a few alternatives, the semantic network behind the *Electronic Yellow Pages* can be used as a guide. For example, grocery stores and restaurants are related in that they share the common ancestor 'business' and both sell 'food'. If a consumer was looking for a restaurant in a specific locale and none existed, the system might present the consumer with names of nearby grocery stores (see Fig. 5.5).

connectivity

The connections among nodes in a semantic net are critical to its functionality. In spreading activation, a concept is identified in a semantic net and then adjacent concepts in the net are visited in the course of solving some problem. The significance of the traversal of the net depends on the net and the way the traversal is used to infer a solution to a problem. In one of its simplest forms,

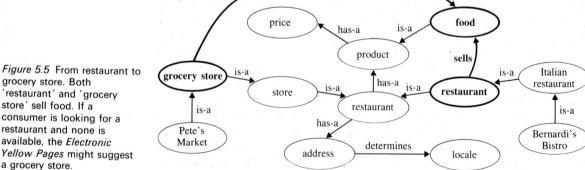

Figure 5.5 From restaurant to grocery store. Both 'restaurant' and 'grocery store' sell food. If a consumer is looking for a restaurant and none is available, the *Electronic Yellow Pages* might suggest a grocery store.

Analogical inheritance

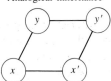

Figure 5.6 *x* is a child of *y*, *y* has attribute *y'*, *x* has attribute *x'*, and *x'* is a child of *y'*.

spreading activation starts from two **nodes** and activates all the nodes connected to each of them. Then all of the nodes connected to each of those are activated, forming an expanding sphere of **activation** around each of the original concepts. When some concept has been activated simultaneously from two directions, a conclusion is drawn (Fikes and Hendrix, 1977).

ANALOGICAL INHERITANCE

One key feature of the semantic net representation is that important associations can be made explicitly and succinctly. Relevant facts about a concept can be inferred from the nodes to which they are directly linked. Given that Tweety is a canary and that a canary is a bird, one can use the property of **inheritance hierarchies** to infer that Tweety is a bird. Semantic nets facilitate representation and reasoning with inheritance hierarchies, and such hierarchies are particularly germane to hypertext.

inheritance

To say that a concept inherits the attributes of its parent concept is only to characterize the **attributes** which the two concepts have in common. There is a structure-function relationship in semantic nets which allows a special kind of inheritance called analogical inheritance. Assume that every concept has both **hierarchical** and non-hierarchical relations. In one example of analogical inheritance each attribute $f(x)$ of a concept x would have a child relationship to the attribute $f(y)$ when x is the child of y (see Fig. 5.6). More generally, analogical inheritance means that a concept x which is a child of a concept y will have an attribute x' which is related in some systematic way to the corresponding attribute y' of y (see Exercise 5.1).

analogical structure

If an author has developed part of a semantic net and has a fragment but does not know where to connect that fragment to the rest of the network, analogical inheritance might provide a guide. An example of how this **insertion** might occur is in the placement of the 'Chairperson of the Mathematics Department' into the hierarchy about the administration of the university (see Fig. 5.7). If one knows that the 'Chairperson of the Mathematics Department' has an office in the 'School of Natural Sciences', then one might expect that the Chairperson reports to the 'Dean of the School of Natural Sciences' rather than to the 'Dean of the School of Engineering'. The computer can keep track of the semantic net that has been created and make suggestions to the author about patterns.

insertion

To what extent does a document **outline** constitute a semantic net (see Exercise 5.2)? Imagine an outline as a special binary tree. For every pair of siblings the first entry is meant to relate to the second entry by implication (see Fig. 5.8). For instance, if the first section of a document is called 'Assumptions'

outline

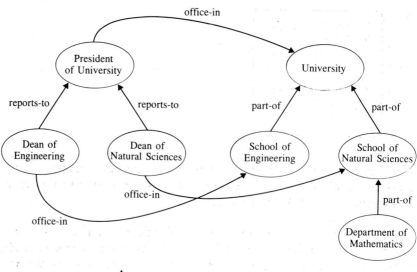

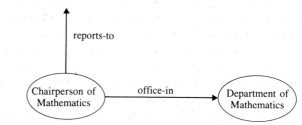

Figure 5.7 Insertion by analogical inheritance. To whom should the 'Chairperson of Mathematics' report? Reasoning by analogical inheritance.

Figure 5.8 Patterns in outline. Example of an outline viewed as a semantic net.

and the second section is called 'Demonstration', then the 'Assumptions' imply the 'Demonstration'. Likewise, the 'Assumptions' section may be divided into a 'Problem' and 'Hypothesis' section in which the 'Problem' implies the 'Hypothesis'. These patterns demonstrate analogical inheritance.

BOOK OUTLINES

models of books

Non-fiction writers appeal to a number of models of their areas of discourse. Such **models** are reflected in the structure of their books. Inherent to the outline of a book are two kinds of relationships:

Section number	Logic
...	...
4.	**D**
4.1.	**A**
4.2.	**A → B**
4.3.	**B → C**
4.4.	**C → D**
...	...

Figure 5.9 Logic in outline.

1. precedence relationships as reflected by the sequence of subsections, and
2. hierarchical relationships of textual containment between a section of text and its subsections (Mili and Rada, 1990).

Precedence relationships   The precedence relationships usually embody one of three ordering relationships: incidental, logical, or temporal. In an **incidental** or non-essential ordering, the ordering of subsections within a given section is arbitrary, and the subsections can be read in any order. In a **logical ordering**, the ordering of the subsections within a given section corresponds to the overall scheme of a proof procedure. For example, to prove D, knowing A, A → B, B → C, and C → D, an outline for the section about D might look like Fig. 5.9. Also, back chaining may be used, in which case the author may chose to prove C → D before proving B → C, and so forth. More complex proof patterns may occur, as in A → B, A → C, B AND C → D, where to prove D knowing A the two subsections A → B and A → C may be presented in any order.

incidental and logical orderings

In a **temporal ordering**, the subsections of a given section may be used in describing dynamic or time-evolving concepts. This is a recurrent pattern in medicine where the subject is often the description of the different stages of a biological process. For example, Pauerstein's *Clinical Obstetrics* has chapters organized along a time line (see Fig. 5.10). A similar time-line is evident in other books about pregnancy, such as *Pregnancy and Childbirth*, a book by Tracy Hotchner aimed at the expectant mother.

temporal orderings

Containment relationships   **Textual containment relationships** include hierarchical relations and frame/slot relations. Hierarchical relationships are usually based on a specific model of the topics covered. For example, a **taxonomy** of diseases may be based on a taxonomy of organs (see Fig. 5.11).

hierarchy

Chapter headings
Early development of the fetus
Physiological reactions of the mother
Care before labor
...
Labor
Management of the mother after labor
Care of the newborn

Figure 5.10 Chapters in an obstetrics book. These chapter headings indicate the time line which the book follows.

Section number	Section heading
...	...
8.	Diseases of the organs
8.1.	Diseases of the lungs
8.2.	Diseases of the liver
...	...

Figure 5.11 In a medical textbook, chapters on diseases may be organized by organ system, as illustrated here.

Section number	Section heading
...	...
8.1.2.	Chronic bronchitis
8.1.2.1.	Causes
8.1.2.2.	Manifestations
8.1.2.3.	Diagnosis
8.1.2.4.	Treatment
8.1.2.4.	Prognosis
...	...

Figure 5.12 Outline by slots. A section about a given disease may contain subsections dealing with its various aspects as in this outline from a medical textbook.

frame/slots

In the case of **frame/slot relationships**, each subsection corresponds to a slot of the frame represented by the section. For example, a disease may be characterized by its cause, manifestation, diagnosis, treatment, and prognosis (see Fig. 5.12). The breakdown of a requirements document into environment, system functions, and logistics is another example of a frame/slot decomposition.

comparison of hierarchy and frame

Semantically, there are two major differences between hierarchical relations and frame/slot relations:

1. With hierarchical relations, the concepts represented by a section and its subsections belong to the same **semantic category** (e.g. diseases), and the same relation holds between each subsection and the section.
2. With frame/slot relations, the concepts represented by the subsections generally belong to different semantic categories than the semantic category of the section.

guidance in outline construction

Textual containment and textual precedence interact in many ways to convey a document's semantic structure or map. Factors, such as the consistency of lengths between different subsections, may lead authors to organize sections in a way that corrupts containment or precedence relations. For example, in Hotchner's *Pregnancy and Childbirth* a time line is prominent at the chapter level, except that care during pregnancy is treated in three different chapters entitled 'Care of the Mind', 'Care of the Body', and 'Care of the Emotions'. There is no time precedence between these three topics as the pregnant woman should care for all three aspects simultaneously. An alternative organization that would preserve the temporal ordering at the top level would be to indent the care subsections under one section (see Fig. 5.13). Thus attention to patterns

---

Pregnancy and childbirth
1.   Before you get pregnant
2.   Difficulties getting pregnant
3.   Care during pregnancy
3.1. Care of the body during pregnancy
3.2. Care of the mind during pregnancy
3.3. Sexuality during pregnancy
4.   Labor
5.   Delivery
6.   Post-partum care

Figure 5.13 Reorganization of sections. This revised outline of the book would improve its regularity as a semantic structure.

---

in the outline can guide the organization of the outline. One might expect that readers would benefit from a **consistent organization** of an outline.

5.1.1.2 Logic

Expert systems have become the popular way of applying artificial intelligence to practical problems. The representation of knowledge in **expert systems** is often as 'rules'. A rule is essentially a logical statement of the form 'if A, then B'. Logical representation schemes combine predicates and logical operators in statements. An example of a rule is 'IF likes(Judy, cheese) AND have(pizza, cheese), THEN wants(Judy, pizza)'. In this statement 'likes(Judy, cheese)' is an example of a predicate and 'AND' is a logical operator. — rules

The text of documents themselves may provide evidence on which **rules** operate in order to determine which documents are relevant to a query. The rules may be provided by the user and define a hierarchy of topics. By naming a topic, the user invokes the rules. The lowest-level topics are defined in terms of patterns in the text itself. Thus the system ultimately depends on a string search of text. But once a pattern in the text is detected, other rules may operate on those patterns in the course of inferring that higher-level concepts characterize a document (Tong and Shapiro, 1985). The results of the **string searching** are combined in a more sophisticated way than is typically allowed in a string-searching system. Assume one has a query for documents about 'machine learning' and that the following rules are used: — retrieval

1. If 'machine' and 'learning', then 'machine learning'.
2. If 'computer' or 'hardware', then 'machine'.
3. If 'learning' or 'adaptation' or 'acquisition', then 'learning'.

A document with the three terms 'computer', 'knowledge', and 'acquisition' would activate first rules 2 and 3 and then rule 1, and the document would be returned to the query 'machine learning'.

FLOW CONTROL

A flow control model is a special graph whose two node types are **places** and **transitions**. The model includes functions which map transitions to places. A **marking** of a flow control model assigns a number of tokens to each place in the — definition of flow control graph

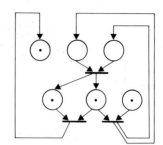

Figure 5.14 A flow control graph before and after transition firing. The bold, short lines are transitions. The circles are places. The small dots are tokens.

graph. To change the marking of a flow control graph, one must first select a transition each of whose input places has, at least, one token. Then this transition is fired by removing one token from each place in the input of the transition and by adding one token to each place in the output of the transition (see Fig. 5.14). The marking of a node may be viewed as a predicate and the transition as an implication.

hypertext model

With a flow control graph one can model hypertext and control browsing (Stotts and Furuta, 1989). The model

- associates a **text block** with each place in the flow control graph, and
- associates a **link** with each transition in the flow control graph.

The model also includes display functions which dictate how the text blocks and links are presented on a display device.

browsing

Activation of a link causes the current display to change in a specified way. During **browsing**, the current marking of the net determines what is viewable. The transitions enabled under the marking determine which links are visible. Selection of a link fires one of the enabled transitions and causes the display to change correspondingly.

security

In order to make a certain path within a flow control graph accessible only to privileged classes of browsers, a transition in that path may be **locked**. To implement a lock, the system marks a place, call it the status place, with exactly one token when a privileged user enters the system (Rada *et al.*, 1990a). When a restricted user enters the system any token is removed from the status place. The use of the status place can be illustrated in the browsing of a textbook. In Fig. 5.15 the teacher is allowed to access the exercise answer. All users of the textbook can access the exercise. If the initial marking of the place 'teacher' is 1, then whenever a token is present at the place 'exercise', the transition leading to 'answer' can fire. Conversely, if the user is *not* the teacher, then that place has a marking of 0, and the transition leading to 'answer' can never fire.

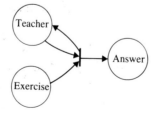

Figure 5.15 Access control. 'Exercise' is accessible to everyone; if someone is a 'teacher', then they have access to the, otherwise restricted, 'answer'.

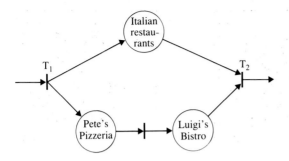

Figure 5.16 Display control. 'Italian restaurants' will remain displayed while first 'Pete's Pizzeria' and then 'Luigi's Bistro' are shown.

A flow control system could place or remove windows from the computer screen. For instance, 'Italian Restaurants' could be a high-level node or place which would appear in one window, while first 'Pete's Pizzeria' and then 'Luigi's Bistro' would appear in another window (see Fig. 5.16).

multiple windows

QUERY PROCESSING

A modified flow control scheme can be used to represent arbitrary logical statements (Rada *et al.*, 1990a). Places in the flow control graph correspond to **predicates** (equivalently relations), with no predicate labeling more than one place. Tokens occupying a place indicate that the predicate is true for the arguments represented by the token; unless the token is negated in which case it indicates that the predicate is false. The input (output) edges of a transition are also labeled with tokens (see Fig. 5.17). Transitions represent logical implication.

extended flow control and logic

The logic, flow control scheme can be illustrated with a directory access problem. The following data might be parts of two blocks of text within an **Electronic Yellow Pages**: Grand Store sells books and newspapers and is open from 7 a.m. to 7 p.m., and Super Store sells newspapers, magazines and paperbacks and is open from 9 a.m. to 11 p.m. From these two blocks of information come the following facts:

Electronic Yellow Pages example

- Grand Store sells books and Grand Store sells newspapers.
- Grand Store opens at 7 a.m. and closes at 7 p.m.
- Super Store sells newspapers, magazines and paperback books.
- Super Store opens at 9 a.m. and closes at 11 p.m.

Now suppose a user browsing the *Electronic Yellow Pages* asks the following question:

'From whom can I buy a newspaper after 10 p.m.?'

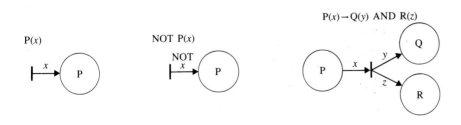

Figure 5.17 Logic flow control. Flow control graphs for (i) $P(x)$, (ii) NOT $P(x)$, and (iii) $P(x) \rightarrow Q(y)$ AND $R(z)$.

Then this can be answered by encoding the following information:

- sells (G,N) (i.e. Grand Store sells newspapers)
- sells (S,N) (i.e. Super Store sells newspapers)
- closes (G,7) (i.e. Grand Store closes at 7 p.m.)
- closes (S,11) (i.e. Super Store closes at 11 p.m.)
- later (11,10) (i.e. 11 p.m. is later than 10 p.m.)
- NOT later (7,10) (i.e. 7 p.m. is not later than 10 p.m.).

To pose the question in logical form one may make a statement whose truth would have to be checked against the other statements of the problem. The query may be translated into the following statement:

- closes (x,y) AND later $(y,10) \rightarrow$ sells(x, N)

which may be interpreted as 'if store x closes at time y and y is later than 10 p.m., then does store x sell newspapers?' The value of x which is consistent with the other information in the directory will be the name of the store that answers the query. A logic, flow control graph for these premises can be drawn (see Fig. 5.18). After processing the tuple $\langle S,N \rangle$ resides in the place sells and the text block for Super Store can be displayed.

browsing and queries

In the normal view of hypertext the reader sees a set of buttons and on selecting a button is shown another window. In the logic-based approach, a query is posed as a logic statement and the **resolution** of the query leads to a series of transitions which result in the display of text blocks (see Exercise 5.4). Text blocks may be associated with each transition or inference, and thus a sequence of text blocks may be offered to the user as a kind of guided tour of the information system in response to the user's input. Each query initiates a kind of browsing.

navigation

The **navigation** of hypertext can be achieved by using the inference engine to construct paths in the hypertext in response to the user's queries. Sections of the

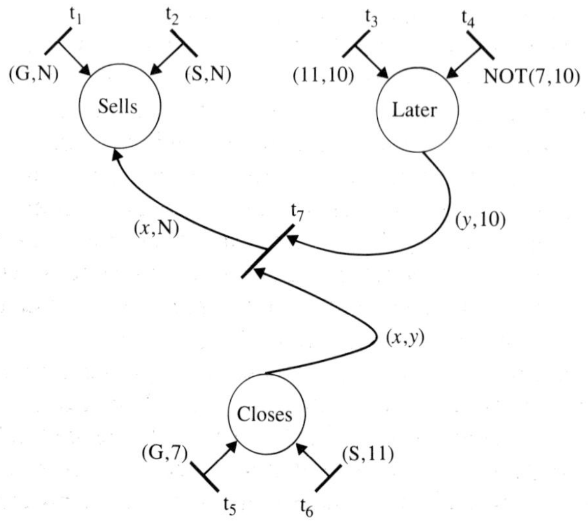

Figure 5.18 Electronic Yellow Pages logic. Reasoning net to determine which store sells newspapers after 10 p.m.

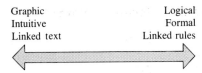

Graphic   Logical
Intuitive   Formal
Linked text   Linked rules

Figure 5.19 Continuum for expertext. Hypertext system characteristics are shown at the left end as graphic and intuitive, while expert system characteristics are shown at the right end as logical and formal.

hypertext may be used to illuminate the rules across which logical inferencing has arrived at particular conclusions. In one application, a medical expertext incorporates an expert, diagnostic, rule system and a hypertext representation of a medical textbook. In explaining how a particular conclusion has been reached the inference system interacts with the hypertext and highlights the textual sources for the various **inferences**. The facts utilized by the rules are available in an expanded and more accessible (to a reader) form within the hypertext.

While the logic capabilities of expert systems can provide powerful flexibility to a hypertext system, there are also costs. The greatest cost concerns the different character of the two technologies which makes them appropriate for different purposes. Hypertext systems appeal to one's **intuitive** and graphic faculties, whereas expert systems appeal to one's formal, logical faculties (see Fig. 5.19). In converting a hypertext system into something more **formal**, one must be careful not to destroy its intuitive or graphic power. Conversely, in converting an expert system into hypertext, one does not want to lose the robust inferencing facilities of logic (see Exercise 5.5).

intuitive versus formal

5.1.1.3 Procedures

The links in a logical model of hypertext can be extended to support procedures. When procedures are included on the links of a graph, the graph is sometimes called an **augmented transition network**. Mathematicians have proven that this can represent any computable algorithm; thus the augmented transition network model can simulate any other model.

theory

A **taxonomy** of **procedure** types could be based on the primitives used in the procedures (see Exercise 5.6). The procedure language is bound to include primitives which correspond to initiating a conditional jump, to storing information, to retrieving information, and to performing a computation on information. Each of these primitives can be further decomposed. For instance, the retrieving information procedure could retrieve information from the screen or from the computer disk memory. Retrieving information from the screen can be broken into types according to whether the user is first asked to provide some specific information in an input statement or whether the computer simply gathers information about where the user has left the cursor.

taxonomy

Initially, workers in artificial intelligence focused on representing knowledge in logic and semantic nets. Questions about how the knowledge would be manipulated were considered secondary. In the 1970s procedural representations became popular. Those who prefer procedures over logic and semantic nets argue that the useful knowledge of a domain is intrinsically bound

procedural approach history

with the specialized knowledge about how it is used. In the **procedural approach** control knowledge about how inferences should be made can be attached to the facts on which the inferences will be made. The current interest in object-oriented approaches is a return to a procedural approach but with certain structuring of the procedures.

informal processing

The procedural requirements for expertext can be effectively viewed in object-oriented terms. An expertext system should

- represent and automatically process certain information in formally specified ways,
- represent and make it easy for humans to process information in ways that are not formally specified, and
- allow the boundary between formal processing by computers and informal processing by people to be easily changed.

Representations which can facilitate such processing include objects and messages, which are extensions of the procedural approach to knowledge representation. Users of hypertext should be provided with menus and templates for freely examining and modifying the description of an object. **Messages** can be triggered by such events as the arrival of computer mail. The user should easily be able to change the rules which activate messages.

frames

Frame representations combine semantic network and procedural representations. A frame may be viewed as a complex data structure for representing a stereotypical situation, such as being in a certain kind of living room. The frame has **slots** for the objects that play a role in the stereotypical situation as well as relations between these slots. Attached to each frame are different kinds of information, such as how to use it, what to do if something unexpected happens, and default values for its slots. Programming with frames is a kind of object-oriented programming.

5.1.2 Distributed expert principles

multiple knowledge sources

The distributed expert approach to hypertext may use semantic nets, logic, or procedures, but also employs other more complex structures, such as models of users and natural language processors. The emphasis is on incorporation of robust **knowledge** in the hypertext system, which facilitates intelligent interaction with the user.

5.1.2.1 Natural language processing

lexical, syntactic, semantic, and pragmatic levels

One of the key challenges to the improvement of hypertext systems is to make the interface accept queries posed in something close to natural language and to make the database encode documents automatically by processing the natural language of the documents. Natural language processing requires a **lexicon**, a **syntax**, a **semantics**, and a **pragmatics**.

- The lexicon gives for each word in the language its part of speech and definition.

- The syntax defines the legitimate ordering of words in a sentence according to their part of speech. For instance, a noun followed by a verb constitutes a valid sentence.
- The semantics addresses the meaning of a sentence and may also be used to check for semantically legitimate constructions. For instance, the statement 'fish flew' is syntactically correct but semantically incorrect.
- A semantic analysis would note that the statement 'fish flew' contradicts the normal understanding of how fish transport themselves.
- The pragmatics is a level above the semantics and accounts for the context in which the natural language occurs.

The challenge in the development of robust semantics or pragmatics is to build a knowledge base. The network of a hypertext can be used as a knowledge base by a natural language processor (Marsh and Friedman, 1985).

Syntax, semantics, and pragmatics should be exploited in the interaction with a user. For instance, the system may know that

$$\langle sentence \rangle \rightarrow \langle new\text{-}word \rangle \text{ is a } \langle known\text{-}word \rangle$$

is a semantically valid construction where the terms within brackets refer to classes of terms. If the user types 'A length is a measure', and the system knows the word 'measure' but not the word 'length', then the system may conclude that 'length' is a synonym of the known word 'measure' (Haas and Hendrix, 1980). In the interaction with the user (and herein lies the pragmatics) the system could then confirm its interpretation of the meaning.

Language processing techniques may extensively exploit **hierarchically structured knowledge**. For instance, if document types have been characterized based on the presence or absence of proper names, then a natural language processing system that knows it is dealing with a document can next look for proper names. If an incoming document has proper names, then the document may be classified into its specific type (Schank, 1982).

5.1.2.2 Access and creation

In an ill-structured domain there are many potentially useful actions at any point. Selecting the most appropriate direction may require extensive computing that is supported by various knowledge sources. The communication among these knowledge sources can be facilitated with an architecture that is referred to as **distributed computing**. To focus control in a distributed system, blackboard architectures may be useful (Filman and Friedman, 1984). In a blackboard system, knowledge sources communicate by reading and writing on a blackboard. The knowledge sources use pattern-action rules: if the information on the blackboard matches the pattern of a knowledge source, then its action can be executed.

An access system helps users search, browse, or read information. A distributed, expert **access system** includes modules for processing documents and modules for interacting with users (see Fig. 5.20). The system uses knowledge bases and blackboards (Fox, 1987). Typically, an interface manager and a blackboard are assigned to each user. A blackboard architecture is

interaction with user

hierarchy

blackboard architecture

access model

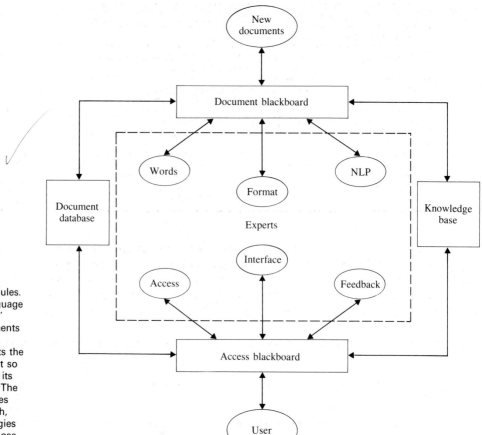

Figure 5.20 Expert modules. NLP means natural language processing. The 'Words' module analyzes documents at the word level. The 'Format' module exploits the markup of the document so as to decompose it into its logical, structural units. The 'Access' module includes information about search, browse, and read strategies so as to help users in those activities.

appropriate because multiple strategies are required, and there is no analytic way of determining which choice of strategies is best.

role of knowledge

The **knowledge bases** may include general and specific knowledge at varying levels of abstraction. Although natural language processing techniques are not likely to provide the basis for a complete understanding of **documents** for some time, resources at a lexical level may help identify the information documents contain. The documents and users are likely to focus on a domain. If the system contains legal documents for legal personnel, the knowledge base should emphasize legal knowledge.

functionalities

An **information system** needs to have (Belkin *et al.*, 1984):

- an understanding of the state of the user,
- an idea about what kind of response or system capability is appropriate,
- a model of the user, including goals, intentions and experience,
- a description of the situation the user is facing and the user's knowledge about it, and
- a hypothesis about what sort of dialogue mode is appropriate.

Components	
Name of function	Description
Problem state	Determine position of user in problem treatment process, e.g. formulating problem
User model	Generate description of user type, goals, beliefs, e.g. graduate student, thesis
Dialogue mode	Determine appropriate dialogue type for situation, e.g. natural language, menu
Retrieval strategy	Choose and apply appropriate retrieval strategies to knowledge resource, e.g. best match
Explanation	Describe mechanism operation and capabilities to user as appropriate

Figure 5.21 Functions behind intelligent macrotext interface.

This information will be gained through interaction with the user, which will require analysis of the user's part of the dialogue so that it can be used by the other functions (see Fig. 5.21). The results can then be used to specify what aspects of the knowledge base or database are relevant to the user and to generate a response. Finally, the system may need to explain its operation to the user.

In a distributed expert creation system, a user interacts with a host of expert   document creation

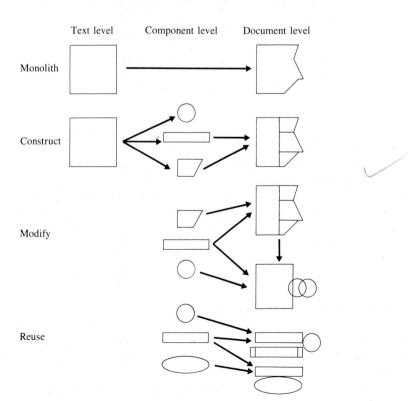

Figure 5.22 Creation approaches (Fischer, 1987). The 'Document level' is the finished product. The 'Text level' involves a sequential, word-by-word view. At the 'Component level' large, logical components of a document are manipulated.

modules. An explanation module is able to retrace what the system has done and explain the system actions to the user. A creation module helps the user create new systems or applications (Fischer, 1987), different creation modules supporting **monolith**, **construct**, **modify**, and **reuse** approaches (see Fig. 5.22). In monolithic creation a new document is created directly from scratch. In the construct approach intermediate units are first created and then subsequently organized into a document. In the modify approach, units from an existing document are replaced with units from another document. In the reuse approach existing intermediate units are combined into a new document. Reuse has high costs. Knowing about the existence of components is not trivial, especially as the number of components grows.

idea processing

Authors must both process ideas and design documents. In idea processing an author creates and augments a set of ideas and relations. The operations include creating a **node** in the semantic net and linking nodes via a predefined set of semantic relations. The author must be able to indicate that a particular topic is part of a broader topic and be able to indicate that one topic sequentially precedes another.

5.1.2.3 Machine learning

models

An expertext system may support machine learning functions. In one model of a learning system the **environment** supplies information to a **performance element** which uses a knowledge base to perform its task (Forsyth and Rada, 1986). A learning element uses this information to make improvements in the knowledge base (see Fig. 5.23). To extend this model for hypertext, the environment is seen as providing text and requests to a performance element which must first represent text and requests in a manner that matches the representation of the knowledge base. The performance element then tries to respond to the request. An evaluate element examines the performance relative

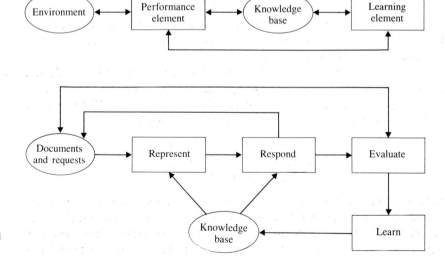

Figure 5.23 A simple model of learning systems.

Figure 5.24 Expertext model in a learning system.

to the environment and provides evaluation information to the environment and to a learning element. The performance element relies on a knowledge base, while a learning element operates on the knowledge base so as to produce better knowledge (see Fig. 5.24).

WEIGHT ADJUSTMENT

One of the first, and most famous, machine learning programs is a checker-playing program from the late 1950s. The learning algorithm basically adjusted **numeric weights** on feature detectors and slowly but methodically improved its checker-playing ability. Adjusting numeric weights easily leads to success when the feature detectors are well-chosen, but choosing the feature detectors is difficult.

success adjusting weights

If documents could be meaningfully represented as **numbers**, then a machine learning expertext system could compare numbers in performing its tasks. The learning element would suggest changes to weights on documents or requests. While such a scenario of numeric representation is impractical for text in general, there may be cases where numeric manipulations are valuable.

weights and text

Documents and queries may be represented as weighted vectors of terms. Retrieval is determined by matching the query vector to document vectors. The **learning algorithm** may change the query weights based on feedback and must choose which weight changes to make. For a given query the documents are retrieved which best match that query. The retrieved documents are then divided by the searcher into relevant and not relevant sets. The learning algorithm moves the weights on the query so that they are more like the weights on the relevant documents (see Exercise 5.7). In a universe with two documents (document_1 and document_2) and two terms (term_1 and term_2) the weights might be

weight adjustment

$$\text{document}_1 = (0 \ \text{term}_1, 1 \ \text{term}_2)$$
$$\text{document}_2 = (1 \ \text{term}_1, 0 \ \text{term}_2).$$

With a query,

$$\text{query} = (0.5 \ \text{term}_1, 0.5 \ \text{term}_2),$$

the system may return both document_1 and document_2. But the user may want only document_2. To achieve this result the weight on term_1 should be raised, or the weight on term_2 should be lowered.

It may not be possible, for an arbitrary set of documents, to find a set of query weights such that all the documents judged relevant by the person are retrieved by the computer in response to the **query** (Minsky and Papert, 1969). Assume that the documents are indexed each with just one weight:

separability

$$\text{document}_1 = (0.11 \ \text{term}_0)$$
$$\text{document}_2 = (0.99 \ \text{term}_0)$$
$$\text{document}_3 = (0.01 \ \text{term}_0)$$

Assume that the query is some weight on term_0 and that documents are returned to the query, if the difference between the document term weight and the query term weight is under some threshold. If the user wants exactly document_2 and document_3, there is no query, represented as a weight on term_0, that will allow that retrieval. The criterion of success for adaptive queries should recognize that a perfect retrieval may not be possible within the confines of the weighted scheme. The numeric description of documents may not allow certain sets of documents to be separated from one another.

real-world difficulty

The attractiveness of working with numbers is that they have a natural metric of similarity (they have a total ordering). A state which includes numbers may be slightly changed by slightly changing a number, and the resultant effect on the distance to the goal may well be small. In other words, the search space is smooth. On the other hand, the ease with which **real-world problems** can be represented so that changes on weights are meaningful is less clear.

RECOMBINING DESCRIPTIONS

genetic algorithm

The **genetic algorithm** is a machine learning strategy based on the principles of genetics. The algorithm separates the more useful descriptions from the less useful and then forms new descriptions from the existing ones. The algorithm is designed so that the good parts of an original description will be recombined in ways likely to generate new descriptions which are better.

iterative process

The genetic algorithm uses an iterative three-phase process and operates on strings (Holland, 1975). **Strings** are the basic data structure of the genetic algorithm, which, biologically, are interpreted as chromosomes. For an artificial intelligence application the strings may be interpreted as rules. In phase one of the three-phase process each string is assigned a value based on its **performance** in some environment or on some task. In phase two, the strings are copied in proportion to the value of their performance. In phase three, parts of one string are exchanged with parts of another string (see Fig. 5.25).

document retrieval

Suppose there is a document which a significant number of searchers would judge relevant to their information need, if it were presented to them. Despite this agreement among the **searchers** about the relevance of this document, searcher indeterminacy suggests each of them will ask for it differently. Suppose also that the document has several descriptions. When a query is matched against a document, the query is matched against each description of the document. The retrieval performance is evaluated. Next, the document descriptions are reproduced in numbers proportional to their relative fitness. Then the recombination process randomly pairs reproduced descriptions and interchanges their components. This process repeats. Experiments demonstrate good performance of the genetic algorithm in the context of information retrieval (Gordon, 1985).

Figure 5.25 Genetic algorithm recombination. Two strings have had good enough performance value that they are used as the basis for new strings.

Recombination	
Old strings	New strings
□□□□□□□□	□□□□○○○○
○○○○○○○○	○○○○□□□□

5.2 Systems

Expertext principles show how links of hypertext can be 'enlivened'. To what extent have the principles been applied in the construction of systems? There are instances of expertext in all the major areas of hypertext—namely, **microtext**, **macrotext**, and **grouptext**.

micro, macro, and group

5.2.1 Intelligent microtext

The most widely used microtext system is **HyperCard**. It is attractive in part because it supports procedures on its links and thus has great flexibility from the expertext perspective. What application areas have been suitable for the addition of enlivened links to a single text? Systems for **computer-assisted instruction** have a long history and in their robust forms are examples of small-volume expertext.

tools and applications

5.2.1.1 Procedures

When a button is activated in HyperCard, another card is usually brought to the screen. However, the designer of a HyperCard document has the option of attaching a **procedure** to a button. Procedures are written in an object-oriented programming language which treats each card as an object. The HyperCard procedures get invoked whenever the button with the procedure is activated. The system can incorporate expertise of the author in the procedures and thus respond to the human browser in tailored ways. In one example, an explanation is to be offered about the meaning of a computing concept. If the user has a good background in computer science, then the explanation can incorporate references to such things as 'Turing Machine equivalent' but if the user has no formal training in computer theory, then the explanation should have a different slant (see Fig. 5.26). This example of guidance does not exploit the full power of the procedures, as within the link any amount of **computation** can be initiated.

example

The programming language of HyperCard is **HyperTalk**, which has some 'object-oriented programming' features. There are five types of objects in HyperTalk: stacks, backgrounds, cards, buttons and fields. All these objects can send and receive messages and they all can have a procedure associated with them.

HyperTalk

If clicking on a button should do something, then one needs a procedure in the button. A message travels through the Hypercard hierarchy from button to background to card to stack until it finds the appropriate procedure. A **procedure** starts with the keyword 'on' and ends with 'end'. The commands between these words are executed whenever the object receives the message whose name follows the keyword. Most messages are user generated, e.g. mouseUp, OpenCard, and Idle. A procedure such as 'On mouseUp... code...end' in a button's script would execute 'code' when the mouse was released. If this procedure were present in a card, then the actions would be obeyed from this card, while procedures in different cards or buttons would not be activated.

messages

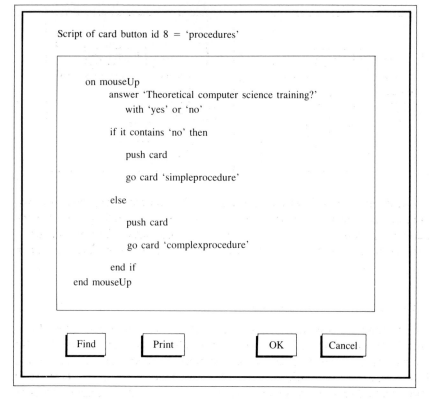

```
Script of card button id 8 = 'procedures'

    on mouseUp
        answer 'Theoretical computer science training?'
            with 'yes' or 'no'

        if it contains 'no' then

            push card

            go card 'simpleprocedure'

        else

            push card

            go card 'complexprocedure'

        end if
    end mouseUp
```

| Find | Print | OK | Cancel |

Figure 5.26 HyperCard procedure on link. This figure shows a screen of HyperCard that appears when a procedure is to be created or amended. The buttons at the bottom are for the author. The procedure itself is in the inner box. If the user answers 'no' to the question 'Theoretical computer science training?', then the next card gives a simple explanation; otherwise a complex explanation is provided.

5.2.1.2 Browsing

phone number example

In one application, the users of an expertext may ask for the phone number of an individual by clicking first on an icon representing the individual and then on the 'phone number please' option. Alternatively, since the information has been stored in a **database** as well as connected to the icons on the screen, the user can directly interact with a query front-end and request by name the person's phone number. Furthermore, the database supports queries which would not be supported in normal microtext. For example, a user who wants to know which people share a phone number, can easily get this information from the database.

dynamic routing

An expertext system may dynamically generate user-tailored maps. In one university guide system, the user has options to request certain traversals by indicating some starting point and query. For instance, if one is in the Chemistry department and wants to know the best route to the Psychology department, then by clicking on both departments on the map and then choosing the 'best route' query from a menu, the user can initiate an expertext process which will produce a best route on the screen (see Fig. 5.27). The logical representation of the map allows inferencing to determine what connections must be made to get from one department to the other. The hypertext tools then facilitate **dynamically displaying** this route to the user.

loading database

The Glasgow On-Line project produced a beautiful hypertext guide for tourists to Glasgow but several person-years of effort were required to build the

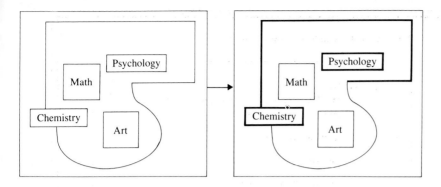

Figure 5.27 Dynamic routing. The user has requested to see the best route from the Chemistry department to the Psychology department. The screen on the left shows the original map; the screen on the right shows how the system updates the map in response to the user's input.

hypertext database and it was soon outdated. Furthermore, the careful hand-crafting did not facilitate subsequent maintenance. If new information for the Glasgow guide was readily available, then some automatic procedure might be used to maintain the database. With such **automatic** procedures, the system can be easily updated.

5.2.1.3 Computer-assisted instruction

The first computer-assisted instruction system was developed by B. F. Skinner in the 1950s (Skinner, 1958). The teaching approach adopted in his programs was drill-and-practice whereby subject material was presented to the student followed by questions. On the student correctly responding to a question, textual reinforcement was issued by the program. Incorrect responses by the student were ignored. The teaching material was divided into such small sections that appropriate answers were easy to produce. These programs might be called **looping programs** because of the loop a student takes through the material on incorrectly answering a question (see Fig. 5.28).

looping programs

In branching computer-assisted instruction programs, information is presented to the student followed by questions. On the selection of a response, the program comments on its appropriateness (see Fig. 5.29). In this way the student gets specific feedback for specific mistakes. In branching computer-assisted instruction, the extent of learner **control** and characteristics of the interface can be tailored by the author or teacher to match the requirements of the student.

branching

The Drexel Disk includes simple examples of branching computer-assisted instruction. For example, if the user chooses the 'Truth and Consequences' option from the 'Rights and Responsibilities' screen (Hewett, 1987), he is then taken to questions which test his knowledge of the subjects offered elsewhere

Drexel Disk example

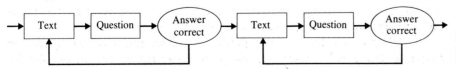

Figure 5.28 Looping computer-assisted instruction.

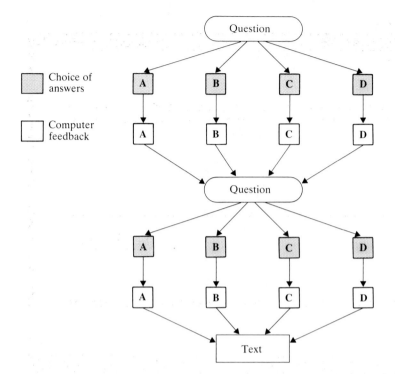

Figure 5.29 Branching
computer-assisted
instruction.

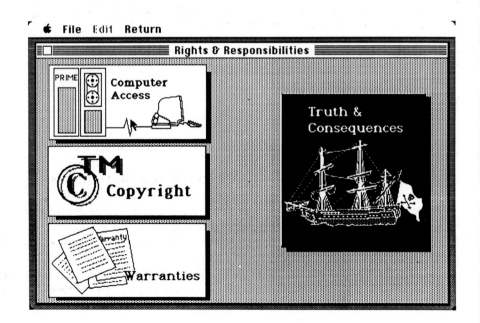

Figure 5.30 Start with truth
and consequences.

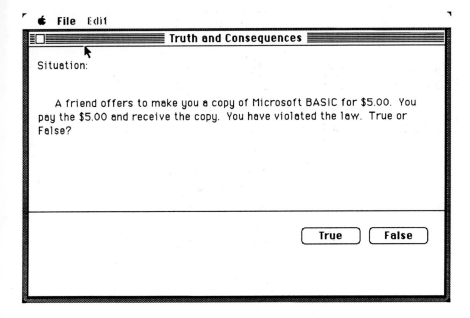

Figure 5.31 Drexel question.

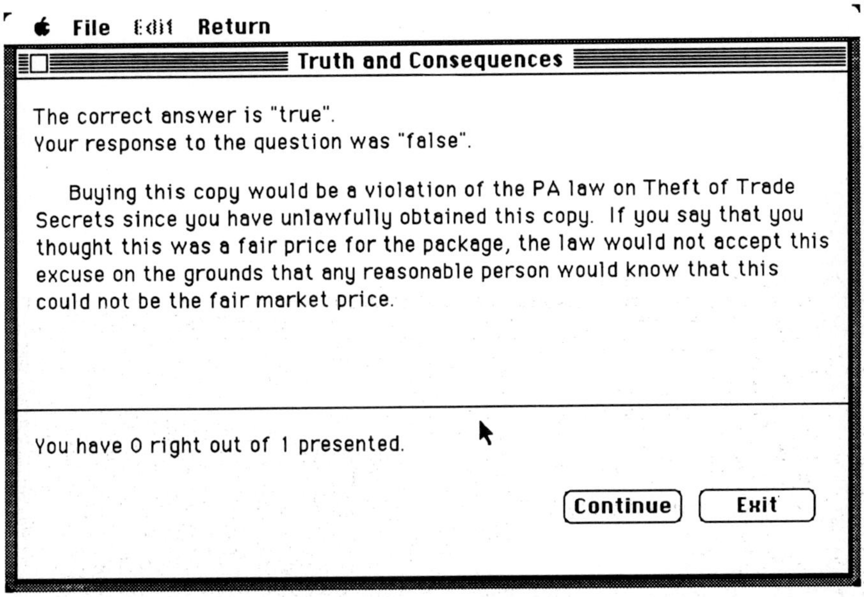

Figure 5.32 Drexel answer.

(see Fig. 5.30). The next screen is a question about buying a piece of software from another student for very little money (see Fig. 5.31). If the user answers 'false', then the computer notes that this answer is incorrect and informs him or her accordingly (see Fig. 5.32).

Computer-assisted instruction can be markedly enhanced by incorporating additional knowledge models of who was being taught, what was being taught, and how to teach (see Exercise 5.8). The Neomycin system takes advantage of a knowledge base for diagnosing infections (Clancey, 1983), but in addition, has **student models** and knows how to conduct a dialogue. It conveys general medical knowledge to a student, who takes the role of physician, through the discussion of a patient case. Comparison of the student's medical diagnosis and the system's diagnosis forms a basis for the discussion.

intelligent textbook

The **Oxford System of Medicine** is an expertext system based on the *Oxford Textbook of Medicine* (Gordon *et al.*, 1990). In addition to the information of the textbook itself, knowledge bases have been incorporated into the system. One knowledge base is about selecting an investigation for an ill patient. Another knowledge base is about the presentation of information so as to make the most sense. A medical knowledge base exists as a partial abstraction of the textbook to support reasoning with the textbook information. The various display and editing modalities are integrated into a uniform interaction style.

5.2.1.4 Document design

construction kits

The document design process can be supported by **construction kits**. These need knowledge to distinguish good designs from bad designs and the ability to explain decisions. **Rules** use knowledge of design principles and detect and criticize partial solutions constructed by the designer. If designers want more information, they can make requests for explanations.

weakness

Tests of one construction kit revealed that it did not go far enough toward achieving its goal of informing users about construction. The rules for the design were intended to be rules of thumb. While users were free to ignore the system's criticism, in practice they had difficulty judging when and how to do so. The system's brief explanations failed to reveal the complex **argumentative** background—including assumptions, conditions, and controversies. Without this background it was difficult for users to make the intelligent exceptions characteristic of good design.

connecting design and argument

The construction kit was improved by connecting the brief explanations to a hypertext network. The design rules thus provide the designer with entry into the exact place in a text relevant to the current design task (Fischer *et al.*, 1989). The rules serve as the mechanism linking construction to hypertext. The rules invoke display messages, if design principles are violated. In doing so they also identify the argumentative content from hypertext. The user may interpret the information in a rich way that would be difficult to achieve with a normal **expert system** or **hypertext system**.

5.2.2 Intelligent macrotext

definition of large-volume expertext

Intelligent macrotext includes a database with numerous documents that are richly identified and connected. The interface supports activities in a more salient fashion than it would in a macrotext system. The **intellectual processes** of contributors, searchers, or system maintainers are, in intelligent macrotext, done partially by the computer.

rules

The **rules** or logic which may be added to the database to facilitate **retrieval** go beyond what indexing would normally add to a document database. A user

---

IF

(a) documents about a ship at a certain location are requested

(b) the system doesn't have the current location explicitly stored, and

(c) the system knows where ships were yesterday and knows the average speed at which each ship travels,

THEN

with knowledge of travel and a map of the seas, the system computes where each ship is today and returns relevant documents.

Figure 5.33 Rule for retrieval from ship document database.

may pose a query for documents about an entity whose description the system does not recognize. If the system has rules which allow it to infer what that entity might be, then the system could more effectively carry out retrieval. For instance, access to a ship document database involves large amounts of information and intelligent processing (Schutzer, 1985). An example of a rule for the ship document database is shown in Fig. 5.33.

The **ship document database** system might store information about ships in predicates, such as 'docked(Titanic, pier 13)'. Rules in the system may operate on these **predicates** in supporting the retrieval of documents. For example, a rule might say 'if arrived(ship y) and empty(pier z) and type-pier(ship y, pier z), then pier-assignment(ship y, pier z)'. This rule basically says that a ship will be assigned to the appropriate, vacant pier. If a user asks for documents about the ship that will be assigned to a certain pier, the rule might help to find the right ship.

predicates

5.2.2.1 Blackboard architecture

An expertext system supports cooperative effort between the user and the system. The activity of distributed experts may be controlled by an agenda mechanism. Typical agenda management involves ordering posted actions and then selecting the one on the top. A scheduler controls the **agenda** by determining what experts can post actions and in what order those actions are executed. The basis for the scheduler's decisions is derived from the analysis of user dialogues. The dialogue structure is reflected directly in the structure of the scheduler.

agenda mechanism

In one intelligent macrotext system, called I³R (for intelligent, interface information retrieval) the scheduler structure is essentially a goal tree with extra transitions (see Fig. 5.34). What transition to take is determined by the rules associated with each **goal**. For example, say the user was familiar with the system, was an expert in the subject area of the search topic, and wanted a precision-oriented search, then the system might set the expectations of the system to be: five documents required and two searches allowed. If, after two searches, five documents were not found, the scheduler would take the transition from 'Search for relevant documents' to 'Get information need' and initiate further dialogue with the user (Croft and Thompson, 1987).

scheduler structure

In typical blackboard systems the experts can be implemented in any manner

I³R system

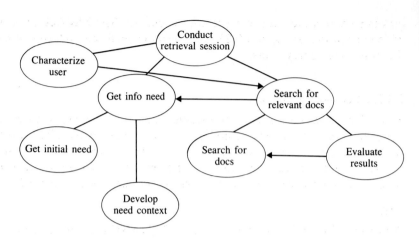

Figure 5.34 Scheduler structure. Each node in the graph is a goal of the scheduler. The lines between nodes indicate transitions which the scheduler may follow. The lines without arrows are part of the tree, while the lines with arrows cut across the tree. (Info is short for information, and Docs is short for documents.)

as long as they conform to the interface defined by the blackboard structure. In I³R the expert control knowledge is represented as rules. The rules provide a uniform control knowledge representation but not a uniform data representation. The data is structured in ways most suitable for each expert's function. For instance, in I³R the Domain Knowledge Model is conceptually viewed as a semantic net and implemented as a hash table of structures.

CODER document sources

The CODER system emphasizes the use of knowledge and document sources (Fox, 1987). Several major reference documents have been stored in the CODER system after having been parsed so that their contents can be easily manipulated. One of the reference documents is a dictionary; another is the *Handbook of Artificial Intelligence*, Volumes 1, 2, and 3; another is all the messages on the electronic newsletter called *AIList*. By taking advantage of structures in these reference works, the CODER system is better able to answer queries about other documents it stores.

menus and hierarchies

A menu-based interface can exploit an existing hierarchical indexing language. One such system, **CANSEARCH**, takes advantage of an existing hierarchy, called MeSH, for classification of information in its course of leading users to the proper formulation of their query (Pollitt, 1986). The system was designed to provide access to cancer therapy literature indexed using **MeSH**. The object is therefore to help construct an appropriate search query, with proper terms and structure. The underlying system structure is a rule-base designed to lead the user, via touch-screen menus, through a **hierarchy** of frames. The main areas of the hierarchy deal with cancer and its sites, types and therapies. The rules for selecting frames and processing term choices are associated with specific frames, so a frame can be thought of as having its own rule packet. The rules communicate via blackboards, one for each aspect of a query. The system supports clarifying dialogue when the user has made inconsistent menu selections.

use indexing languages

The main source of knowledge for CANSEARCH is the indexing language **MeSH**, which gives the set of available concept labels and their hierarchical structure. The indexing language allows the retrieval system to seem intelligent and flexible. Other intelligent hypertext systems also exploit the indexing languages which are used to represent documents. The MedIndex system has added knowledge on top of MeSH and supports intelligent indexing of medical literature (Humphrey, 1989).

5.2.2.2 Spreading activation

Spreading activation can support document retrieval. A query is represented as nodes in a semantic net whose nodes also point to documents. The transitivity of hierarchical relations is important for the effectiveness of this **retrieval** method. Heuristics can be added to the spreading activation algorithm to improve its effectiveness in solving retrieval problems (see Exercise 5.9).

document retrieval

DISTANCE

A variant of spreading activation, called **DISTANCE**, is designed to measure the distance between terms that characterize a document and a query or, more generally, between any two sets of terms in a graph. The design of DISTANCE was guided first by the observation that the conceptual distance between two nodes is often proportional to the number of edges separating the two nodes (Rada *et al.*, 1989b). To calculate DISTANCE, all pairwise **combinations** between two sets of terms are generated. If set X is {$term_{X,1}$, $term_{X,2}$}, and set Y is {$term_{Y,1}$, $term_{Y,2}$}, then the four pairwise combinations are {($term_{X,1}$, $term_{Y,1}$), ($term_{X,1}$, $term_{Y,2}$), ($term_{X,2}$, $term_{Y,1}$), ($term_{X,2}$, $term_{Y,2}$)}. For each pairwise combination, the algorithm calculates the minimal number of relationships that must be traversed in a network (in either direction) to get from one term to the other. These distances are summed to create a metric over sets of terms in the network (see Exercise 5.3).

formula

How can one test whether DISTANCE is useful in practical situations? Semantic nets were designed as psychological models of associative memory. DISTANCE between sets of nodes in a semantic net should simulate human performance on a cognitive task. One of the virtues of DISTANCE is that it produces numbers that, supposedly, represent the conceptual distance between its arguments. Given a query represented as a set of nodes and a set of documents, each represented by a set of nodes, by applying DISTANCE to the query and each of the documents, one can rank the documents based on their distance to the query. The smallest value presumably corresponds to the most relevant document to the query. To test this hypothesis, one could compare the **ranks** produced by DISTANCE to those produced by **people** when given the same query and same collection of documents.

how to evaluate?

Hierarchical semantic nets support the ranking of documents by DISTANCE in a way that significantly agrees with the ranking of experts. Experiments on different hierarchical semantic nets and with different queries and documents have supported this conclusion. What happens when non-hierarchical relations are added to the semantic net? For instance, in addition to having 'cow is animal', a semantic net may say that 'cow makes milk'. Surprisingly, hierarchies augmented with **non-hierarchical** relations led to rankings by DISTANCE that did not significantly correlate with the rankings of experts.

hierarchical versus non-hierarchical

DISTANCE treated non-hierarchical relationships no differently than it

lack of transitivity

would handle hierarchical relationships. Hierarchical relationships such as 'is-a' are **transitive**: the fact that juvenile rheumatoid arthritis 'is-a' rheumatoid arthritis 'is-a' arthritis also means that juvenile rheumatoid arthritis 'is-a' arthritis. For measures of conceptual similarity the spreading activation should traverse one kind of relationship. For instance, if x is a y, y is a z, and y causes w, then x is a z but may or may not cause w (Groot, 1983).

restrained spreading activation

DISTANCE has been revised to take advantage of non-hierarchical relations. This **neo-DISTANCE** can only follow a non-hierarchical relationship when the query explicitly refers to that non-hierarchical relationship. For example, a query for arthritis treated by drug can follow the drug treatment relationship from arthritis to aspirin, but a query for arthritis alone cannot follow the link from arthritis to aspirin. The application of neo-DISTANCE produced rankings similar to those of people on a semantic net with hierarchical and non-hierarchical relations (Rada, 1985).

GRANT

heuristics

Spreading activation algorithms can include multiple **heuristics** that exploit the differences in relationships in the semantic net. Weights or endorsements can also be placed on the network, and the spreading activation algorithm can adapt its behavior to these weights. An example of heuristic spreading activation for document retrieval in the GRANT system shows the utility of this approach.

semantic net

The GRANT system uses spreading activation to retrieve relevant documents to a query (Cohen and Kjeldsen, 1987). The domain is **research funding**. The system's architecture includes a semantic net with nodes that represent the research interests of funding agencies (see Fig. 5.35). Nodes are added to the network by linking them to other nodes with one or more distinct relations. All relations are directional and have inverses; for example, the inverse of has-setting is setting-of and the inverse of is-a is has-instance.

constraining activation

During a run of the GRANT system, activation spreads from the topics stated in a proposal to agencies. Some **constraint** is required so that not too many agencies in the network are activated. Graph structure can be exploited

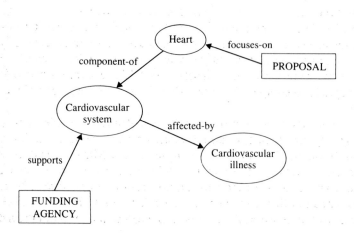

Figure 5.35 Semantic net for heuristic retrieval. Depiction of part of semantic net for GRANT. The box PROPOSAL represents a query for information. The box FUNDING AGENCY represents a document which describes the characteristics of a funding agency.

by requiring that activation cease after some aspect of the graph has been recognized. For instance, the system may require that activation cease at a certain distance from a research topic mentioned in the query. Alternatively, activation might cease at nodes that have high connectivity or **fan-out**. For example, disease and science had high fan-out nodes in the network, but an agency that funds disease research may not fund science research and vice-versa.

endorsements

The likelihood of an agency funding a proposal depends on the nature of the relationships between the agency's interests and those of the researcher. If one would ask an agency to fund research on hypertext hardware and hypertext hardware is a part of hypertext systems, then one stands a reasonable chance of obtaining funding from an agency that funds hypertext systems. The above rule constitutes a positive path **endorsement**. On the other hand, some associations are not appropriate to follow. For instance, a hardware institute may be interested in funding research on hypertext hardware but not on cognitive aspects of hypertext systems. A query for funding on 'hypertext systems' that did not specify 'hardware' should not take the path from 'hypertext systems' to 'hypertext hardware'—a negative path endorsement is attached. As the spreading activation mechanism collects path endorsements, and a negative path endorsement will curtail a search, negative path endorsements act as constraints.

results

In terms of usage, the GRANT system proved most helpful in those cases where the likely funding agencies did not come to mind quickly. In terms of the semantic net, those nodes with more than 15 branches emanating from them contributed adversely to the performance of the system. The nodes with **branching factors** of about 8 were most helpful. Nodes with very high branching factors suggest a lack of specificity in the semantic net. Those who develop semantic nets for document retrieval applications should try to avoid large branching factors.

5.2.3 Intelligent grouptext

An intelligent grouptext system should include a model of authoring and of group communication (Hahn *et al.*, 1989). In a collaborative environment the **knowledge base** related to the ideas behind the document can serve as a **communication device**. One might suspect that collaborative writing would be easier for hypertext than for text since people use networks of ideas. If author Y wants to modify the text of author X and has no explicit network, then Y would have to make the inverse translation of X's text into a network form before being able to compare X's network of ideas to Y's network of ideas (see Fig. 5.36).

communication

The requirements of an **intelligent writing tool** might include allowing the writer to specify constraints, to switch easily among writing strategies, and to have multiple views of the material (Sharples and O'Malley, 1988). A sample screen for one system is shown in Fig. 5.37. In the network version of the document, every node is a note with an arbitrary amount of text. Notes can have direct links to other notes and may be collected into bins. The linear view is a traversal of the network. As each note is created, it appears in the network

screen

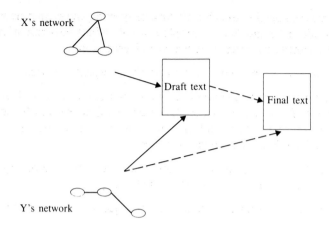

Figure 5.36 Collaborative hypertext. If writer Y is to modify the text of writer X, then Y might benefit by seeing the network of ideas behind the writing of X.

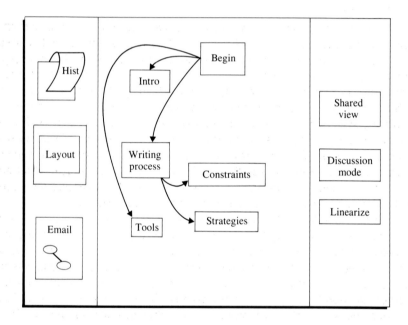

Figure 5.37 Intelligent writing interface. Mock screen display for writing system (Sharples and O'Malley, 1988).

window as a box with a title and any links to other notes. To the left of the screen are icons that indicate some of the available operations. On selecting the 'history' icon, the user is given the history of changes to a node based on author name and date. The 'layout' icon activates a formatting of the text according to the layout rules in the attributes of the nodes. Choice of the 'shared view' allows the user to share his screen with another user. The 'discussion mode' option brings forward a screen through which the user can post comments into an issue-based discussion system.

constraints

To implement constraints in an authoring environment, the components of a document can be viewed as objects with attached rules. The rules implement the constraints. Each rule has a condition and procedure part. The **condition** is a pattern that is matched against the object's own properties; the procedure is run whenever the condition is satisfied. A simple example might be a rule within a sentence object to notify the user of repeated adjacent words:

'if $word_1$ adjacent $word_1$, then tell author about repeated words'.

In other words, when the user finishes writing a sentence, the sentence is stored in a sentence object. The rule attached to the sentence object checks whether the sentence has two adjacent words that are the same. Similarly there may be a document object. One document constraint says:

'if not (title followed by author followed by abstract followed by body), then warn author of abnormal structure.'

When the user saves the document, the document object checks its constraints.

5.2.3.1 Annotations

Annotations are guides to changing a document. Intelligent processing of annotations requires knowing who is supposed to do what with what annotation at what time. Quilt is an example of an annotation system which incorporates some intelligent processing (Fish *et al.*, 1988). It allows users to change and annotate a document electronically, with the history of these notes attached to arbitrary regions of the document. Each user is assumed to have a specific role and categories of privileges are associated with these roles. The base document can be annotated and each annotation can be annotated. **Procedures** may interpret annotations as initiating actions. For example, the action associated with a comment about a deadline might be to notify a co-author that action needs to be taken, remind the co-author before the deadline, and report to the initial author at deadline whether the document has been modified.

 Quilt

As one example of the use of Quilt, Anne and Bill have started to write collaboratively a document on the topic 'Log Cabins'. A table-driven interface displays options to the users (see Fig. 5.38). The system style will determine basic **privileges**. The role of each person is identified, and this, in turn, constrains that person's privileges. Anne selects a sharing style which means that any co-author can modify any section. The students who are working on the project are classified as commenters, which means that they can add annotations but not change the base document.

 Quilt example

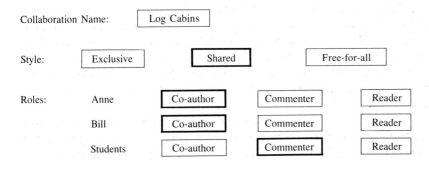

Collaboration Name:	Log Cabins		
Style:	Exclusive	Shared	Free-for-all
Roles:	Anne	Co-author	Commenter	Reader
	Bill	Co-author	Commenter	Reader
	Students	Co-author	Commenter	Reader

Figure 5.38 Sample screen from Quilt.

5.2.3.2 Messaging

computer supports
communication

Communication among people may be supported by the computer. This support can be indirect, as when noting to users that an inter-person conflict has occurred which the people may want to address. On the other hand, the support can be direct, as when messages are routed to the right people (see Exercise 5.10).

task monitoring

A message system may allow messages to be categorized as to whether they request an action or a commitment. One application of intelligent message processing is to **track message** types and determine what **tasks** have or have not been done. An intelligent grouptext system could answer questions such as what tasks have which people requested or are any of these tasks overdue.

Message processing can apply to the **routing of messages**. If a user wants to store all messages from the company president in a special file, then a procedure can be developed to do this. The **procedure** will cause the 'From' field of incoming electronic mail to be copied. Then the name in the 'From' field is checked against the objects in the knowledge base and with the attribute of position in the company. If the attribute is 'president', then the message is stored in a special file. Conversely, the system can determine to whom a message should be sent. The sender can place a description of the type of person to receive the message, such as 'people who have finished their work', and the system will check its information base and determine to whom exactly the message needs to be sent.

5.2.4 Expertext systems for software requirements

motivation for software
engineers

The need for expertext can be seen in many applications, such as software engineering, law, and medicine. In these application areas a group of people are responsible typically for maintaining documents which are critical to the functioning of the enterprise. Expertext systems are frequently applied to **software engineering** environments because software engineers are bound to the computer, unlike lawyers or physicians. One of the documents of the software life cycle which has proven most resistant to formal or mathematical analysis has been the requirements document. However, impressive expertext tools have been developed to support the collaborative development of requirements documents.

informality

The earliest phase of requirements acquisition involves a discussion, the goal of which is to achieve consensus among end users about what they want. The requirements analyst's main role in this phase involves his interpersonal skills. The end product is typically an **informal description**, which is characterized by incompleteness and ambiguity. This is not because of laziness but is an essential characteristic of the human thought process. Informality is a powerful debugging strategy for dealing with complexity. One starts with an almost-right description and then modifies it incrementally until it is acceptable. Much work on software requirements focuses on validating formal descriptions. This does not, however, address the key question of first, how an informal description is obtained, and then of how an informal description becomes a formal description.

Compared with implementation and design systems, a requirements system needs a wider range of domain knowledge (Rich and Waters, 1988). The requirements document constitutes the first bridge from the language and needs of the real world to that of the computer world. In principle, any part of the **real world** may be relevant. An expert requirements system would know in detail about the application for which requirements are being written. In the dialog between a person and an intelligent requirements system, the person presents various definitions and actions, while the system collects and analyzes the information and, if it sees an inconsistency, notifies the person and requests clarification. For instance, in describing a library system, a person may say that the 'acquire transaction' tracks the addition of a book, the 'checkout transaction' tracks the removal of a book, and the 'return transaction' is the inverse of the 'checkout transaction'. If the system had the right knowledge, it would note an overlap of the return and acquire transactions and ask the person for clarification. Clarification might be that 'acquisition' means 'library purchase', while 'return' means 'patron returns borrowed book'.

One intelligent requirements tool (called ASPIS) helps refine requirements by exploiting methodical and domain knowledge (Puncello *et al.*, 1988). The methodical knowledge specifies the possible ordering of statements and tells the user what must be described in each phase, from which viewpoint, and at what level of detail. By exploiting **domain knowledge** the system can verify the accuracy of some components. Methodical and domain knowledge are organized at two levels of abstraction so that domain knowledge can be seen through methodical knowledge. Semantic nets with productions are used. Because domain knowledge is specialized **methodical knowledge**, the classes representing domain knowledge are connected with 'is-a' links to their related methodical knowledge classes (see Fig. 5.39). To exploit the knowledge contained in these classes, the system navigates the method classes according to

domain knowledge

method knowledge

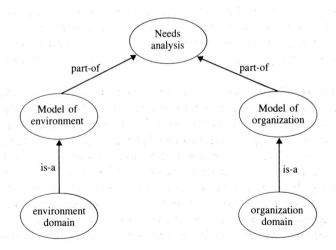

Figure 5.39 Method versus domain. An example of domain classes that are a specialization of method classes.

their links. With inheritance, the domain knowledge is exploited by focusing on the domain classes that are specializations of the current method step.

intelligent notepad

The Knowledge-Based Requirements Assistant (KBRA) emphasizes intelligent assistance for incrementally refining requirements and strives to present a natural communication medium (Czuchry and Harris, 1988). Natural language processing techniques are exploited. System engineers use an intelligent notepad to jot requirements ideas. Within sentences, the system examines each word and responds by underlining when encountering specific words in a lexicon. Words in the lexicon include typical requirements verbs like 'update' and 'generate' and names of reusable library items. These words are thus directly linked to the evolving library. The **intelligent notepad** includes natural language processing facilities and recognizes some sentences. If it cannot interpret a sentence, it is still entered as a node in a text network. Diagrams which show some of the system functions can be initialized and updated from the intelligent notepad.

reuse

The systematic reuse of software components can make a significant contribution to reducing software costs. Reuse should be considered from the early stages of software development rather than only at the code stage. A reusable requirements library enables **engineers** to incorporate commonplace solutions into an evolving system description. Engineers often gather, merge, and modify requirements from several existing systems. In a software engineering environment, engineers should have access to cut and paste facilities for moving information from one window to another. To simplify reuse, selection should be available by explicit naming through a linguistic interface. In addition, the system should provide graphical browsing capabilities of taxonomies within the library; engineers should be able to move up and down the **taxonomy** to find what they want (Czuchry and Harris, 1988).

5.3 Epilogue

synergy of intuitive and formal power

Logic, semantic nets, and procedures are representations which can be useful in hypertext. Expert systems reason with such representations. By combining the techniques of expert systems with those of hypertext, one may build expertext systems which combine both the **intuitive power** of hypertext systems and the **formal power** of expert systems.

semantic net patterns

An expertext system should be able to reason with the **semantic net** of hypertext. Spreading activation should be provided as a search mechanism. Analogical inheritance should be supported so that users can be helped in finding or creating meaningful patterns in the network of the hypertext.

procedures

The user should be able to embed **procedures** on links, and the expertext system should be able to execute these procedures. The language might be object-oriented, such as that of HyperTalk but needs to be easily learned and have general-purpose capabilities, as well as to be tailored for hypertext. The effects of the procedures can not only change the screen and vary what the user sees based on various circumstances, but can also constitute significant dynamic changes to the hypertext system itself.

collaborative authoring

The writing of documents involves constraints and procedures. While many of these constraints and procedures are useful both in solo and collaborative authoring, some are most applicable when more than one writer is working on the same document. In **collaborative authoring** the heuristics for making decisions are more likely to become explicit as colleagues explore what needs to be done and why. To the extent that heuristics can be specified for guiding the collaboration and can be placed in the computer, the computer can support collaboration. This help could apply to the organization of ideas, to the handling of annotations, or to the routing of electronic mail.

Building a network of links for a hypertext is typically a labor-intensive job. Furthermore, the network needs to be updated, as text is updated. Finally, a new network often repeats substantial amounts of material already present in existing networks (Dextre and Clarke, 1981). For these reasons, partial automation of the building of hypertext nets is desirable. **Natural language processing** might support the building of hypertext nets by automatically suggesting terms and relationships from a text block. Given that large lexicons and grammars are now readily available, a simple natural language processing system should be part of a hypertext system.

building networks and natural language processing

Hypertext is text plus an abstraction of the text. By reasoning with this abstraction, a hypertext system can better guide its users. An expert system that includes text may offer better explanations to its users. The combination of hypertext and expert system features gives rise to expertext systems. When the abstraction of a text is a semantic network, spreading activation and inheritance methods may help people to appreciate the structure of the text. When predicates and implications are included in the abstraction, logical deductions can be performed, and queries can be answered with relevant passages of text. Distributed expertext systems use knowledge bases about the domain of the text and about the users. The many and varied functions of a robust, distributed expertext system require not only very sophisticated software but also extensive knowledge bases and text bases. While people are not yet skilled at developing the knowledge bases which underlie expertext, the hope is that, by combining expert systems with hypertext systems, development of the **knowledge bases** and the **text bases** will be easier. By developing the expertext as one product rather than separately developing a knowledge base and a text base, one might exploit a synergy between the two. The range of applications of expertext is so great that, despite the complexity of the problem area and the difficulty of formalizing what can and cannot be done, many people are now actively working with expertext.

role of knowledge bases and text bases

5.4 Exercises

5.1 An isomorphism is a mathematical concept which means that two functions have the same form. For example, if

isomorphism

$f(x) = a,$
$f(y) = b,$
$g(x) = y,$ and
$g(a) = b,$

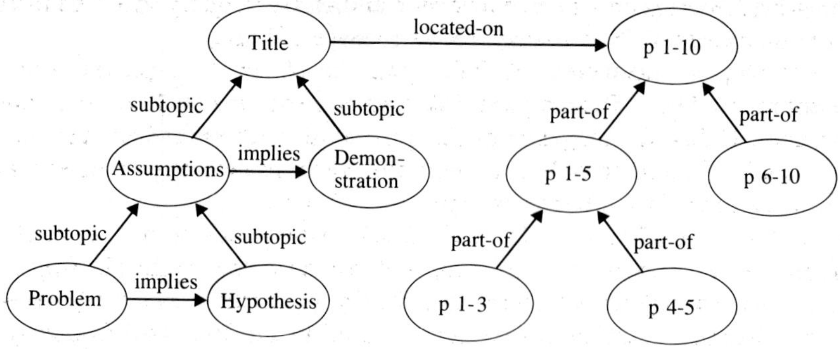

Figure 5.40 Example of an outline viewed as a semantic net. The spline labeled 'located-on' from 'Title' to 'p 1-10' could be copied between other pairs of topics and page ranges, such as between 'Assumptions' and 'p 1-5'.

then the isomorphism is $g(f(x)) = f(g(x))$. Analogical inheritance may be viewed as an isomorphism. Give an example of an isomorphism in which f, g, x, y, a, and b form a semantic net. (20 minutes—assumes mathematical background of student)

5.2 Semantic nets may be formally represented as directed, labeled graphs G with:

vertices $V = \{\text{unknown}, v_0, v_1, ..., v_n\}$ and
edges $E = \{(v_i, v_j, l_k) \mid v_i, v_j \in V; l_k \in \text{labels}\}$ with labels $= \{\text{is-a, part-of, ..., cause}\}$. $P(v_i, v_j, l_k)$ is a predicate which is true, if and only if, $(v_i, v_j, l_k) \in E$.

Analogical inheritance means (Rada and Mili, 1989):

$$\text{Inh}_{x,y,z} \ G \equiv (\forall v_i, v_j, v_{i'}, v_{j'} \in \{V - \text{unknown}\})$$
$$(P(v_i, v_j, x) \wedge P(v_i, v_{i'}, z) \wedge P(v_j, v_{j'}, z)) \rightarrow (P(v_{i'}, v_{j'}, y) \vee P(v_{i'}, \text{unknown}, y))$$

What analogical inheritance is present in the outline in Fig. 5.40? (2 hours—assumes mathematical background of student)

5.3 Define a **metric** between sets X and Y of nodes in a semantic net. A function $f(X,Y)$ is a metric if the following properties are satisfied:

1. $f(X,X) = 0$ (zero property),
2. $f(X,Y) = f(Y,X)$ (symmetry property),
3. $f(X,Y) + f(Y,Z) > f(X,Z)$ (triangular inequality).

Hint: given any two nodes in the semantic net, the minimal path distance between them is useful. (3 hours—assumes mathematical background of student)

5.4 The method of reasoning with the logic, flow control model can be formalized. Given a set of premises, one can pose a query as a negative statement and try to prove with the **resolution algorithm** that the premises along with the query lead to opposite statements. Firing rules in the logic, flow control graph can implement a resolution algorithm. Suggest a method of implementing the resolution algorithm. (3 hours—to do this exercise one needs to understand the resolution theorem proving method)

5.5 Obtain a portion of a semantic net for a microtext. What would be required to convert this representation into predicates which support **deductive**

inferencing? Make such a small conversion and answer a query with a deduction on the predicates. (2 hours—requires knowledge of logic)

5.6 Develop a **taxonomy of link types** based on a representation of procedures on links. The simplest link type is associated with a 'go to node' procedure. Define the language of the procedures with primitives such as 'go to', 'node', 'if', and 'read'. Then note the combinations of primitives which make most sense in the hypertext context. (2 hours)

procedural taxonomy

5.7 Index a set of text blocks and initially assign each term the weight 1. Arrange some queries, do retrieval, and evaluate the retrieval. Apply an **adaptive weight adjustment** algorithm. Will your method eventually retrieve relevant documents which did not get retrieved in the first case? (3 hours)

adaptive weights

5.8 Give an example of a student model which might be integrated with a branching **computer-assisted instruction program** so as to give more intelligent guidance to students. (1 hour)

computer-assisted instruction

5.9 Develop a semantic net for a small hypertext. Describe a query processing strategy which allows a user to ask for parts of the hypertext as a set of query terms and which uses simple spreading activation to facilitate retrieval. Test the method by constructing some queries and manually implementing the spreading activation method. The test will require deciding what would constitute good **retrieval**. (2 hours)

spreading activation

5.10 Various kinds of **messages** may be sent among colleagues as part of the annotation process. If the collaborators are part of a hierarchical administrative structure, how might the processing of messages be facilitated? (30 minutes)

messaging

Good chapter for "??" or "Book" "Hypertext"

6

Conclusion

Figure 6.1 Cemetery. When people die, they are often buried under a tombstone with an inscription about their role in the world. As text on stone marked the beginnings of civilization (see Fig. 1.1), so for each individual, text on stone often marks the end of life.

extra dimensions

Hypertext is a popular term with an unclear meaning. In the literal sense the term implies extra **dimensions** to text; in practice, the term is often applied to computer systems which allow a person to browse a document by gracefully jumping from text block to text block. Yet this 'browse' dimension alone is limiting. The argument advanced here is that hypertext is most profitably viewed as a **combination** of dimensions that extends across large document collections, across collaborative work, and across artificial intelligence. One must start with an understanding of text and from there develop the perspectives that will allow the specification of new hypertext systems for the 1990s.

6.1 From text to expertext

links

Text must be linked to other text and to people (see Fig. 6.2). The holistic view of **hypertext** focuses on **links**: links within a document (microtext), links among documents (macrotext), links among people (grouptext), and dynamic links (expertext). The principles and systems which are relevant to creating and

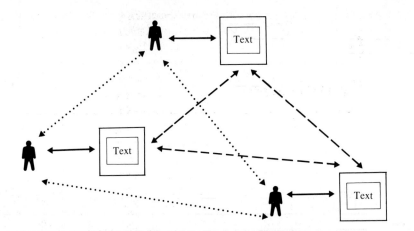

Figure 6.2 Links among people and text. People interacting with computers to create and access text.

accessing hypertext can be usefully presented under the headings of text, microtext, macrotext, grouptext, and expertext (see Exercise 6.1).

6.1.1 Text

Hypertext is an extension of text, but to understand hypertext, one must first understand text. Text is a recorded body of information. The terms **text** and **document** are synonymous, and while text contains predominantly natural, written language, it may contain graphics.

definition of text

Six thousand years ago in the cradles of civilization, people were recording information on clay or papyrus. Thousands of years passed before significant libraries were created. The introduction of the **printing press** in the Middle Ages took a century to influence the distribution of documents. New technologies for text take root gradually.

history

The words that form a text are the raw material from which a mental representation of the meaning of that text is first constructed. Local **coherence** is then established across sentence boundaries. Language users must establish coherence quickly. The language user makes preliminary hypotheses about local coherence from the title and first words of the text and from knowledge about global situations.

reading and coherence

Readability means the relative ease with which texts can be read and remembered. Traditional readability models deal primarily with surface variables, such as sentence length. An adequate model of readability must account for the cost of constructing complex memory structures.

readability

A good writer must produce a coherent text, but the process of writing is otherwise not necessarily like the process of reading. The three phases of writing a document are **exploring**, **organizing**, and **encoding**. On paper, these correspond to notes, outlines, and prose, respectively. Authors like to move freely from one phase to another and are influenced by their own memory, the writing assignment, and the evolving text.

writing process

To convert the abstract form of a text into a concrete visualization the author needs a **layout language**. The languages for the specification of layout come in

layout language

two generic forms. One requires commands embedded within text, while the alternative involves the direct manipulation of the physical appearance with a 'What You See Is What You Get' environment.

writing tools

Tangibility is important to readers, and the tangibility of paper is greater than that of computer screens. While reading is typically easier on paper than on computer, the same does not apply to writing. The features of a computer tool for writing are often more attractive than that of a paper and pen tool. **Writing tools** have evolved from editors to word processors to outliners to desktop publishers. Outliners help the writer organize thoughts and attach text to the thoughts. Desktop publishing systems facilitate the addition of graphics and the layout of text.

logical structure

To make electronic information more exchangeable, standards of logical document structure are useful. The **Standard Generalized Markup Language** is a language for logical document structure and is an international standard for publishing. It is based on the principles of generic encoding of documents and marks a document's logical structure, such as section headings, and not the document's physical presentation.

6.1.2 Microtext

definition of microtext

Microtext is text with explicit links among its components. A microtext system provides a computer medium for manipulating the links of microtext and supports authoring and browsing, whereas a macrotext system principally supports searching. The first microtext system, the Augmentation System, was developed in the 1960s, but HyperCard, the first widely-popular, microtext system, did not appear till the late 1980s.

6.1.2.1 Principles

levels of description

Microtext may be described from various levels, including **screen**, **internal**, and **logical**. What the user sees on the screen is often a combination of windows and buttons, and selection of a button often causes a jump to another window. Inside the computer the information may be stored as files whose markup indicates the actions which the computer program can take on the files, or the information may be stored in some more structured form, such as a relational database. The computer internal representation may also be viewed from a logical perspective. The logical perspective addresses the conceptual units of the microtext and their relations. This logical structure is often described in terms of nodes, links, and attributes.

independent versus embedded semantic net

The network of microtext may be viewed as a **semantic net** which models human memory. The nodes and links of the net are labeled with terms that represent concepts. The semantic net of microtext may be independent or embedded. In the independent case, the nodes and links are tagged with terms that represent concepts (per the usual semantic net), but each node or link may point to text blocks. When a user is presented with an independent semantic net microtext, he may traverse the semantic net without seeing a text block. In the embedded case, a text block is at the end of a link. In traversing an embedded semantic net, the user must visit text blocks.

The principles of microtext must also cover the **psychological** or ergonomic issues of human–computer interaction. A novice user wants clear options and simple instructions, while an expert user may place a premium on a powerful command system. For certain tasks and certain users, certain microtext strategies are appropriate. For instance, the task of guiding lay people to the resources of a city via hypertext may benefit from the use of tourist metaphors. An example of a tourist metaphor is an icon of a tour bus which when selected leads the user through a tour of the hypertext.

appropriateness depends on task and user

6.1.2.2 Systems

All of the popular microtext systems are of the embedded, rather than independent, semantic net type. NoteCards, HyperCard, and HyperTies emphasize the connecting of one text block to another. The user selects a highlighted term in one text block in order to see another text block. Guide, KMS, and Emacs-Info follow the model of highlighted terms in one text block pointing to other text blocks, but these microtext systems indirectly provide an independent semantic net. In Guide, KMS, and Emacs-INFO outlines are critically important, and these have an implicit **independent semantic net** character. An outline is a restricted type of semantic net.

popular systems

The importance of giving users an overview of the network of concepts was not lost to the developers of NoteCards, which provides special cards with a semantic net whose nodes point to text blocks. The developers of HyperTies have realized the importance of **outlines** and are incorporating features to facilitate their management.

outlines

6.1.2.3 Text and Microtext

In **translating** between text and microtext, one should distinguish between two classes of text: clearly-structured and implicitly-structured. The links of clearly-structured text can be readily extracted from the markup commands in the text, while the links of implicitly-structured text must be extracted manually. Examples of clearly-structured text are technical manuals, dictionaries, encyclopedias, and course catalogs. Essays and novels are examples of implicitly-structured text; the logical structure is not suggested by markup commands in the text.

clear versus implicit structure

Converting text to microtext has immediate economic importance because of the vast amounts of text that could be treated in this way. The reverse process of converting microtext to text will become more important as the amount of available microtext increases. A **traversal** of the network of a microtext that prints every text block once, and only once, has effectively linearized the text. For a hierarchically structured microtext like Guide or KMS, translation of microtext to text is straightforward. The hierarchy is traversed in a depth-first fashion. If the hierarchy was designed with a sequence in mind, as is often the case, the resulting sequence tends to make sense. For a complex, non-hierarchical network a meaningful traversal is less obvious.

traversals

NOW GO. TO SYSTEMS
P. 39 – 46 Brief then
Guide & HyperTies

6.1.3 Macrotext

definition of macrotext

Macrotext is essentially hypertext, with emphasis on the links that exist among many documents, rather than within one document. Typically, many people have contributed documents to macrotext and an institution maintains a macrotext system. Both the interface to the document collection and the links among documents must be maintained. The user is searching for a few documents from a large set. A macrotext system does not support the browsing of a single document—that is a microtext system facility. Traditionally, the term 'information storage and retrieval' was used when talking about storing and retrieving many documents.

history

Vannevar **Bush** argued as early as the 1930s for the importance of using modern technology to turn text into macrotext. He described a scenario in which one individual dealt with the text of many other individuals by placing connections among the text items. The National Library of Medicine in the United States of America built the first major macrotext system in the mid-1960s; in its first year it stored citations for over 100 000 documents and handled several thousand queries.

6.1.3.1 Principles

queries and documents

If the **language** of queries and documents is not unified at some point, a match cannot be made between queries and documents. The traditional way of representing the content of documents in a macrotext system is to label each document with a handful of terms from an indexing language. An alternative strategy is to represent a document by the words which occur with significant frequency within the document.

thesaurus

One of the most popular forms for an indexing language is a thesaurus. While in the lay use the term suggests an alphabetically-sorted list of terms with attached synonyms, in the context of macrotext a thesaurus is far more. A **thesaurus** is a set of concepts, each represented by synonymous terms, broader concepts, narrower concepts, and related concepts. The broader and narrower concepts form a hierarchical semantic net. This hierarchy helps users find terms to represent their query.

query logic

In the simplest **query**, the user presents a single term to the system, which returns those documents which have been indexed with that term. More generally, index terms are combined with operators, such as AND. If one asks for all the documents that have been indexed with the term 'optical disk' AND 'encyclopedia', one would get the documents which had been assigned both of the index terms. This notion of operators between terms of the semantic net to support querying is not part of the microtext system armamentarium. A macrotext system will also typically allow a user to request all documents indexed by a term or indexed by any of the terms narrower than that term in the thesaurus—this is another instance of exploiting the hierarchical structure of the indexing language.

word patterns

For maximum exploitation of the computer, methods have been developed to index and retrieve documents based on **word patterns**. A document may be perceived as being about the subject symbolized by a certain word, if that word occurs more frequently in that document than could be expected in a randomly chosen document. To reduce search time, documents may be clustered according to their word patterns. By then clustering the clusters, a hierarchy is created. A search can thus start at the root cluster and proceed in a depth-first manner to the cluster which best matches the query.

When a very large thesaurus is accessed via a computer screen, the user may need to change the contents of the screen many times to find the terms for a query. As the number of hierarchical levels increases, users take longer and make more errors. Accordingly, parallel modes of presentation should be provided so that users can get quickly and easily to the places they desire. These insights about the **user interface** for macrotext systems also apply to microtext systems.

thesaurus presentation

6.1.3.2 Systems

The **1970s** witnessed a rapid growth in the availability of macrotext via telephone lines and time-sharing computers. By the late 1970s over 300 macrotext systems were operating, providing access to over 60 million document citations and processing over 5 million queries a year. In the **1980s** optical disks became cheap enough to impact substantially on the method of delivering macrotext. Now, an entire macrotext system can be supported by one personal computer with an optical disk.

growth in systems

The National Library of Medicine **MEDLINE** system which was developed in the 1960s remains one of the salient macrotext systems, and now contains citations to over 6 million biomedical articles. While it remains accessible via telephone lines, optical disk versions of its database are becoming increasingly popular.

MEDLINE history

One of the latest developments in macrotext is the merging of macrotext with microtext. The IDEX system allows users to search massive document databases through a thesaurus and by author, title, and date of publication. Additionally, once a document is found which seems interesting, the user can stay in the same system with the same interface and proceed to browse the entire document with the Guide microtext system. Several groups are exploring the combination of word-frequency strategies of **macrotext** with network strategies of **microtext**. In such systems the user first locates a block of text within a document by searching for a text block that has a certain pattern of words in it. Having found such a text block, the user then browses from that point along the network of the document.

combining micro and macro

Whereas for microtext the connection of text to microtext is a current research problem, methods of automatically or systematically moving texts into macrotext have been well-established. In many ways, macrotext systems have features which microtext systems may eventually emulate. The most fascinating of these features concerns the connection of one body of text to another. The Vocabulary Switching System was developed in the early 1980s to connect the indexing languages of 15 different macrotext systems. This system depends largely on lexical matching of terms. The United Nations, the American

macrotext to macrotext

National Institutes of Health, and many other organizations have sponsored work to connect indexing languages. No comparable effort has occurred within the microtext arena, but the dream of hypertext is to **connect text** across more than one document boundary. One can predict that macrotext methods will be explored for connecting one microtext to another.

6.1.4 Grouptext

Grouptext is text which is created or accessed by several people collaboratively. A database is needed to keep track of which author made what changes to the text and when. Collaborators may want to communicate synchronously or asynchronously, and screen sharing is critical to synchronous communication.

One compelling argument for **collaborative writing** is that good writing requires an understanding of the reader, and a collaborating author can serve as a reader. Expert writers differ from novice writers in the extent to which they have sophisticated models of the reader. Experiences with children suggest that their writing and reading abilities improve more quickly under collaborative than under solo conditions.

Whereas in traditional databases a primary concern is to lock a record during use by one person so that it cannot be changed by other persons, at the same time, the character of transactions for authoring may call for a different paradigm. Rather than a central server controlling all events, each user can have a copy of the database on his workstation, and his changes to the database may be broadcast from his workstation to a central server which subsequently checks for conflicts. In the case of conflict, the central server notifies those who participated in the conflict, and they then must discuss among themselves how to resolve the conflict. This process of **social mediation** is contrary to the norm for databases, but supports very rapid access for each user to arbitrary amounts of text.

In collaborative work another key ingredient is synchronous communication. The speed of electricity is so fast compared to the speed of human senses that a local network of computers can give every user the sense of sharing the same screen. Such **What You See Is What I See** screen treatment allows action that would not be possible on paper, two people can write on the same file at the same time and see what each is doing (see Fig. 6.3). Furthermore, other media can be mixed with that of the computer. Video and audio can be carried with the data signals and allow people to see and hear one another simultaneously as they share the workspace of the screen.

Despite the flexibility of high technology to simulate the sense of being together without being physically close, studies suggest that people find **physical proximity** to be especially important in creating and maintaining collaborative efforts. New methods are needed to assess the impact of electronic media on work and to determine the conditions under which the computer can help people work together. There are many examples, such as the PicturePhone, where although technologists thought society ready for a new medium or way of work, people preferred the traditional methods.

definition of grouptext

compelling argument

databases and social mediation

synchronous communication

physical proximity

Figure 6.3 Two screens and people. Two people would have difficulty writing at the same time on the same piece of paper, but the computer can support such behavior. Here two people are working on the same document at the same time.

One analog of reading in the grouptext domain is **annotation**. As a group of people read a document on the computer, they can add notes that explain their reaction to the text. Not only might this help the authors revise the document, it might also help other readers appreciate the various messages which the document contains. Group annotations on paper are difficult to manage, but with the computer many people can make simultaneous comments, which others can elect either to see, or not see. Furthermore, the look and feel of paper can be simulated with modern workstation software that allows the annotator to have a red pen and to write on the document. These annotations are, however, stored separately from the document, and any reader can elect to see them merged in various ways with the document or to ignore them entirely.

annotation

6.1.5 Expertext

While links within and among documents are critical to hypertext, its future may depend on links that support complex computations. This computation capability converts hypertext into **expertext** as expertise is incorporated in the hypertext. The Dynabook microtext system of the 1970s had dynamic links; the user could cause different information to appear within a text block as a function of the traversal followed to that text block. Some of the most famous expert systems of the 1970s, such as MYCIN and INTERNIST, have been converted into systems that combine the facilities of expert systems and of hypertext systems.

definition of expertext

The **patterns** in hypertext semantic networks can be exploited. One example of such a pattern is **inheritance**. If a node is connected by a hierarchical relation to another node, then the child node can be expected to inherit attributes of the

inheritance

parent node. A different kind of pattern is that exploited by spreading activation. In retrieval, one may want text blocks associated with nodes near another node. The computer can follow the links from a node and collect information from the user, based on the assumption that two connected nodes are likely to have related information which the user may want.

logic

Logic formalisms can be incorporated into the network representation so as to give hypertext the power of logic systems. If a node corresponds to a predicate and a link to an implication, then when the predicate at the node is true, the implication is activated. Rule-based expert systems are **logic systems** which can be represented as networks with nodes that are predicates. By associating text with the network, one converts an expert system into an expertext system; a product called Knowledge Pro does just this. While on the one hand, the conversion of hypertext into a logic system provides inferencing capabilities, the logic approach also has its costs. Hypertext is intended to appeal to one's intuition—to be simple to create and to access. Logic systems are formal and not intuitive.

procedures

Procedures may be embedded in the links of hypertext. HyperCard is the most prominent example of a hypertext system that supports procedures on the links. The simplest procedure simply says to go to a certain card, but the procedures may be arbitrarily complex. For instance, the procedure may first ask the user about his background and then branch to one card or another, based on the user's response.

knowledge sources

Expertext systems will ultimately need to reference many different **knowledge sources**. For instance, one knowledge source may support the parsing of natural language queries. Another may model user backgrounds and modify the interface style based on predictions of what the user wants. Yet, another may observe behavior across the population of users and make modifications to the knowledge of the system in accord with what users seem to want.

intelligent micro-, macro-, and grouptext

Expertext can be applied to microtext, macrotext, and grouptext. Some computer-assisted instruction programs are examples of **intelligent microtext**. **Intelligent macrotext** systems may handle natural language queries and search for documents based on knowledge about those documents. **Intelligent grouptext** systems have been built to monitor annotations or electronic mail and to notify participants when actions of one person should lead to responses by another.

software engineering

Software engineering environments are a major application area for all of hypertext. For one example of microtext, the definition of a subroutine in a program may be linked to the places in the program where the subroutine is called. The program may be connected with the requirements document and the user's manual and with other programs that serve related purposes—this is macrotext. Since groups of people inevitably write, read, and modify the documents of the software life cycle, grouptext is needed. In each of these areas, knowledge can be incorporated into the system to try to increase the productivity of the software engineers. Since **software engineers** naturally use computers as tools anyhow, the opportunities for improving those tools by incorporating expertext capabilities are ripe.

6.2 The environment

The model of an individual and his or her place in the world is relevant to an **society** understanding of hypertext. The processes of an individual creating and accessing text occur within a social context. The economic analysis of hypertext also depends on such a **model** of the individual and his or her role in society.

6.2.1 System model

Text is a fundamental medium of influence. To make precise the notion of **influence as copying** influence, assume that each person is described by a set of bit strings and each **strings** bit can be assigned a unique tag. When a string is copied, all the tags associated with its bits are also **copied**. Production of a document involves the copying of strings from the person into the document. When another person accesses or reads a document, the strings are copied from the document into that person, and **influence** occurs (see Exercise 6.2). People who want influence will read documents that will further their own influence.

A **writer** must build on the structures in text which the audience is prepared **writing for an audience** to understand. Radical departures from the expected structure are unlikely to be understood. Similarly, the impact which the text is expected to have on its audience must be one which the audience was almost ready to bear anyhow—otherwise, the writer will not succeed. A good writer must understand the audience.

Dealing with text invokes enormously complex psychological and social **creating and accessing** processes. In a simplified **model** of cognition, a person uses a process bank and

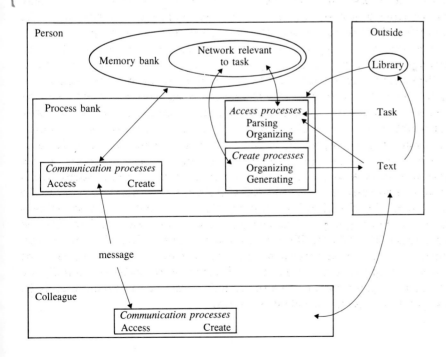

Figure 6.4 Model of text creation and access.

a memory bank. A task which motivates text creation or access also primes memory with a network of relevant concepts (see Fig. 6.4).

hypertext needs special access cues

In parsing and organizing text a person immediately needs local **coherence cues**. As access continues, structures that provide global coherence become important. Accessing text on paper is already a resource-consuming task. If having to deal with hypertext requires new cognitive resources and does not remove any of the old need for resources, then people will be unlikely to use hypertext. If hypertext searching, browsing, and reading are to be feasible, the reader must easily gain helpful cues about coherence at the local and global levels—cues which would not be available with text alone.

authoring assistance

In generating and organizing a network of concepts and text, the creator also accesses that text to test how well it satisfies the task. The global structures generated in writing are not fixed properties of the memory system, but are generated on demand in some particular **task** context. People need **help** in combining locally coherent structures into globally coherent structures. By serving as an intelligent database machine, the computer may be able to provide some of this help. Furthermore, if the computer can facilitate collaboration among people, then the most potent aid to good writing will have been stimulated.

6.2.2 Economies

history of mass production

Although the printing press of the 1400s is often viewed as beginning the revolution in publishing and as marking the advent of literacy, the size of libraries did not substantially change for many decades after the invention of the printing press. It was only after the methods and markets for the mass production of books were established that libraries grew substantially in size and literacy became more prevalent. The implications of this history for hypertext are that the existence of a **technology** does not necessarily imply its widespread availability.

cost versus benefit questions

The power of hypertext comes at a price (Scacchi, 1989). The cost can be expressed in the terms of the technological and social resources that get displaced to accommodate the use of hypertext. Society has made an enormous investment in paper processing techniques, but if companies abandon paper in favor of computer media, do they lose their and society's investment in paper media? A business must make substantial new **investments** in equipment and training to make hypertext work (see Fig. 6.5). Will the profits derived from hypertext more than compensate for the new start-up costs?

coordination economies

Hypertext and **electronic mail** may help a group work together, but the potential of hypertext systems as coordinating mechanisms depends on the continuity of staff participation. If one person of the group does not use the new technology, then an additional channel of communication must be retained for that one person. For instance, if the best way to reach people who do not use the computer network is through a paper memo, then the cost of preparing such a memo and waiting for it to reach its audience by the normal paper routes must still be borne.

Figure 6.5 Resistance to new technology. The elderly executive is annoyed at the telephone salesman and says 'do you expect me to fiddle about with my little finger and select the right number? What do you take me for—the educated pig at the circus?'

Professional enrichment may emerge from mastery of hypertext techniques. However, as with text processing systems, technical staff may broaden their skill base downward through the assimilation of more **clerical responsibilities**. Hypertext skills may enable increased workloads but little or no new upward mobility. For instance, the professional who previously wrote a report in draft on paper and then asked the secretary to polish and distribute it, may, with the new computer resources, also feel obliged to polish the document and distribute it electronically. What has the professional gained from being able to polish and distribute so easily? **downward mobility**

The combination of a hypertext system with a particular application provides a framework for organizing information processing work in a systematic manner. Standardized document contents and structures support the cataloging and reuse of information. The links of hypertext support the organization of work and information. This leads in turn to improved communication and productivity. A **domain-specific** hypertext system incorporates information about the domain and is tailored to help a particular group of users with a particular class of text-related tasks. This kind of facility has not been adequately available in pre-hypertext technology. **domain-specific help**

In the late 1960s and early 1970s, programs were developed which could generate teaching materials. Part of the teaching took the form of the student answering problems set by the program. The problems were not prestored by the course designer, but generated by the program. The teaching of mathematics is particularly well suited to such **generative** programs, since the student can generate new examples by varying the parameters of a mathematical model (Dickinson and Ingram, 1979). This kind of hypertext goes beyond what a textbook can offer and illustrates a domain-specific application. **novel functionality**

The extension of hypertext to hypermedia increases the marketability. The **extend to videos**

Figure 6.6 Patrons of this store are attracted to videos in part by the images on the cover of their boxes. A computer system could help people find and use videos.

average person is now more likely to watch television than to read a book. But computer technology for manipulating videos may build on the principles of hypertext. For instance, the libraries of videos which are now readily available (see Fig. 6.6), could be stored on computers, and people could search the computer database for the videos they require. Furthermore, links could be built into the video; by interacting with a computerized video projector, the viewer could jump from one part of the video to another, as might a browser of hypertext.

6.3 Directions

information explosion

The amount of text in the world is growing rapidly. A Second World War fighter aircraft had 1000 pages of documentation, a Korean War aircraft had 10 000 pages of documentation, and a Vietnam War aircraft had 100 000 pages of documentation. Yet, more dramatic than the growth in the size of individual documents is the growth in the total number of documents. Each individual with a desktop publishing system can now create text which looks as if it came from a professional publisher—and in high-technology societies every professional has access to desktop publishing systems. Unfortunately, while creating new text may be easy, making it understandable and available remains difficult. New structures and methods are needed to deal with the **information explosion**.

6.3.1 New structures

selection and Vannevar Bush

Vannevar Bush argued that knowledge that could not be selected was lost (Bush, 1945). His thoughts about **selection** were so vital to his thinking that the following two paragraphs appeared in each of his published papers about his now famous memex (*mem*ory *ex*tended) system (see Nyce and Kahn, 1989).

> The real heart of the matter of selection, however, goes deeper than a lag in the adoption of mechanisms by libraries, or a lack of development of devices for their use. Our ineptitude in getting at the record is largely caused by the artificiality of systems of indexing. When data of any sort are placed in storage, they are filed alphabetically or numerically, and information is found (when it is) by tracing down from subclass to subclass. It can be in only one place, unless duplicates are used; one has to have rules as to which path will locate it, and the rules are cumbersome. Having found one item, moreover, one has to emerge from the system and re-enter on a new path.

> The human mind does not work that way. It operates by association. With one item in its grasp, it snaps instantly to the next that is suggested by the association of thoughts, in accordance with some intricate web of trails carried by the cells of the brain. It has other characteristics, of course; trails that are not frequently followed are prone to fade, items are not fully permanent, memory is transitory. Yet the speed of action, the intricacy of trails, the detail of mental pictures, is awe-inspiring beyond all else in nature.

Bush was explicitly thinking about a personal machine in which an individual would record associations of significance to that individual.

idiosyncratic associations

How do different readers take advantage of the **associations** that the author or other readers have made? Early objections to memex anticipated this problem of idiosyncratic associations. In 1945 Bush received a letter from John Weakland containing the following questions (Nyce and Kahn, 1989):

> (1) Wouldn't the fact that association patterns are thoroughly individual make a general use of the memex difficult? (2) How would the tremendous bulk of information already recorded be made usable, especially for a searcher who wants to branch into lines of thought and knowledge that are quite new and unfamiliar to him?

This kind of problem anticipates one of the greatest problems of hypertext. If an individual does not take advantage of existing associations, then how can access to new literature be provided? If the associations of others are to be followed, then what conventions or rules will allow these associations to be commonly understood?

classification systems needed

While Bush's dream was to connect the world's literature, his approach to this suffers from some naivety. He felt that the existing **classification** systems were too cumbersome for people to use. Yet, his proposal that each person should build a network of connections among documents would require each person to find documents and connect them. The advantage to a standard classification and its usage in indexing text is that people looking for text can learn about the classification and then find text which they have not previously seen.

guidance on link types

The general link in hypertext is unlabeled and does not give the browser enough information about what to expect. It is like a **goto** in computer programming and creates a similar 'lost in space' or 'spaghetti tangle' feeling in the reader. Hierarchical links seem particularly useful as people have heuristics for anticipating hierarchical structures. Other link structures or navigation aids are needed. Furthermore, guidance is needed as to the types of links which are appropriate for a given type of text and a particular type of audience.

limit the number of link types in one text

A novice hypertext author may introduce many different types of links and nodes. Experience suggests, however, that one document should contain a relatively small number of different **styles**—otherwise, readers will be confused. Consider by analogy the case of typesetting. When authors start to use computerized document formatters to drive laser printers, the authors tend to use many different fonts and character sizes. Later they realize that when many typesetting changes are introduced on one page, the page looks fragmented.

virtual structures

In authoring, a global structure is not given a priori but evolves dynamically. With current hypertext tools, however, authors may stick to inadequate structures because the effort to change the initial global structure is too large (Fischer *et al.*, 1988). NoteCards, for instance, requires its users to segment ideas into labeled cards that are placed in fileboxes. However, a user in the early stages of writing may not know what the labels should be. **Virtual links** make hypertext more flexible. A link could, for example, specify the source extensionally but the destination intensionally. Thus one could link 'Claim X' to the 'node containing the strongest evidence for Claim X' (Halasz, 1988).

6.3.2 New methods

new representations are needed

Hypertext, in its current form, is a scheme of representation largely short of **supporting processes**. As a consequence, the work needed to take advantage of its representation features must be expended by its users, through some division of labor between creator and accessor. Processes must be developed whereby the computer can assume a larger role in transforming the information of the author into forms that are usable by readers.

guidance

One of the founders of hypertext has said that despite the positive claims made by various groups about hypertext,

> By and large the hypothesis remains unproven that, with little guidance, people can construct really good trails, really good webs that help them and help other readers. I think we still need to test that hypothesis in a major way (Dam, 1988).

The question is not whether links can be helpful, but what guidance is needed in the creation and access of links. A hypertext network may look like a complex map (see Fig. 6.7), which people need help in navigating. This **guidance** could

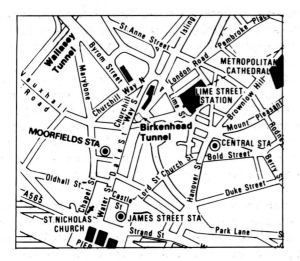

Figure 6.7 Map. This sketch of the roads and transportation centers in one area of Liverpool is typical of those used around the world.

come in the form of knowledgeable assistance, although the necessary knowledge is only partly identified (Frisse and Cousins, 1990). Some knowledge has **global** relevance and applies to all documents; for example, outlines should have a handful of elements under one heading. Some knowledge pertains to the structure of a **class** of documents; for instance, a budget report must include a section that summarizes inflow and outflow of cash. All document tools should contain knowledge of global import, while tools for dealing with one class of documents should have knowledge about that class.

Artificial intelligence and hypertext have complementary strengths and weaknesses. One of the major shortcomings of artificial intelligence is that people have difficulty building **knowledge bases**, though, once built, these are supposed to be easy to use. A major difficulty with hypertext is that text bases are difficult for readers to browse. People create massive text bases more easily than massive knowledge bases. If people created text bases which had some knowledge base features, would access be easier? Would the extra effort of adding artificial intelligence features to the text be rewarded by an increased impact on the audience of the resulting text plus knowledge base?

artificial intelligence versus hypertext

6.3.3 Requirements

Links are the essence of hypertext. In microtext the links are within a document. Links among documents via an intermediary representation constitute macrotext. Links among people and among versions of text are essential to grouptext. Enlivening the links makes expertext. What are the requirements for a hypertext system that supports these links?

links

A hypertext **interface** should be responsive to users who have varying levels of ability. The user interface should be modeless and never report an unrecoverable error. The number of items from which to choose at any given juncture should be small. Different perspectives should be available for different situations.

tailored to user and situation

extensible like Emacs
and HyperCard

Hypertext systems should have **extension facilities** analogous to those currently found in Emacs and HyperCard (Halasz, 1988). Without those facilities, many potential users will discover that the problems of dealing with hypertext systems outweigh the benefits. Both Emacs and HyperCard are built around an interpreter for a general-purpose programming language that also has special features for handling hypertext objects. Moreover, the language has a kind of scalability, as simple things can be done using single commands, yet complex programs can also be written.

Intermedia: strengths
and weaknesses

One of the most powerful, commercially available hypertext systems is **Intermedia**. What are its strengths and weaknesses? Intermedia's modeless interface supports flexible manipulation of objects and links. The system supports interactions as on paper and also beyond those which one could get on paper. While discussion, authoring, annotation, searching, browsing, and reading can be done on the system, the semantic support for these activities is not specific. Intermedia also does not address the problems of translating text into hypertext, or hypertext into text.

text to hypertext

Before the potential of hypertext can be realized adequately, tools to facilitate the **conversion** of text to hypertext must be robust and generally available. A marked-up text only explicitly specifies some of the links important for hypertext. A text-to-hypertext conversion tool should help people add links that were not explicit in the text. One such conversion tool uses, at least, two windows for displaying chunks of text and suggesting links between those chunks. Natural language processing tools could suggest the meaning of blocks of text and the links between blocks. While natural language processing is a notoriously difficult computational problem, the requirements for text to hypertext conversion are much more relaxed than those for many other natural language processing applications.

semantic net

The conceptual structure and function of hypertext might be seen from the semantic net perspective. **Semantic nets** are simple enough to be intuitively understandable, and yet sophisticated enough to support certain aspects of hypertext. The semantic net representation may be seen as instance of an object-oriented representation and, within the broader framework of object-oriented representations, all of hypertext can be handled.

writing

The **writing process** should allow notes, paragraphs, semantic nets, and outlines to be manipulated (see Fig. 6.8). Textual notes can be expanded into paragraphs and indexed in a semantic net, which can be traversed to create an outline. A document can be automatically generated from the outline and paragraphs, and conversely, a document with markings for section headings can be automatically translated into paragraphs and an outline.

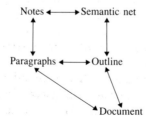

Figure 6.8 Writing forms.

A hypertext authoring system should support discussing, writing, and annotating. Particularly, for **discussion** and **annotation**, the date and author of a text block should be recorded and displayed. The network structure for the discussion and annotation phases should be handled in the same way as that for the writing phase.

For reading, browsing, and searching many access points should be supported by a hypertext system. The system must respond to queries for objects based on authorship and date. The semantic network which represents the text must be eminently accessible. Users must be able to pose **queries** of logical combinations of terms from the semantic net. When a new document enters the system, that document's semantic net must be automatically connected with the system's existing semantic net so that retrieval can go across all documents.

The first generation hypertext systems included at least some support for medium to large teams of workers sharing a common computer network. Oddly enough, many of the systems of the 1980s were designed for single users and do not support collaborative work. As text is a social phenomenon, hypertext should deal with **groups** of people.

In microtext, links among small blocks of text within a document are explicitly available to users. Macrotext is a collection of documents with links among the documents. Grouptext connects people and the portions of the document which the people are modifying. Expertext has augmented links which support intelligent computations. Measures of recall and precision are well accepted as reflecting the search effectiveness of a macrotext system. No formulas for **evaluating** text, microtext, grouptext, or expertext are widely accepted. Perhaps this imbalance is because macrotext systems are the most mature of the computerized hypertext systems, but until rigorous evaluation standards are available for microtext, grouptext, and expertext, their developments as scientific disciplines will be stunted.

The hypertext systems of the future will support all of the following:

- an individual writing or reading a single document,
- a group creating or accessing a few documents,
- institutions creating massive libraries, and
- dynamic text that adapts to input.

A paper document cannot **respond** to one reader differently than it does to any other reader. But a hypertext system can collect information from the user, and generate new presentations that suit the user.

An image may carry a valuable message (see Fig. 6.9), and a video may carry more. With the improvements in electronic storage and networking, the incorporation of audio and video into hypertext has become commercially viable. It is now possible to watch a show and interact with it as with a hypertext. Links from one part of the show go to other parts, and the viewer decides which path to take. Given the society's reliance on **television**, the potential influence of hypermedia is awesome.

The future of hypertext depends on developments in hardware, information science, human–computer interaction, and artificial intelligence. Hardware developments determine what is physically possible. The sciences of in-

Margin notes: creation phases; access through semantic net; collaboration; evaluations; dynamic; hardware and multimedia; future

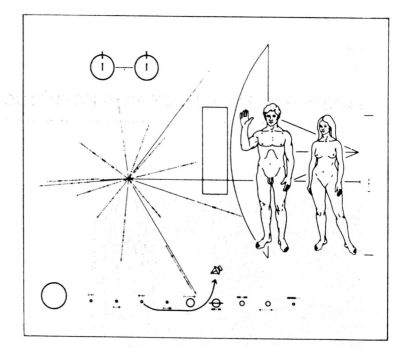

Figure 6.9 Message to outer space. This image was etched on a gold-coated aluminum plaque and attached to the Pioneer 10 space probe which flew past the planet Jupiter and into outer space. The image shows the path of the space craft, scaled drawings of people, and the earth's position relative to pulsars. Space scientists expected that intelligent life would decipher this message.

formation, human–computer interaction, and artificial intelligence provide powerful theories and software tools for hypertext. To the extent that people can control the **tools**, they will want to use them.

6.4 Exercises

integrated

6.1   Assume that an integrated microtext, macrotext, grouptext, expertext system is available. Describe possible everyday uses of this **hypertext system**. (30 minutes)

influence

6.2   A person may be described by a set of bit strings. Production of a document involves the copying of strings from a person into the document. For another person to be influenced by a document, the strings from the document must be copied into that person. Describe conditions under which three people might produce documents and be influenced by them so that one document has **perpetual influence**. (90 minutes)

7

Answers to selected exercises

Figure 7.1 The exhausted exerciser wants the answers.

In this chapter answers to some of the exercises in the book are provided. The exercises themselves appear at the ends of Chapters 1 to 6. Exercises give one the opportunity both to apply, and also to advance one's knowledge. The exercises in this book are intended to provoke thought—to complete some of them requires a major mental effort. In no case is the answer given here the only correct answer. Answers by readers should, in general, be more detailed and show other avenues of approach.

other answers are possible

7.1 Text answers

1.2 Part of the difficulty in answering this question is that standards for hypertext are lacking. If one assumes that a Guide-like hypertext is the target,

layout

then one answer to the question might be that the language or architecture would need added to it:

- an outline facility for displaying selected levels of the outline,
- pop-up displays for the temporary display of additional information,
- folding to hide sections behind a button, and
- a linkage facility to enable users to follow links automatically.

7.2 Microtext answers

independent versus embedded

2.2   If the author of the independent semantic net microtext assures that the term to label a node also occurs exactly once within the associated text block, then translation from the independent-net representation to the embedded-net representation is straightforward. In the **translation** of independent to embedded, the node is simply shown within the text itself, rather than independently. In general, an embedded semantic net microtext cannot be translated automatically into a meaningful independent semantic net microtext.

natural language

2.4   A system relying upon device-dependent syntactic knowledge needs to be regularly used to prevent that knowledge from fading from memory. An infrequent user would prefer to converse in a method that is stable in memory; such a method would involve semantics rather than syntactics. Natural language interaction is the semantically richest interaction style for people.

museum layout

2.6   To find a certain guidebook in a museum one might follow these steps:

(a)   look at the map of the museum and find the visitor information desk,
(b)   move to the visitor information store using the mouse and directional commands,
(c)   select the guidebook section,
(d)   from the menu of available guidebooks choose one.

visual formalisms

2.7   In the traditional **layout** the child x of y appears beneath y and to the right of y. An alternative layout would place children within their parent (see Fig. 7.2).

meaning of Previous

2.8   The Previous link may go from a node to the sequentially preceding node. For instance, in a book with a node for page i, the Previous link may point to page i-1. Alternatively, a Previous link may point to the beginning of a section or to the outline. For instance, a Previous link at a node within Section 2.3 might point to the beginning of Section 2. Last, but most interesting from

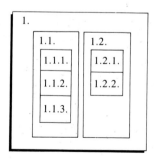

Figure 7.2 Visualization determined by relationships. Another way to represent an outline that the computer generates based on the outline relationships.

a microtext perspective, a Previous link may point to the node which the user last visited. This is a dynamic link, since where it points depends on the latest history.

2.10 The breadth-first traversal gives a broad overview from one topic and then gives a broad overview about each subtopic. The depth-first traversal goes deeply into the topic's first subtopic before later proceeding to another subtopic.

depth versus breadth

2.11 The algorithm to traverse the graph and print the document can be sketched in this pseudo-code form:

depth-first algorithm

```
traverse (edge)
    to-visit-list ← visit (edge)
    mark edge as visited
    while to-visit-list is non-empty
        choose edge
        {if edge deadend value is yes
            then do not visit
        else if edge has already been visited
            then do not visit
        else traverse (edge)}
        remove edge from to-visit-list
visit (edge)
    insert edge and its paragraph(s) in the document
    identify and return edges whose source equals target of edge
```

2.13 The 'he' in the second sentence refers to Bluto and not to Popeye. This use of a pronoun binds the two sentences together. There is a further tie inferred by the two names. Though not explicitly mentioned, Popeye and Bluto are, within some cultures, well-known cartoon enemies, and readers from those cultures mentally create the tie because of a global, mental model of the characters.

pronoun references

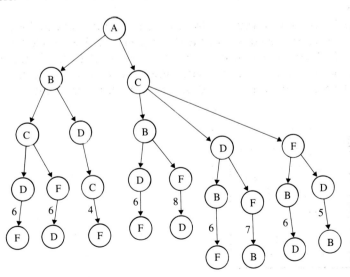

Figure 7.3 Costs of traversals. The numbers at the last edge of each path indicate the cost. For example, the cost of the path A–B–C–D–F is 6.

path costs

2.14 The costs of the traversals are indicated in the graph (see Fig. 7.3). The depth-first searches are consistently less costly than the breadth-first searches in this graph.

7.3 Macrotext answers

set and logical operators in queries

3.1 A query for 'boy $\cap$ dog' retrieves exactly the document {boy, dog}, while a query for 'boy $\cup$ dog' returns all three documents. The analog of the set operations 'intersection', 'union', and 'complement', are the Boolean operators 'and', 'or', and 'not', respectively.

a relevance formula

3.3 One popular relevance measure between a document and a query is the **cosine** function (Salton and McGill, 1983):

$$\text{cosine}(\text{document},\text{query}) = \frac{\sum\limits_{k=1}^{m} (\text{doc}_k \times \text{qu}_k)}{\left[\sum\limits_{k=1}^{m} (\text{doc}_k)^2 \times \sum\limits_{k=1}^{m} (\text{qu}_k)^2\right]^{0.5}}$$

All documents whose cosine(document,query) value are greater than some threshold are considered relevant to the query and retrieved.

discrimination analysis

3.4 Say that the distance between two vectors V_1 and V_2 is given by distance(V_1, V_2). The document space will be maximally separated, when the average distance between each document and the centroid is maximized, that is when

$$\sum_{i=1}^{n} \text{distance}(C,D_i)$$

is maximum.

hierarchy search benefit

3.5 For a collection of n documents about n comparisons are required to determine the documents closest to a query. If hierarchies are determined, then the number of comparisons required is the logarithm of n. In other words, the unordered collection requires exponentially more search effort than the hierarchically ordered collection. The search over the hierarchy concludes with a cluster of documents which are close to the query.

validity of indexing

3.7 For each document there is a test set of descriptors

$$A = a_1, a_2, ..., a_n$$

and an ideal set of descriptors

$$B = b_1, b_2, ..., b_m.$$

The following steps produce a numerical measure of the **validity** of the indexing for a given document (Wessel, 1979):

(a) Pair identical terms and remove them from the test set and the ideal set. For each pair score one point. If that pairing produces p pairs, then p is added to the validity of the indexing.

(b) Pair off remaining terms (in the test set) one level apart from any terms in the original ideal set and remove them from the test set. For each pair score one half point and if there are q such pairs, then add $\frac{q}{2}$ to the validity score.

(c) If there are remaining terms in the test set that are one level apart from any

terms in the original ideal set remove them from the test set and add 0 points to the final tally.
(d) Score $-1/2$ for all remaining terms in the indexer's set. If there are r such terms in the indexer set, then subtract $r/2$ from the validity score.
(e) In the last step the preceding terms are summed and divided by the number m of terms in the ideal set:

$$\text{validity} = \frac{p + \dfrac{q}{2} - \dfrac{r}{2}}{m}$$

This measure has intuitively appealing characteristics to it. It takes account of the similarity between terms rather than just the absolute agreement.

3.10 The word frequency formulas are amenable to many equally valid variations. The logarithm (log) is frequently used to dampen the effect of a variable, as is the case in this answer. *(searching for paragraphs)*

$$\text{WEIGHT}_{ij} = \text{FREQ}_{ij}[\log(n) - \log(\text{BLOCKFREQ}_j) + 1]$$

where FREQ_{ij} is the number of occurrences of term j in block i, n is the number of blocks in the collection, and BLOCKFREQ_j is the number of blocks containing j. In order to incorporate the intrinsic and extrinsic weights TOTALWEIGHT is proposed:

$$\text{TOTALWEIGHT}_i = \sum_j \text{WEIGHT}_{ij} + y^{-1} \sum_d \text{TOTALWEIGHT}_d$$

where y is the number of immediate descendants of block i, j is a query term in i, and d is an immediate descendant of block i (Frisse, 1988). This propagation function can be called recursively from the leaf blocks to the root block of the document to determine the most relevant block to a given query.

3.11 In addition to the ways described in the exercise, the group language and the common language may be related by the superset and the intersection relation. *(translations)*

3.12 One could change one semantic net so that both have 'hand injury' under 'arm injury'. More careful examination reveals, however, another problem. In one anatomy section 'arm' is broader than 'hand'. A pattern has been maintained between the disease and anatomy sections. Thus to change the disease section without also changing the anatomy section, would introduce a second-order inconsistency (Rada and Martin, 1987). *(inconsistency)*

7.4 Grouptext answers

4.1 One might agree that node names should all be nouns and in singular form. In a hierarchy, if one term is of a certain type, then its descendant terms should be of the same type. *(node types)*

4.2 A reference to an entity may refer to a specific version of that entity along a specific branch of the version graph or to the latest version of the entity that matches some particular description. *(versions)*

4.3 A group of users are going to be identified to a database program (called *(cooperative database)*

database$_{program}$). All users have a copy of the database on their workstation and initiate a program on their workstation (called workstation$_{program}$) that notifies the file server when a file has been changed. The database$_{program}$ will be told when the users started editing the file. When the users request through workstation$_{program}$ that they want to save changes, the database$_{program}$ will check whether anyone has written the file since they started editing. If yes, then their file will be stored under a temporary name, else database$_{program}$ overwrites the original file with their new file. The database$_{program}$ and the workstation$_{program}$ may send notice to the users involved in a conflict. In other words, if user$_1$ started work on file$_{permanent}$ at time time$_1$, user$_2$ started work on a copy of the same file at time $t_{1+delta}$, user$_2$ saved changes to the file at time $t_{1+delta+epsilon}$, and user$_1$ tried to write to the file at time $t_{1+delta+epsilon+gamma}$, then user$_1$ and user$_2$ should be told that user$_1$'s file is in file$_{temporary}$ on the file server, while user$_2$'s changes are in file$_{permanent}$.

acetate mode

4.4   An appropriate decomposition of a document into objects and harmonization with the special annotation operations would allow a form of acetate annotation that did not require freezing of the source document. In this case, the users of the system could decide whether or not to incorporate the annotations in the document and whether to return to authoring mode.

capitalist versus communist

4.5   The advantages of collaborative authoring are concerned with using resources efficiently. A group of people has varying skills. This is analogous to division of labor when making anything in a 'production line' environment. The disadvantages of collaborative authoring include the administrative overhead, and that specialization results in boredom. In money terms the profits are split equally between the participants, and one person's share may be quite small. One can compensate for this by charging a higher price to represent the increase in quality. In so doing, however, one would reduce the quantity sold and the profits, unless the demand curve is 'inelastic', i.e. does not respond to price changes. Forced collaboration may also discriminate against the person who could write a document alone and thus gain all the benefits.

student collaboration

4.6   Collaborative writing is impeded by the relative lack of a mechanism in the school for students to interact and work together. Writing tools in a school may be difficult to share and products may be difficult to reproduce. Teachers are not trained in instilling collaboration in students. When the process can be managed it has the advantages that the teacher can supervise others (namely, the students themselves) in the process of teaching one another. For short essays about personal experiences, a student may be best writing alone and then doing revisions with the help of feedback from a peer. For large, factual documents which can be prepared over a long period of time, collaboration may motivate and guide people.

scientist evaluation

4.7   In the first instance the Dean might promote the academic who had authored the most papers in the database. But this might give preference to quantity over quality. One person may have written 100 papers which hardly anyone else has read, whereas another person may have written only one paper but it may be referenced by every other paper in the database. Surely, the second person has a legitimate claim to be the one to be promoted? In this style, each academic is assigned a score equal to the number of times that his papers are cited in the database. This method is, however, flawed in several ways, one of which is similar to the flaw of simply counting publications, namely, the references may come from papers which themselves are important or from ones which are unimportant. (N.B.—the above strategy for evaluating people is actually used in some institutions of higher learning.)

4.8   A task specification must match with the **memory** of the authors in order that the writing **task** can be performed. Given writing $task_X$ and $memory_X$, then the writing task can be finished in one step, but given writing $task_Y$ and $memory_X$, writing $task_Y$ cannot possibly be done with $memory_X$. When two people collaborate, they must communicate, which takes time. For $task_Y$ with two authors each having complementary halves of $memory_Y$, the writing can now be done, if and only if collaboration occurs. If writing now takes one-half a step, then if the cost of communication is less than one-half a step, the two writers have an efficiency greater than one.

efficiency exceeds one

7.5 Expertext answers

5.1   An example of an isomorphism is given for a semantic net about viral infections, but many other examples can be readily imagined:

isomorphism

- cause(flu) = virus,
- cause(infection) = infectious agent,
- parent(flu) = infection, and
- parent(virus) = infectious agent,

then the isomorphism is parent(cause(flu)) = cause(parent(flu)).

5.2   Analogical inheritance of various kinds is present in the outline. In particular:

outline

$Inh_{x,y,z}G$, where x = subtopic, y = part-of, and z = located-on.
$Inh_{x,y,z}G$, where x = subtopic, y = (subtopic^2)$^{-1}$, and z = implies.
$Inh_{x,y,z}G$, where x = subtopic, y = (subtopic^2)$^{-1}$, and z = implies^{-1}.

5.3   The definition is

metric

$$DISTANCE(X,Y) = \frac{1}{n,m} \sum_{t_i \in X} \sum_{t_j \in Y} d(t_i, t_j)$$
$$= 0, \text{ if } X = Y.$$

Here m is the cardinality of X and n is the cardinality of Y (Rada *et al.*, 1989b).

resolution algorithm

5.4   No initial marking is associated with the graph, except that 'source' transitions (which are always enabled) will deposit tokens in their destination places. These source **transitions** represent the initial facts. The full firing algorithm follows (Rada *et al.*, 1990a):

(a)   Fire all source transitions.
(b)   For all places, p: If p contains a tuple α and there is an edge (t,p) labeled $\neg \beta$, where β negates α, replace this edge by an edge (p,t) labeled β.
(c)   Fire every enabled transition with exactly one output place. A transition,

t, is enabled, if and only if, for all places p which are inputs of t should (p,t) be labeled β there is a token α which matches β resident in p. Firing of such a transition does not remove tokens from places and results in the corresponding output token being placed in the unique output for t.

(d) Repeat from step(b) until: some place contains identical tuples of opposite polarity (in which case the set of premises encoded are inconsistent); or every transition has fired at least once; or no transition can be enabled. In the last two cases the set of premises encoded are consistent.

messaging

5.10 Messages from the supervisor must be given high priority for processing. For example, if the supervisor has sent a message which requires action in a fixed time, then those who received the message might be reminded before the deadline about the requirement.

7.6 Conclusion answer

influence

6.2 Suppose that the universe consists of three people, and each month each individual produces a document of the same length (i.e. the same number of bits). It is these bits from these documents on which influence will be calculated. Documents A and B are ignored after having been written, and document C is read by all three people. The three people now write documents and base them on the document C. These three documents face a similar fate in that two of the three are ignored, while the third again is incorporated by all three people (see Fig. 7.4). The following situation obtains:

(a) At any time t there exists a document C that represents one-third of the system's bits.
(b) For all times after t, the descendants of C occupy all of the population.
(c) This process repeats indefinitely.

In this closed world, perpetual influence has been achieved through document C.

Figure 7.4 Influence. In the upper diagram A, B, and C represent documents. In the lower diagram new documents appear but all have been influenced by, and only by, document C.

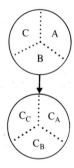

References

The growth of interest in hypertext is indicated by the abundance of new literature on the subject.

- Several new books, such as *Hypertext/Hypermedia* (Jonassen, 1989), *Hypertext and Hypermedia* (Nielsen, 1990b), and *Hypertext Hands-On!* (Shneiderman and Kearsley, 1989), emphasize small-volume hypertext. *Hypertext Hands-On!* is advertised as the first book available both in hypertext and on paper.
- There are many textbooks about macrotext systems, such as *Introduction to Modern Information Retrieval Systems* (Salton and McGill, 1983).
- Several conference proceedings have appeared as books, such as *Text, Context, and Hypertext*, and tie together a wide variety of research-oriented papers.
- A few of the many journals which contain relevant information are *Journal of American Society of Information Science, Journal of Documentation, Hypermedia, Information Processing and Management Systems, Interacting with Computers, International Journal of Man–Machine Studies*, and *IEEE Transactions on Man, Systems and Cybernetics*.

Akscyn, Robert, Donald McCracken, and Elise Yoder (1988) 'KMS: a distributed hypermedia system for managing knowledge in organizations', *Communications of the Association of Computing Machinery*, **31**, 7, 820–835.

Allen, Thomas J. (1980) 'Communication networks in R and D laboratories', in *Key Papers in Information Science*, Belver C. Griffith (ed.), Computational Environment, Knowledge Industry Publications, White Plains, New York, 66–73.

Allinson, Lesley and Nick Hammond (1989) 'A learning support environment: the hitch hikers guide', in *Hypertext: Theory into Practice*, R. McAleese (ed.), Intellect Books, Oxford, 45–61.

Arefi, Farahangiz, Charles Hughs and David Workman (1990) 'Automatically generating visual syntax-directed editors', *Communications of the Association of Computing Machinery*, **33**, 3, 349–360.

Austin, Derek (1984) *PRECIS: A Manual of Concept Analysis and Subject Indexing*, British Library, London.

Bachrach, Cliff and Thelma Charen (1978) 'Selection of MEDLINE contents, the development of its thesaurus, and the indexing process', *Medical Informatics*, **3**, 3, 237–254.

Bain, Malcolm, Richard Bland, Lou Burnard, Jon Duke, Colin Edwards, David Lindsey, Nicholas Rossiter and Peter Willet (1989) *Free Text Retrieval Systems: a Review and Evaluation*, Taylor Graham, London.

Baird, Patricia and Mark Percival (1989) 'Glasgow on-line: database development using Apple's HyperCard', in *Hypertext: Theory into Practice*, R. McAleese (ed.), Intellect Books, Oxford, 75–92.

Baker, T. F. (1972) 'Chief programmer team management of production programming', *IBM Systems Journal*, **11**, 1.

Barrett, Edward and James Paradis (1988) 'The on-line environment and in-house training', *Text, ConText and Hypertext*, E. Barrett (ed.), MIT Press, Cambridge, Massachusetts, 227–249.

Begoray, J. A. (1990) 'An introduction to hypermedia issues, systems and application areas', *International Journal of Man–Machine Studies*, **33**, 2, 121–148.

Belkin, N. J., R. D. Hennings and T. Seeger (1984) 'Simulation of a distributed expert-based information provision mechanism', *Information Technology*, **3**, 3, 122–141.

Bigelow, James (1988) 'Hypertext and CASE', *IEEE Computer*, **21**, 3, 23–27.

Blair, David and M. E. Maron (1985) 'An evaluation of retrieval effectiveness for a full-text document-retrieval system', *Communications of the Association for Computing Machinery*, **28**, 3, 289–299.

Blake, John B. (1980) 'Billings and before: nineteenth century medical bibliography', in *Centenary of Index Medicus*, J. Blake (ed.), National Library of Medicine, Bethesda, Maryland, 31–52.

Borgman, Christine L. (1986) 'The user's mental model of an information retrieval system: an experiment on a prototype online catalog', *International Journal of Man–Machine Studies*, **24**, 47–64.

Bovey, J. D. and P. J. Brown (1987) 'Interactive document display and its use in information retrieval', *Journal of Documentation*, **43**, 2, 125–137.

Brailsford, D. F. and R. J. Beach (1989) 'Electronic publishing—a journal and its publication', *The Computer Journal*, **23**, 6, 482–493.

Brooks, F. (1975) *The Mythical Man-Month*, Addison-Wesley, Reading, Massachusetts.

Brown, Heather (1989) 'Standards for structured documents', *The Computer Journal*, **23**, 6, 505–515.

Brown, Peter J. (1987) 'Turning ideas into products: the guide system', *Hypertext '87*, University of North Carolina, Chapel Hill, North Carolina, 33–40.

Brown, Peter J. and M. T. Russell (1988) 'Converting help systems to hypertext', *Software Practice and Experience*, **18**, 2, 163–165.

Bush, Vannevar (1945) 'As we may think', *Atlantic Monthly*, **176**, 1, 101–108.

Campbell, Brad and Joseph M. Goodman (1988) 'HAM: A general-purpose hypertext abstract machine', *Communications of the Association of Computing Machinery*, **31**, 7, 856–861.

Campbell, Robert M. and Barrie T. Stern (1987) 'ADONIS: A new approach to document delivery', *Microcomputers for Information Management*, **4**, 2, 87–107.

Carlson, David and Sudha Ram (1990) 'HyperIntelligence: the next frontier', *Communications of the Association of Computing Machinery*, **33**, 3, 311–322.

Case, Donald, Christine L. Borgman and Charles T. Meadow (1986) 'End-user information-seeking in the energy field implications for end-user access to DOE RECON databases', *Information Processing and Management*, **22**, 4, 299–308.

Catlin, T., P. Bush and N. Yankelovich (1989) 'InterNote: extending a hypermedia framework to support annotative collaboration', *Proceedings Hypertext '89*, Association of Computing Machinery, New York, 365–378.

Clancey, William (1983) 'The epistemology of a rule-based expert system—a framework for explanation', *Artificial Intelligence*, **20**, 3, 215–251.

Cohen, Paul R. and Rick Kjeldsen (1987) 'Information retrieval by constrained spreading activation in semantic networks', *Information Processing and Management*, **23**, 4, 255–268.

Collier, George (1987) 'Thoth-II: hypertext with explicit semantics', *Hypertext '87*, University of North Carolina, Chapel Hill, North Carolina, 269–289.

Conklin, Jeff and Michael Begeman (1989) 'gIBIS: A tool for all reasons', *Journal American Society Information Science*, **40**, 3, 200–213.

Cove, J. F. and B. C. Walsh (1988) 'Online text retrieval', *Information Processing and Management*, **24**, 1, 31–37.

Crane, Diana (1980) 'Social structure in a group of scientists: a test of the '"invisible college" hypothesis', in *Key Papers in Information Science*, Belver C. Griffith (ed.), Knowledge Industry Publications, White Plains, New York, 10–27.

Croft, W. Bruce and Roger H. Thompson (1987) 'I³R: A new approach to the design of document retrieval systems', *Journal American Society Information Science*, **38**, 6, 389–404.

Curtis, Bill, Herb Krasner and Neil Iscoe (1988) 'A field study of the software design process for large systems', *Communications of the Association of Computing Machinery*, **31**, 11, 1268–1287.

Czuchry, Andrew J. Jr. and David R. Harris (1988) 'KBRA: A new paradigm for requirements engineering', *IEEE Expert*, **3**, 4, 21–35.

Dahlberg, Ingetraut (1980) 'The broad system of ordering as a basis for an integrated social sciences thesaurus', *International Classification*, **7**, 2, 66–72.

Dahlberg, Ingetraut (1983) 'Conceptual compatibility of ordering systems', *International Classification*, **10**, 1, 5–8.

Dam, Andries van (1988) 'Hypertext '87 keynote address', *Communications of the Association of Computing Machinery*, **31**, 7, 887–895.

Darby, Jonathan and Peter Miller (1990) 'LinkWay—a review', *The CTISS File*, University of Oxford, Oxford, 24–26.

Dextre, S. G. and T. M. Clarke (1981) 'A system for machine-aided thesaurus construction', *ASLIB Proceedings*, **33**, 3, 102–112.

Dhawan, S. M., S. K. Phull and S. P. Jain (1980) 'Selection of scientific journals: a model', *Journal of Documentation*, **36**, 1, 24–41.

Dickinson, C. J. and D. Ingram (1979) 'Review of educational applications of four models of circulation, respiration, body fluids, and drug absorption', in *Proceedings Medical Information Berlin*, B. Barber (ed.), 471–478.

Dijk, Teun van and Walter Kintsch (1983) *Strategies of Discourse Comprehension*, Academic Press, New York.

Dillon, Andrew, Cliff McKnight and John Richardson (1990) 'Navigation in hypertext: a critical review of the concept', *Proceedings Third International Conference on Human–Computer Interaction*, North-Holland, Amsterdam, 587–592.

DiSessa, A. (1985) 'A principled design for an integrated computational environment', *Human Computer Interaction*, **1**, 1–47.

Egan, D. E., J. R. Remde, L. M. Gomez, T. K. Landauer, J. Eberhardt and C. C. Lochbaum (1989) 'Formative design-evaluation of "SuperBook"', *ACM Transactions of Information Systems*, **7**, 1, 30–57.

Egido, Carmen (1988) 'Videoconferencing as a technology to support group work: a review of its failure', *Second Conference on Computer-Supported Cooperative Work: CSCW '88*, Association of Computing Machinery, New York, 13–24.

Engelbart, Douglas (1984) 'Authorship provisions in augment', *Proceedings Compcon Conference*, IEEE, New York, 465–472.

Engelbart, Douglas C. and W. K. English (1968) 'A research center for augmenting human intellect', *American Federation of Information Processing Societies Conference Proceedings of the Fall Joint Computer Conference*, **33**, Thompson Book Company, Washington, DC, 395–410.

Farradane, Jason (1977) 'A comparison of some computer produced permuted alphabetical subject indexes', *International Classification*, **4**, 2, 94–101.

Fidel, Raya (1984) 'Online searching styles: case-study-based model of searching behavior', *Journal of the American Society for Information Science*, **35**, 4, 211–221.

Fikes, R. E. and G. Hendrix (1977) 'A network-based knowledge representation and its natural deduction system', *Proceedings Fifth International Joint Conference Artificial Intelligence*, William Kaufmann, Los Altos, California, 235–246.

Filman, Robert and Daniel Friedman (1984) *Coordinated computing: tools and techniques for distributed software*, McGraw-Hill, New York.

First, M. B., L. J. Soffer and R. A. Miller (1985) 'QUICK (QUick Index of Caduceus Knowledge): using the internist-1/caduceus knowledge base as an electronic textbook of medicine', *Computers and Biomedical Research*, **18**, 137–165.

Fischer, Gerhard (1987) 'Cognitive view of reuse and redesign', *IEEE Software*, **4**, 4, 60–72.

Fischer, Gerhard, Stephen A. Weyer, William P. Jones, Walter Kintsch, Alan C. Kay and Randall H. Trigg (1988) 'A critical assessment of hypertext systems', *Proceedings CHI '88*, Association of Computing Machinery, New York.

Fischer, Gerhard, Raymond McCall and Anders Morch (1989) 'JANUS: integrating hypertext with a knowledge-based design environment', *Proceedings Hypertext '89*, Association of Computing Machinery, New York, 105–118

Fish, Robert S., Robert E. Kraut, Mary D. P. Leland and Michael Cohen (1988) 'Quilt: a collaborative tool for cooperative writing', *Proceedings Conference on Office Information Systems*, Association Computing Machinery, New York, 30–37.

Forsyth, Richard and Roy Rada (1986) *Machine Learning: Expert Systems and Information Retrieval*, Ellis Horwood, London.

Fox, Edward A. (1987) 'Development of the CODER system: a testbed for artificial intelligence methods in information retrieval', *Information Processing and Management*, **23**, 4, 341–366.

Frederiksen, Carl H. and Joseph F. Dominic (1981) 'Introduction: perspectives on the activity of writing', in *Writing: the Nature, Development, and Teaching of Written Communication*, Volume 2, J. F. Dominic (ed.), Lawrence Erlbaum Associates, Hillsdale, New Jersey, 1–20.

Frisse, Mark (1988) 'Searching for information in a hypertext medical handbook', *Communications of the Association for Computing Machinery*, **31**, 7, 880–886.

Frisse, Mark and Steve Cousins (1990) 'Guides for hypertext: an overview', *Artificial Intelligence in Medicine*, **2**, 6, 303–314.

Furuta, Richard (1989) 'An object-based taxonomy for abstract structure in document models', *The Computer Journal*, **23**, 6, 494–504.

Furuta, Richard, Catherine Plaisant and Ben Shneiderman (1989a) 'A spectrum of automatic hypertext constructions', *Hypermedia* **1**, 2, 179–195.

Furuta, Richard, Catherine Plaisant and Ben Shneiderman (1989b) 'Automatically transforming linear documents into hypertext', *Electronic Publishing: Origination, Dissemination and Design*, **2**, 4, 211–230.

Gale, Stephen (1990) 'Human aspects of interactive multimedia communication', *Interacting with Computers*, **2**, 2, 175–189.

Garfield, Eugene (1985) 'Journal selection for current contents: editorial merit versus political pressure', *Current Contents/Life Sciences*, **11**, 3–11.

Gehani, Narain (1986) 'Tutorial: UNIX document formatting and typesetting', *IEEE Software*, **3**, 5, 15–24.

Ghaoui, Claude, Steven George, Roy Rada and Martin Beer (1991) 'Text to hypertext and back again', in *Computers and Writing: The State of the Art*, Patrik Holt (ed.), Intellect Books, Oxford.

Glushko, Robert K. (1989) 'Transforming text into hypertext for a compact disk encyclopedia', *Proceedings of CHI '89*, Association of Computing Machinery, New York, 293–398.

Goodman, Danny (1987) *Complete HyperCard Handbook*, Bantam Books, New York.

Gordon, Colin, John Fox, Andrzej Glowinski and Mike O'Neil (1990) 'Design of the Oxford system of medicine: an overview', in *Lecture Notes in Medical Informatics: Proceedings Medical Informatics Europe '90*, Springer-Verlag, Berlin.

Gordon, Michael (1985) 'A learning algorithm applied to document redescription', *Proceedings of Eighth Annual Association Computing Machinery Special Interest Group in Information Retrieval Conference*, 179–186.

Green, T. R. (1982) 'Pictures of programs and other processes, or how to do things with lines', *Behavior Information and Technology*, **1**, 1, 3–36.

Greif, Irene and Sunil Sarin (1987) 'Data sharing in group work', *ACM Transactions on Office Information Systems*, **5**, 2, 187–211.

Griffey, Quentin (1986) 'Word processing for LD college students', *Academic Therapy*, **22**, 2, 61–67.

Groot, A. M. B. de (1983) 'The range of automatic spreading activation in word priming', *Journal of Verbal Learning and Verbal Behavior*, **22**, 417–436.

Haas, Norman and Gary Hendrix (1980) 'An approach to acquiring and applying knowledge', *Proceedings National Conference Artificial Intelligence*, American Association Artificial Intelligence, 235–239.

Hahn, Udo, Matthias Jarke, Klaus Kreplin, Marisa Farusi and Francesco Pimpinelli (1989) 'CoAUTHOR: A hypermedia group authoring environment', *Proceedings of First European Conference on Computer Supported Cooperative Work*, Computer Sciences Company, Slough, 226–244.

Halasz, Frank G. (1988) 'Reflections on NoteCards: seven issues for the next generation of hypermedia systems', *Communications of the Association of Computing Machinery*, **31**, 7, 836–855.

Hall, James L. and Marjorie J. Brown (1983) *Online Bibliographic Databases*, ASLIB, London.

Hansen, Wilfred J. and Christina Haas (1988) 'Reading and writing with computers: a framework for explaining differences in performance', *Communications of the Association of Computing Machinery*, **31**, 9, 1080–1089.

Hardman, Lynda (1988) 'Hypertext tips: experiences in developing a hypertext tutorial', *Proceedings of People and Computers IV*, British Computer Society Human–Computer Interaction, 437–451.

Harel, David (1988) 'On visual formalisms', *Communications of the Association of Computing Machinery*, **31**, 5, 514–530.

Hayes, John R., Linda Flower, Karen A. Schriver, James F. Stratman and Linda Carey (1987) 'Cognitive processes in revision', in *Advances in Applied Psycholinguistics*, Sheldon Rosenberg (ed.), Cambridge University Press, Cambridge, 176–240.

Hayes-Roth, F., D. Waterman and D. Lenat (1983) *Building Expert Systems*, Addison-Wesley, Reading, Massachusetts.

Hewett, Tom (1987) 'The drexel disk: an electronic "Guidebook"', *People and Computers III*, Cambridge University Press, Cambridge, 115–119.

Hewett, Tom (1990) 'Update on the drexel disk: handout for SIGGraph 1990 annual conference', *Technical Report from Department of Psychology*, Drexel University, Philadelphia, Pennsylvania.

Hewitt, Carl (1986) 'Offices are open systems', *ACM Transactions on Office Information Systems*, **4**, 3, 271–287.

Holland, John (1975) *Adaptation in Natural and Artificial Systems*, University of Michigan Press, Ann Arbor, Michigan.

Howell, Gordon (1990) 'Hypertext meets interactive fiction: new vistas in creative writing', *Hypertext: State of the Art*, R. McAleese (ed.), Intellect Books, Oxford, 136–141.

Humphrey, Susanne (1989) 'MedIndex', *IEEE Expert*, Fall, 25–38.

Humphrey, Susanne and Biagio Melloni (1986) *Databases: A Primer for Retrieving Information by Computer*, Prentice-Hall, Englewood Cliffs, New Jersey.

International Standards Organization (1988) *Information Processing—Text and Office Systems—Office Document Architecture (ODA) and Interchange Format*, Parts 1 and 2, ISO 8613, Geneva, 4–8.

International Standards Organization (1989) *Information Processing—Text and Office Systems—Standard Generalized Markup Language (SGML)*, ISO 8879, Geneva.

Irish, Peggy and Randall Trigg (1989) 'Supporting collaboration in hypermedia: issues and experiences', *Journal American Society Information Science*, **40**, 3, 192–199.

Jonassen, David (1989) *Hypertext/Hypermedia*, Education Technology Productions, Engelwood Cliffs, New Jersey.

Jonassen, David (1990) 'Semantic network elicitation: tools for structuring hypertext', *Hypertext: State of the Art*, R. McAleese (ed.), Intellect Books, Oxford, 142–152.

Jones, Karen Sparck (1971) *Automatic Keyword Classification for Information Retrieval*, Butterworth, London.

Jones, Karen Sparck (1972) 'A statistical interpretation of term specificity and its application in retrieval', *Journal of Documentation*, **28**, 1, 11–21.

Kane, Beverly (1990) 'LIMES: A hypertext advisory system', *Artificial Intelligence in Medicine*, **2**, 4, 193–204.

Karel, L. (1967) 'Selection of journals for Index Medicus: a historical review', *Bulletin of the Medical Library Association*, **55**, 259–278.

Kintsch, Walter (1988) 'The role of knowledge in discourse comprehension: a construction-integration model', *Psychological Review*, **95**, 2, 163–182.

Klingbeil, W. (1985) 'Phrase structure rewrite systems in information retrieval', *Information Processing and Management*, **21**, 2, 113–126.

Koved, Larry and Ben Shneiderman (1986) 'Embedded menus: selecting items in context', *Communications of the Association for Computing Machinery*, **29**, 4, 312–318.

Kraft, D. and T. Hill (1973) 'A journal selection model and its implications for a library system', *Information Storage and Retrieval*, **9**, 1–11.

Kraut, Robert, Jolene Galegher and Carmen Egido (1988) 'Relationships and tasks in scientific research collaborations', *Human–Computer Interaction*, **3**, 1, 31–58.

Lancaster, F. W. (1972) *Vocabulary Control for Information Retrieval*, Information Resources Press, Washington, DC.

Langer, J. A. (1984) 'The effects of available information on responses to school writing tasks', *Research in the Teaching of English*, **18**, 1, 27–44.

Lee, Eric and James MacGregor (1985) 'Minimizing user search time in menu retrieval systems', *Human Factors*, **27**, 2, 157–162.

Lee, Jinta and Thomas W. Malone (1990) 'Partially shared views: a scheme for communicating among groups that use different type hierarchies', *ACM Transactions on Information Systems*, **8**, 1, 1–26.

Lenat, Douglas B. and R. V. Guha (1990) *Building Large Knowledge-Bases*, Addison-Wesley, Reading, Massachusetts.

Lewis, Brian T. and Jeffrey D. Hodges (1988) 'Shared books: collaborative publication management for an office information system', *Proceedings Conference on Office Information Systems*, Association Computing Machinery, New York, 197–204.

Litoukhin, J. (1980) 'Toward an integrated thesaurus of the social sciences', *International Classification*, **7**, 2, 56–59.

Logan, Elizabeth (1990) 'Cognitive styles and online behavior of novice searchers', *Information Processing and Management*, **26**, 4, 503–510.

Lowe, David G. (1985) 'Cooperative structuring of information: the representation of reasoning and debate', *International Journal of Man–Machine Studies*, **23**, 97–111.

Magill, Frank and Ian McGreal (1961) 'Aristotle's Rhetoric', in *Masterpieces of World Philosophy in Summary Form*, Harper & Row, New York, 169–179.

Marsh, Elaine and Carol Friedman (1985) 'Transporting the linguistic string project system from a medical to a navy domain', *ACM Transactions on Office Information Systems*, **3**, 2, 121–140.

Mazur, Zygmont (1986) 'Organization of the inverted files in a distributed information retrieval system based on thesauri', *Information Processing and Management*, **22**, 2, 243–250.

McCarn, D. B. (1980) 'MEDLINE: an introduction to on-line searching', *Journal of the American Society for Information Science*, **31**, 3, 181–192.

McCracken, Donald and Robert Akscyn (1984) 'Experience with the ZOG human–computer interface system', *International Journal of Man–Machine Studies*, **21**, 293–310.

McCue, G. M. (1978) 'IBM's Santa Teresa Laboratory—an architectural design for program development', *IBM Systems Journal*, **17**, 1, 4–25.

McMath, Chuck, Bob Tamaru and Roy Rada (1989) 'Graphical interface to thesaurus-based information retrieval system', *International Journal of Man–Machine Studies*, **31**, 121–147.

Meehan, J. R. (1981) 'Tale-spin', in *Inside Computer Understanding: Five Programs Plus Miniatures,* C. Shank and C. K. Riesbeck (ed), Lawrence Erlbaum, Hillsdale, New Jersey, 197–226.

Menzel, Herbert (1980) 'Scientific communication: five themes from sociology', in *Key Papers in Information Science*, Belver C. Griffith (ed.), Knowledge Industry Publications, White Plains, New York, 28–38.

Mhashi, Mahmoud, Roy Rada, Geeng-Neng You, Akmal Zeb, Antonis Michailidis and Hafedh Mili (1991) 'Word frequency based indexing and authoring', *Computers and Writing: The State of the Art*, Patrik Holt (ed.), Intellect Books, Oxford.

Mili, Hafedh and Roy Rada (1985) 'A statistically built knowledge base', *Proceedings Expert Systems in Government Conference*, IEEE Computer Society Press, Washington, DC, 457–463.

Mili, Hafedh and Roy Rada (1988) 'Merging thesauri: principles and valuation', *IEEE Transactions on Pattern Analysis and Machine Intelligence*, **10**, 2, 204–220.

Mili, Hafedh and Roy Rada (1990) 'Medical expertext as regularity in semantic nets', *Artificial Intelligence in Medicine*, **2**, 4, 217–229.

Minsky, Marvin and Seymour Papert (1969) *Perceptrons*, MIT Press, Cambridge, Massachusetts.

Mitchell, Christine and R. A. Miller (1986) 'A discrete control model of operator function: a methodology for information display design', *IEEE Transactions on Systems, Man, and Cybernetics*, **16**, 3, 343–357.

Mittman, Benjamin and Lorraine Borman (1975) 'Bibliographic retrieval and data management systems: precursors of personalized data base processing', in *Personalized Data Base Systems*, B. Mittman (ed.), Melville Publishing, Los Angeles, California, 3–33.

National Library and Information Associations Council (1980) *Guidelines for Thesaurus Structure, Construction, and Use*, American National Standards Institute, New York.

National Library of Medicine, Medical Subject Headings Section (1986) *Medical Subject Headings, Annotated Alphabetical List*, National Technical Information Service, Springfield, Virginia.

Nelson, Ted (1987) *Computer Lib/Dream Machines*, Tempus Books of Microsoft Press, Redmond, Washington.

Neuwirth, Christine and David Kaufer (1989) 'The role of external representations in the writing process: implications for the design of hypertext-based writing tools', *Proceedings Hypertext '89,* Association of Computing Machinery, New York, 319–341.

Neuwirth, Christine, David Kaufer, Rick Chimera and Terilyn Gillespie (1987) 'The notes program: a hypertext application for writing from source texts', *Hypertext '87,* University of North Carolina, Chapel Hill, North Carolina, 121–141.

Niehoff, Robert and Greg Mack (1985) 'The vocabulary switching system', *International Classification*, **12**, 1, 2–6.

Nielsen, Jakob (1989) 'The matters that really matter for hypertext usability', *Proceedings Hypertext '89,* Association of Computing Machinery, New York, 239–248.

Nielsen, Jakob (1990a) 'The art of navigating through hypertext', *Communications of the Association of Computing Machinery*, **33**, 3, 296–310.

Nielsen, Jakob (1990b) *Hypertext and Hypermedia*, Academic Press, San Diego, California.

Normore, Lorraine (1984) 'Developing a menu-based interface system for online bibliographic searching: a case study in knowing your user', in *Trends in Ergonomics/Human Factors I*, Anil Mital (ed.), North-Holland, Amsterdam, 89–94.

Nyce, James M. and Paul Kahn (1989) 'Innovation, pragmaticism, and technological continuity: Vannevar Bush's Memex', *Journal American Society Information Science*, **40**, 3, 214–220.

Perry, J. A. (1985) 'The Dillion hypothesis of titular colonicity: an empirical test from the ecological sciences', *Journal of the American Society for Information Science*, **36**, 4, 251–258.

Pollitt, A. S. (1986) 'A rule-based system as an intermediary for searching cancer therapy literature on MEDLINE', in *Intelligent Information Systems: Progress and Prospects*, Roy Davis (ed.), Ellis Horwood, London, 82–126.

Pracht, William (1986) 'GISMO: A visual problem-structuring and knowledge-organization tool', *IEEE Transactions on Systems, Man, and Cybernetics*, **16**, 2, 265–270.

Price, Jonathan (1988) 'Creating a style for online help', in *Text, ConText, and HyperText*, Edward Barrett (ed.), MIT Press, Cambridge, Massachusetts, 329–342.

Price, Lynne A. (1982) 'Thumb: an interactive tool for accessing and maintaining text', *IEEE Transactions on Systems, Man, and Cybernetics*, **12**, 2, 155–161.

Puncello, P. Paolo, Piero Torrigiani, Francesco Pietri, Riccardo Burlon, Bruno Cardile and Mirella Conti (1988) 'ASPIS: a knowledge-based case environment', *IEEE Software*, 58–65.

Rada, Roy (1985) 'Gradualness facilitates knowledge refinement', *IEEE Transactions on Pattern Analysis and Machine Intelligence*, **7**, 5, 523–530.

Rada, Roy (1989a) 'Guidelines for multiple users creating hypertext: SQL and HyperCard experiments', in *Computers and Writing: Models and Tools*, Noel Williams (ed.), Blackwell/Ablex Publishing, Oxford, 61–69.

Rada, Roy (1989b) 'Writing and reading hypertext: an overview', *Journal American Society Information Science*, **40**, 3, 164–171.

Rada, Roy (1990) 'An expert system for journal selection', *IEEE Expert*, **5**, 2, 60–69.

Rada, Roy and Judith Barlow (1989) 'Document creation in offices', in *Computing Technologies: New Directions and Applications*, Peter Salenieks (ed.), Ellis Horwood, London, 43–74.

Rada, Roy and Lynn Evans (1979) 'Automated problem encoding system for ambulatory care', *Computers and Biomedical Research*, **12**, 131–139.

Rada, Roy and Brian Martin (1987) 'Augmenting thesauri for Information Systems', *ACM Transactions on Office Information Systems*, **5**, 4, 378–392.

Rada, Roy and Hafedh Mili (1989) 'A knowledge-intensive learning system for document retrieval', in *Knowledge Reorganization and Machine Learning*, Katharina Morik (ed.), Springer-Verlag, New York, 65–87.

Rada, Roy, Joyce Backus, Tom Giampa, Subash Goel and Christina Gibbs (1987) 'Computerized guides to journal selection', *Information Technology and Libraries*, **6**, 3, 173–184.

Rada, Roy, Barbara Keith, Marc Burgoine, Steven George and David Reid (1989a) 'Collaborative writing of text and hypertext', *Hypermedia*, **1**, 2, 93–110.

Rada, Roy, Hafedh Mili, Ellen Bicknell and Maria Blettner (1989b) 'Development and application of a metric on semantic nets', *IEEE Transactions on Systems, Man, and Cybernetics*, **19**, 1, 17–30.

Rada, Roy, Paul Dunne and Judith Barlow (1990a) 'Expertext: from semantic nets to logic, petri nets', *Expert Systems Applications*, **1**, 1, 51–62.

Rada, Roy, Mahmoud Mhashi and Judith Barlow (1990b) 'Hierarchical semantic nets support retrieving and generating hypertext', *Information and Decision Technologies*, **16**, 2, 117–136.

Raymond, Darrell and Frank Tompa (1988) 'Hypertext and the Oxford English Dictionary', *Communications of the Association of Computing Machinery*, **31**, 7, 871–879.

Reid, Brian K. (1988) 'The USENET Cookbook—an experiment in electronic publishing', *Electronic Publishing: Origination, Dissemination, and Design*, **1**, 1, 55–66.

Resnick, A. and T. R. Savage (1964) 'The consistency of human judgements of relevance', *American Documentation*, **15**, 2, 93–95.

Rich, Charles and Richard C. Waters (1988) 'The assistant approach: a research overview', *IEEE Computer*, **21**, 11, 11–25.

Ritchie, Ian (1989) 'HYPERTEXT—moving towards large volume', *The Computer Journal*, **23**, 6, 516–523.

Roget, Peter (1977) *Roget's International Thesaurus*, Thomas Crowell, New York.

Rosenthal, Steve (1990) 'Doug Engelbart', *Electric Word*, **18**, 20–25.

Salton, G., C. S. Yang and C. T. Yu (1975) 'A theory of importance in automatic text analysis', *Journal of the American Society for Information Science*, **26**, 1.

Salton, Gerard and Michael McGill (1983) *Introduction to Modern Information Retrieval Systems*, McGraw-Hill, New York.

Scacchi, Walter (1989) 'On the power of domain-specific hypertext environments' *Journal of the American Society for Information Science*, **40**, 3, 183–191.

Scardamalia, Marlene and Carl Bereiter (1987) 'Knowledge telling and knowledge transforming in written composition', in *Advances in Applied Psycholinguistics*, Sheldon Rosenberg (ed.), Cambridge University Press, Cambridge, 142–175.

Schabas, Ann (1982) 'Postcoordinate retrieval: a comparison of two indexing languages', *Journal of the American Society for Information Science*, **33**, 1, 32–37.

Schank, Roger (1982) *Dynamic Memory: a theory of reminding and learning in computers and people*, Cambridge University Press, Cambridge.

Schutzer, Daniel (1985) 'Artificial intelligence-based very large data base organization and management', in *Applications in Artificial Intelligence*, Stephen Andriole (ed.), Petrocelli Books, New York, 251–277.

Seppala, Pentti and Gavriel Salvendy (1985) 'Impact of depth of menu hierarchy on performance effectiveness in a supervisory task: computerized flexible manufacturing system', *Human Factors*, **27**, 6, 713–722.

Sharples, M. and C. E. O'Malley (1988) 'A framework for the design of a writer's assistant', in *Artificial Intelligence and Human Learning: Intelligent Computer-Aided Instruction*, J. Self (ed.), Chapman and Hall, London.

Sharples, M., James Goodlet and L. Pemberton (1991) 'The writer's assistant: a computer system to assist the writing process', in *Computers and Writing: The State of the Art*, Patrik Holt (ed.), Intellect Books, Oxford.

Shneiderman, Ben (1980) *Software Psychology*, Winthrop Publishers, Cambridge, Massachusetts.

Shneiderman, Ben (1986) 'Designing menu selection systems', *Journal of the American Association for Information Science*, **37**, 2, 57–70.

Shneiderman, Ben and Greg Kearsley (1989) *Hypertext Hands-On!*, Addison-Wesley, Reading, Massachusetts.

Shneiderman, Ben and Janis Morariu (1986) 'Design and research on The Interactive Encyclopedia System (TIES)', *Proceedings 29th Conference of the Association for the Development of Computer-based Instructional Systems*, 19–21.

Shneiderman, Ben, Dorothy Brethauer, Catherine Plaisant and Richard Potter (1989) 'Evaluating three museum installations of a hypertext', *Journal of the American Society for Information Science*, **40**, 3, 172–182.

Shortliffe, E., A. Scott, M. Bischoff, A. Campbel, W. van Melle, and C. Jacobs (1981) 'ONCOCIN: expert system for oncology protocol management', *Proceedings International Joint Conference Artificial Intelligence*, William Kaufmann, Los Altos, California, 876–881.

Simon, Herbert and A. Newell (1972) *Human Problem Solving*, Prentice-Hall, Englewood Cliffs, New Jersey.

Skinner, B. F. (1958) 'Teaching machines', *Science*, **128**, 969–979.

Slatin, John (1988) 'Hypertext and teaching of writing', in *Text, ConText, and HyperText*, Edward Barrett (ed.), MIT Press, Cambridge, Massachusetts, 111–129.

Smith, Joan M. (1986) 'The implications of SGML for the preparation of scientific publications', *The Computer Journal*, **29**, 3, 193–200.

Soergel, Dagobert (1974) *Indexing Languages and Thesauri: Construction and Maintenance*, Wiley, New York.

Stallman, Richard (1981) 'EMACS manual for TWENEX users', *AI Memo* 555, MIT AI Lab, Cambridge, Massachusetts.

Stanfill, Craig and Brewster Kahle (1986) 'Parallel free text search on the connection machine system', *Communications of the Association for Computing Machinery*, **29**, 12, 1229–1239.

Stanton, Neville A. and R. B. Stammers (1990) 'Learning styles in a non-linear training environment', *Hypertext: State of the Art*, R. McAleese (ed.), Intellect Books, Oxford, 114–120.

Stefik, Mark, Gregg Foster, Daniel Bobrow, Kenneth Kahn, Stan Lanning and Lucy Suchman (1987) 'Beyond the chalkboard: computer support for collaboration and problem solving in meetings', *Communications of the Association of Computing Machinery*, **30**, 1, 32–47.

Sterne, Laurence (1912) *Tristram Shandy*, Dent and Sons, London.

Stonebraker, Michael, Heidi Stettner, Nadene Lynn, Joseph Kalash and Antonin Guttman (1983) 'Document processing in a relational database system', *ACM Transactions on Office Information Systems*, **1**, 2, 143–158.

Stotts, David and Richard Furuta (1989) 'Programmable browsing semantics in trellis', *Proceedings Hypertext '89*, Association of Computing Machinery, New York, 27–42.

Sudarshan, B. (1979) 'Development of reference retrieval system with simultaneous building of thesaurus', *Library Science*, **16**, 3, 77–83.

Sullivan, Michael V., Christine L. Borgman and Dorothy Wippern (1990) 'End-users, mediated searches, and front-end assistance programs on dialog: a comparison of learning, performance, and satisfaction', *Journal American Society Information Science*, **41**, 1, 27–42.

Sullivan, Patricia (1988) 'Writers as total desktop publishers', in *Text, ConText, and HyperText*, Edward Barrett (ed.), MIT Press, Cambridge, Massachusetts, 265–278.

Svenonius, Elaine (1983) 'Compatibility of retrieval languages: introduction to a forum', *International Classification*, **10**, 1, 2–4.

Swanson, D. G. (1960) 'Searching natural language text by computer', *Science*, **132**, 1099–1104.

Swets, John (1969) 'Effectiveness of information retrieval methods', *American Documentation*, **20**, 1, 72–89.

Tichy, W. (1982) 'Design, implementation and evaluation of a revision control system', *6th International Conference on Software Engineering*, Tokyo, 58–67.

Timpka, Toomas (1986) 'LIMEDS knowledge-based decision support for general practitioners: an integrated design', *Proceedings Tenth Annual Symposium on Computer Applications in Medical Care*, IEEE Computer Society, 394–402.

Tong, R. M. and D. G. Shapiro (1985) 'Experimental investigations of uncertainty in a rule-based system for information retrieval', *International Journal of Man–Machine Studies*, **22**, 3, 265–282.

Travers, Michael (1989) 'A visual representation for knowledge structures', *Proceedings Hypertext '89*, Association of Computing Machinery, New York, 147–158.

Trigg, Randall, Lucy Suchman and Frank Halasz (1986) 'Supporting collaboration in NoteCards', *Proceedings of the Conference on Computer Supported Cooperative Work*, Association of Computing Machinery, New York, 1–10.

Watt, James H. (1988) 'Level of abstraction structured text', *IEEE Transactions on Systems, Man, and Cybernetics*, **18**, 4, 497–505.

Wayner, Peter (1988) 'It's APT to write', *Byte*, **13**, 11, 375–384.

Weinberg, G. M. (1971) *The Psychology of Computer Programming*, Van Nostrand, New York.

Wessel, Andrew E. (1979) *The Implementation of Complex Information Systems*, Wiley, New York.

Weyer, Stephen A. and Alan H. Borning (1985) 'A prototype electronic encyclopedia', *ACM Transactions on Office Information Systems*, **3**, 1, 63–88.

Wingert, F. (1986) 'An indexing system for SNOMED', *Methods of Information in Medicine*, **25**, 1, 22–30.

WordPerfect Corporation (1990) *WordPerfect Reference*, Orem, Utah.

Wright, Patricia and Ann Lickorish (1989) 'The influence of discourse structure on display and navigation in hypertexts', in *Computers and Writing*: *Models and Tools*, Noel Williams (ed.), Blackwell/Ablex Publishing, Oxford, 90–124.

Yankelovich, Nicole, Norman Meyrowitz and Andries van Dam (1985) 'Reading and writing the electronic book', *Computer*, **18**, 10, 15–30.

Zipf, G. K. (1949) *Human Behavior and the Principle of Least Effort*, Addison-Wesley, Reading, Massachusetts.

Author Index

Index of terms